SEASHELLS
of the World

Bivalve shell (inside of right valve)

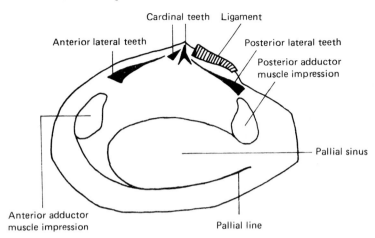

Cardinal teeth   Ligament

Anterior lateral teeth

Posterior lateral teeth

Posterior adductor
muscle impression

Pallial sinus

Anterior adductor
muscle impression

Pallial line

(outside of left valve)

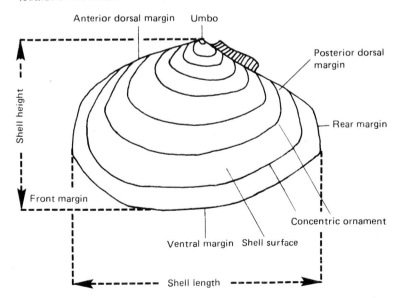

Anterior dorsal margin   Umbo

Posterior dorsal
margin

Rear margin

Shell height

Concentric ornament

Front margin

Ventral margin   Shell surface

Shell length

SEASHELLS
of the World

Gert Lindner

*German, Netherlands, Italian and
Californian Malacozoological Societies*

Translated and Edited by
Gwynne Vevers

*Assistant Director of Science and Curator of the Aquarium,
The Zoological Society of London*

BLANDFORD PRESS

POOLE   DORSET

First published in the English language 1977
Copyright © 1977 Blandford Press Ltd.
Link House, West Street, Poole, Dorset BH15 1LL

ISBN 0 7137 08441

Originally published as German edition
Muscheln und Schnecken der Weltmeere
World copyright © 1975 BLV Verlagsgesellschaft mbH, Munich.

Filmset by Keyspools Ltd, Golborne, Lancashire
Printed in Great Britain by Cox & Wyman Ltd.,
Fakenham, Norfolk

CONTENTS

ACKNOWLEDGEMENTS

All photographs were taken by the author and the following shells were lent for photography:

Perotrochus atlanticus (p. 31) and *Galeodes tyrrhena* (Plate 23/2) from the State Zoological Institute and Museum, Hamburg, Germany.

Scaphella junonia (Plate 40/2) and *Nannamoria parabola* (Plate 40/10) from the private collection of Jens and Chr. Hemmen, Wiesbaden, Germany.

FOREWORD

(with instructions on the use of the book)

This identification guide is intended for use by those interested in beautiful marine mollusc shells. It contains essential information for naturalists and collectors in this field.

Molluscs live in all the seas of the world. Their shells are washed ashore on all coasts, taken from the water by divers and fishermen, and sold commercially throughout the world. They fascinate by reason of their form and coloration, and many people want to know how to obtain them. It would be wrong to think that the whole range will be found on the next holiday trip. Not every stretch of coast will yield a good selection, and shells washed up by the sea are frequently badly eroded. Furthermore, many of the most attractive shells occur only in distant parts of the oceans, and often at great depths. These are usually known to the amateur from pictures. A collector cannot find them personally, but must buy them either from dealers or from fishermen who bring them up in their trawls (see the notes at the back of the book). As one's collection increases the problem arises of how to keep and arrange them. This will entail a knowledge of the scientific classification of the mollusc classes, because without the internationally used scientific nomenclature the collector will be unable to build up and arrange the shells correctly and, just as important, will not be in a position to communicate with other amateurs, collectors, dealers and scientists. This book provides information on all these topics, giving the basic facts on the anatomy of molluscs, on their relationships, habitats, distribution and nomenclature.

The Gastropoda (gastropods, such as snails, winkles, whelks), including those on land and in fresh waters, contain about 105,000 different living species. In addition, the Bivalvia (bivalve molluscs such as mussels, cockles, oysters, clams) have about 20,000 species, the chitons about 1000 species, the scaphopods 350, the cephalopods (octopuses, squids and cuttlefishes) 730. With this wealth of species it is obvious that this book has had to be selective. First, it deals only with marine mollusc and secondly the larger trade lists have been carefully studied to find out which shells are more or less readily obtainable. On this basis shells have been selected which are attractive and relatively inexpensive, and which are, at the same time, representative of the major groups in different parts of the world. Museum rarities and those that reach record prices have not been included. Finally, the book provides a guide to the rich literature of the group (monographs, etc.), which it can in no way replace, but for which it can act as a guide.

The systematic description of the different molluscs extends down to families and subfamilies, and gives some of their representative genera. With the short descriptive text given this part of the book should enable the collector to identify the groups to which his shells belong. For instance, a beginner will not know what type of shell is hidden under the name *Levenia*. Reference to the index of families and genera will lead to p. 60 where the reader will find that *Levenia* is a subgenus of *Cypraecassis* in the family Cassidae, superfamily

Tonnacea. Then, in Plate 23/8, one will find a photograph and description of *Cypraerassis (Levenia) coarctata* (Sowerby 1825).

The systematic position of a shell depends upon having a complete and accurate identification. The scientific name of a shell is followed by the name of the person who originally described the species and in this book this name is written out in full, thus avoiding abbreviations such as 'L.', 'Lam.', 'Sow.' and so on, which are only understood by the specialist. It is also interesting to note that most of the species known today were described by a relatively small number of naturalists. The addition of the date of the original description following immediately after the author's name may seem superfluous, but it will often prove quite essential when dealing with critical points of nomenclature.

Great difficulties often arise, however, when a species has been given more than one name, when the internationally recognised rules of nomenclature have not been adhered to and when specialists in the field have differing views and interpretations. Naturalists in different parts of the world may evaluate the same genera, subgenera and so on in different ways, and even in the same region a shell may be given more than one name.

The systematics used in this book are based primarily on modern monographs, such as R. C. Moore's *Treatise on Invertebrate Palaeonotology*, R. T. Abbott's *Indo-Pacific Mollusca*, together with various specialist papers published in scientific journals.

INTRODUCTION TO MOLLUSCAN SYSTEMATICS

As early as the time of Aristotle and other naturalists of the ancient world, the gastropods and bivalves were grouped together, on the basis of their hard shell, as Testacea or Ostracoderma. At first they were contrasted with another group of soft-bodied animals that lacked shells. This group, containing mainly the octopuses and squids and certain marine slugs without shells, was termed the Mollusca or Malakia. As a result of the comparative anatomical studies of Georges Cuvier (1796–1832), it was found that the internal anatomy of these two apparently dissimilar groups was in fact very similar. Accordingly, they were then placed in a single phylum known as Mollusca.

Mollis is Latin and *malakos* Greek for soft, and the study of molluscs is known as malacology. The study of the shells *only* is known as conchology. At first the families and genera of marine molluscs were, in fact, distinguished on the basis of the external characters of the shells. Hence, the early students of molluscs were known as conchologists and their collections, which were often extensive, as conchological cabinets. As improved methods of capture produced increasing numbers of living molluscs, it was found that very diverse animals might produce and live in similar shells, and conversely. Investigation of the soft parts of molluscs has resulted in improved methods of identification. In addition to the shell, which is as important as ever, studies of the tongue apparatus (radula), gills, reproductive organs, heart and nervous system also play a part. Information on the distribution of molluscs throughout the world comes from zoogeographical studies, and their distribution in geological time from palaeontology. Research on fossil shells provides evidence on the evolution of the species in earlier geological eras.

The purpose of systematics is to produce a method of arranging thousands of different animals, in the present context molluscs, in such a way that those showing similar characters are arranged close together. In some ways this can be compared to a specialised office filing system.

The naming of nomenclature of animals was started by the work of the Swedish naturalist Carl Linné or Linnaeus (1707–1778). He based his system on the species, and introduced what is now known as binomial nomenclature. Each species has two names: the first, denoting its genus (plural, genera) starts with a capital letter, the second or specific name is written with a lower case initial letter. Thus, the black lip pearl shell is *Pinctada margaritifera*. A related species in the genus *Pinctada* is the golden lip pearl shell, *Pinctada maxima* (see Plate 53). Some genera contain large numbers of species, but it is possible to have a genus containing only a single species.

Related genera are grouped together to form a family, and then several families may be classified together as a superfamily. An example of this system for the animal kingdom is shown overleaf in the graded varieties of typographic styles which are used in this book to indicate classification.

SUB-KINGDOM	METAZOA
PHYLUM	MOLLUSCA
Subphylum	Conchifera
CLASS	GASTROPODA
Subclass	Streptoneura
ORDER	MONOTOCARDIA
Suborder	Stenoglossa
SUPERFAMILY	MURICACEA
Family	Muricidae
SUBFAMILY	MURICINAE
Genus	*Murex*
Subgenus	*(Bolinus)*
Species	*cornutus*
Subspecies	*tumulosus*

A species comprises all those individual animals which:
a) under similar external conditions and in a comparable developmental stage show similar anatomical and physiological characters;
b) breed with one other by natural means and over several generations. Individuals of the same species produce offspring similar to themselves and these are fertile; mating between individuals of different species does not normally occur, but when it does the offspring are usually sterile.

RULES OF NOMENCLATURE

The scientific naming of animals and plants, including those that are extinct, is governed by certain rules. In the case of animals there is an International Commission for Zoological Nomenclature, which meets from time to time and issues opinions on ways of improving the details of nomenclature and of settling disputes involving the scientific names of animals.

In contrast to the 'folk' or popular names which are only of local interest, the scientific names of animals are used internationally and they are written in Latin (usually in *italic* type). Normally, the ending of the specific name agrees with the gender of the genus. Specific names ending in -*i* denote a masculine personal name, e.g. *sowerbyi*, of Sowerby or *lamarcki*, of Lamarck. Endings in *ae* denote a feminine name, e.g. *mariae*, of Maria or Mary, those ending in -*orum* denote groups of the male sex or of both sexes, those ending in -*arum* denote groups of the female sex.

When a genus is subdivided into subgenera, the name of the relevant subgenus is placed in brackets immediately after the generic name (and it has a capital initial letter). Example: *Charonia (Cymatiella) columnaria*. Sometimes the subgeneric name is the same as that of the genus. Example: *Charonia (Charonia) tritonis*.

When a species is subdivided into subspecies, the word denoting the subspecies is placed immediately after the specific name, not in brackets and written with a lower case initial letter. Example: *Charonia (Charonia) tritonis variegata*. The subspecies which contains the type specimen (see below) of the subdivided species carries the same name as the species and is known as the nominate subspecies. Example: *Charonia (Charonia) tritonis tritonis*. Subdivisions known as varieties or forms are denoted by inserting var. (= varietas) or f. (= forma) between the specific name and the varietal name. Example: *Oliva (Oliva) reticularis f. olorinella*.

By international agreement, all decisions on the valid name of a given species are based on the rule of priority. The author of the name is the person who first published a proper description of the species. Names given before the publication of Linné's *Systema Naturae*, 10th edition (1758) are invalid, and so are those of more recent date which are not binomial, and therefore transgress the rules of nomenclature. As already mentioned, the author's name is printed immediately after the specific name, and correctly speaking it should be followed by the date of the first description, thus *Haliotis tuberculata* Linné, 1758.

If for any reason the species is transferred to another genus, as the result of new investigations, then the original author's name is retained but it is now placed in brackets. Thus, *Cassis cornuta* (Linné, 1758) for the species which was originally described as *Buccinum cornutum* Linné, 1758.

The names of families end in – idae. This suffix is attached to the stem of the type genus. Thus, genus *Murex*, family Muricidae or genus *Trochus*, family Trochidae.

The names of subfamilies end in – inae, e.g. Muricinae.

Superfamilies end in – acea or – oidea, e.g. Muricacea or Muricoidea, Naticacea or Naticoidea.

TYPE SPECIMENS

When describing a new species the author chooses one of the specimens of the series in front of him and designates this as the 'holotype'. All the other specimens of the same series (type series) are designated 'paratypes'. These are frequently referred to more simply as type specimens or types. Only the holotype is the standard for the valid scientific name. The description of the new species must be published, and furthermore all the type material of the new species must be deposited in a public museum, so that it is available for comparison at a later date. If no holotype is designated and the description is based upon a series of types, then all these type specimens become syntypes. In nomenclatural practice, all the syntypes are of equal validity.

SYNONYMS

When one and the same species has been described under different names, only the older one is valid. The other names are known as synonyms. The most frequent reasons for synonymous designations are when for various reasons one and the same species is described and named twice or sometimes several times. This may be due to ignorance of the previous literature, a lack of specialist knowledge, errors, confusion and so on. Or it may happen because later knowledge has shown that a species originally considered to be uniform actually comprises one or more 'species'. By the strict application of the rule of priority for all species described since 1758, it may happen that a name appears which is practically unknown to anyone. Names from old publications may be accepted as binding by some naturalists, but rejected by others and replaced by new names. Very often the same species may be studied by more than one specialist, without them knowing of each other. Naturally, only the older name has priority. Let us take, for example, a shell that has been labelled as *Polinices pyriformis* (Récluz, 1844). Comparison of the shell itself with drawings in various specialist publications show that it was previously described as *Polinices tumidus* (Swainson, 1840). In view of the rule of priority, the shell should therefore be labelled as *Polinices tumidus*, while the name *P. pyriformis* must be regarded as a synonym. Conversely, it can happen that a given shell has been correctly labelled, but that it appears in the specialist literature under a synonym.

PHYLUM : MOLLUSCA

This phylum has two subphyla – Aculifera and Conchifera – and seven classes – the Aplacophora, Polyplacophora, Scaphopoda, Monoplacophora, Gastropoda, Bivalvia and Cephalopoda.

Molluscs are invertebrate animals with an unsegmented, basically bilaterally symmetrical body, generally consisting of head, foot, visceral hump (or mass) and mantle.

The head, which is not clearly separated from the body in the Polyplacophora and Bivalvia, may, in addition to the mouth, have various highly developed sense organs (eyes, antennae). Just inside the mouth lies the radula, an organ characteristic of most molluscs which, by moving back and forth, rasps off small particles of food. There are several different types of radula, adapted for a variety of feeding habits. Those molluscs which feed by filtering particles from the water do not have a radula.

The foot is a muscular organ used in locomotion. The visceral hump contains the alimentary canal, circulatory, excretory and reproductive organs. It may, as for example in the snails, be spirally twisted towards one side, thus producing asymmetry of the body. The heart lies in the dorsal region and consists of a ventricle and one or two auricles (the number corresponding with the number of gills in the mantle cavity. The ventricle opens posteriorly into a short vessel; this divides almost immediately into a large anterior aorta, which takes the blood forwards, and a smaller posterior vessel, which carries blood to the upper part of the visceral hump. The cavity round the heart is known as the pericardium.

The nervous system consists of interlinked ganglia (collections of nerve cells) which give off nerves to the various organs. The oesophagus is encircled by a ring of six ganglia. Thus, the sense organs of the head are served by the cerebral ganglia, the foot muscles by the pedal ganglia, and the mantle by the pleural ganglia. There are also buccal ganglia serving the mouth region and radula, and other ganglia more posteriorly which innervate the viscera. The nerves connecting the latter and the pleural ganglia form what is known as the visceral loop. In more primitive molluscs (Aculifera and certain gastropods) there are no ganglia, the nerve cells being distributed along the network of nerves. In more highly evolved forms the ganglia are united to form large complexes, and in the cephalopods this has led to the development of a 'brain'.

The integument enclosing the visceral mass forms a wide flap over the foot; this is known as the mantle or pallium. In its simplest form, the mantle hangs down from the back on either side of the back, with an open groove between the mantle edge and the foot. This groove becomes enlarged towards the rear to form the pallial or mantle cavity, which contains the respiratory organs (gills or lungs) and the osphradium, a sense organ thought to function in testing the water. In certain gastropods, torsion of the body results in the mantle cavity coming to lie towards the front of the animal. The alimentary canal and the excretory and reproductive ducts open into the mantle cavity.

The majority of molluscs live in the sea or in fresh water and use gills for respiration. Certain terrestrial gastropods, the pulmonates, breathe by lungs.

The early development varies considerably between the different classes. In most there is a characteristic larval stage (trochophore, veliger), but this may be much modified in some of the pulmonates. The majority of the cephalopods no longer have a free larval stage, and the embryo develops directly into a miniature version of the adult. There are also some live-bearing species among the molluscs.

It is characteristic of the molluscs that they have no internal supporting skeleton. The shell serves to protect the body against the outside world (against the attacks of enemies in the marine molluscs, against desiccation in the land snails), but it does not provide support or rigidity. The shell is, in fact, only a loosely attached part of the body, which has to be carried around. It is a product of secretion which by deposition of material can be thickened, enlarged and if necessary repaired, but it plays no part in the metabolism of the animal. The shell is also that part of a mollusc which lasts long after the animal itself has died, and often it provides the only clue that a species has lived in a given locality. In the case of many mollusc species, only the shell is known (in fossils only the petrified shell or the shell impression), and little or nothing is known of the morphology and habits of the animal.

In spite of advances in our knowledge of the anatomy of the parts, the shells still play an important part in the identification of the vast majority of molluscs; in a relatively small number of molluscs there is no shell.

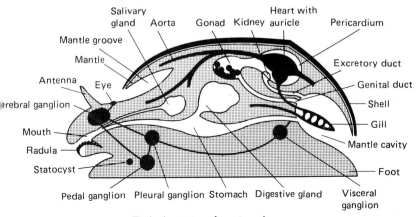

The basic structure of a gastropod.

Subphylum: Aculifera

These are exclusively marine molluscs with well-defined bilateral symmetry, a dorso-ventrally flattened, compressed to worm-like body. They possess no eyes, antennae or organs of equilibrium. The epithelial cells of the mantle form a protective outer skin in which small, pointed calcareous spicules are deposited. In addition, the Polyplacophora have eight calcareous plates on the dorsal side of the body. The subphylum comprises two classes, the Aplacophora and the Polyplacophora, and only the latter is dealt with here.

CLASS: POLYPLACOPHORA (Chitons) See Plate 64

This class contains about 1000 species most of which live in the western Pacific and off the coast of central America. They are more poorly represented in the Caribbean area, and there are a few species in European seas (mostly in the Mediterranean). The body outline is more or less oval, the ventral surface flattened and the dorsal surface arched. The back carries 8 overlapping plates, which have limited movement between one another. The plates are embedded at the edges in tough muscular mantle tissue, forming the girdle. The plates are numbered 1-8 from the front. The surface of the plates is usually sculptured with ridges and knobs, often arranged in distinct areas. On the ventral surface the chitons have a foot with a broad creeping sole. The gills, osphradium and the reproductive and excretory openings are in the mantle cavity. The mouth area is clearly separated from the surface of the foot. The anus lies at the rear. Chitons are mainly found in shallow water, often under rocks and shells. They become active at twilight and move around very slowly in search of food, which consists primarily of small algae. Occasionally they also take small invertebrate animals. The ability to take animal food allows a few species to live at depths down to 4000m (13,000ft).

ORDER: LEPIDOPLEURIDA
Family: Lepidopleuridae: genus: *Lepidopleurus* Leach, 1826; and others.
Family: Chloriplacidae: genus: *Chloriplax* Pilsbry, 1894.
Family: Hanleyidae: genus: *Hanleya* Gray, 1857.

ORDER: ISCHNOCHITONIDA
Family: Ischnochitonidae: genera: *Ischnochiton* Gray, 1847; *Lepidochitona* Gray, 1821; *Tonicella* Carpenter, 1873; and others.
Family: Callistoplacidae: genus: *Callistoplax* Carpenter, 1882; and others.
Family: Callochitonidae: genus: *Callochiton* Gray, 1847.
Family: Chaetopleuridae: genus: *Chaetopleura* Shuttleworth, 1853.
Family: Chitonidae: genera: *Chiton* Linné, 1758; *Liolophura* Pilsbry, 1893; and others.
Family: Mopalidae: genus: *Mopalia* Gray 1847; and others.
Family: Schizochitonidae: genus: *Schizochiton* Gray, 1847; and others.
Family: Schizoplacidae: genus: *Schizoplax* Dall, 1878.

ORDER: ACANTHOCHITONIDA
Family: Acanthochitonidae: genus: *Acanthochitona* Gray, 1821; and others.

Subphylum: Conchifera

This subphylum contains the majority of molluscs, and most of them have a shell. The Gastropoda form the largest class with about 105,000 known species, followed by the Bivalvia with about 20,000 species. The smaller classes are the Cephalopoda with about 730 species, the Scaphopoda with 350 and the Monoplacophora with 6 living species. The latter were first discovered in 1952 off the west coast of central America by the Danish Galathea Expedition, and further specimens were taken in 1958 and 1967 in the Red Sea and central Pacific in depths of about 3500m (11,500ft) (genus: *Neopilina* Lemche, 1957, about 30mm or 1·2in). Previously the Monoplacophora had only been known as fossils.

FORM AND COMPOSITION OF THE SHELL

The shell is secreted by the outer surface of the mantle, or more exactly by the mantle epithelium, a layer of cells with mucus-producing and secretory functions. The shell consists of varying proportions of organic and inorganic material, and is deposited in several layers. The outer layer or periostracum (often lacking) is a thin or thick, horny layer covering the other parts of the shell. It consists mainly on conchiolin, an organic substance related chemically to the chitin found in the exoskeletons of insects and crustaceans. The shell layers beneath the periostracum also contain some conchiolin.

The final shell contains about 10% (or less) organic matter and 90% (or more) inorganic deposits, mainly calcium carbonate which crystallises out as aragonite or calcite. Magnesium carbonate, phosphate and silicate occur in small amounts. These substances are removed from the surrounding water mainly by the outer surface of the mantle and the gills (in land snails they are acquired in the food and by absorption at the surface of the foot). The shell has a complex structure, with crystalline prisms of calcite and layers of mother-of-pearl. The material secreted at the mantle edge has crystals lying obliquely or at right angles to the shell surface, whereas the inner mother-of-pearl layer has thin flat plates of aragonite deposited in the conchiolin and parallel to the surface. The iridescent colours of mother-of-pearl are due to optical interference by these thin layers.

SHELL GROWTH AND ORNAMENT

The mollusc shell does not grow continuously, but periodically (at certain intervals of time). The upper layers are formed by tissue at the mantle edge, while the inner layers, overlain by the whole mantle surface, are secreted by all parts of the mantle surface. Growth therefore takes place in two directions – parallel to the edge (growth in size) and at right angles to the surface (growth in thickness). Growth at the edge proceeds at a faster rate in the young mollusc than in the old. The repeated periods of growth are recorded in the lines or ridges that lie parallel to the edge. At certain times it can be observed that shell formation has stopped or that new structural elements (folds or tubercles) have been secreted. As growth continues, these irregularities may produce what is known as ornament, or sculpture, on the upper surface of the shell. In the bivalves, the ornament may take the form of thickened concentric lines or ridges; in the gastropods it often occurs as axial ribs or varices (singular: varix). Smooth intermediate spaces show that during active shell deposition the mantle edge was lying unfolded over relatively wide areas of shell. Usually, however, the mantle lies in folds, so that in addition to the concentric and axial ornament just mentioned there may also be radial ribs (in the bivalves) or spiral stripes (spiral ornament) in the gastropods. When both axial and spire sculptural features are deposited, the result is a net-like pattern (reticulation).

In some gastropod groups (Cypraeidae, Olividae, Marginellidae), the two lateral lobes of the mantle extend so far over the shell that they almost completely enclose it. In this way, shell substance is secreted on to the surface of the shell in the form of a smooth enamel-like layer, which frequently shows a colour pattern. As the mantle lobes almost completely enclose the shell, they prevent further growth, and the shiny enamel-like surface layer is retained throughout life.

Shell surfaces. Left: strongly ornamented wi' varices *(Hexaplex)*. Below left: no ornament, b with fine growth lines *(Natica)*. Below right: with very shiny enamel-like layer *(Cypraea)*. For spir axial and reticulate ornament, see photographs c pages 30, 31, 33 and 37.

Many details concerning the periodicity of this growth process are still not understood. For instance, the relationship between the number of lines of growth and the age of the shell is not clear. It is known, however, that the growth periods sometimes follow one another very rapidly (in the dog whelks every two days under favourable conditions). In addition, shell formation may be stimulated or inhibited by external and internal factors, such as temperature, nutrition and egg formation. When conditions are unfavourable shell formation stops completely.

Damage to the shell can be repaired provided the relevant mantle tissue has not been destroyed and the affected area is still within reach of the mantle. During the period of repair, calcium and other materials are transported from other parts of the body to the epithelial cells of the repairing mantle.

COLOUR AND PATTERN FORMATION

During the growth of the shell, pigments produced in a special part of the mantle epithelium, are deposited in the calcareous layer lying directly beneath the periostracum. Pigment formation is partly dependent upon the food. The pigments of molluscs include melanins and porphyrins. As in the case of the shell ornament so the colour pattern may also be the result of periodic activity. If the epithelial cells of the mantle edge secrete pigment continuously then spiral or radial lines or bands will be laid down, but if pigment secretion is periodic then spots and flecks will appear on the shell. When the whole of the mantle edge is secreting pigment at the same rate the shell will acquire uniform coloration, but if this process is interrupted at intervals then axial or concentric lines of pigment will appear. If the zonal pigmentation changes during growth then colours will be deposited in wavy bands or as angular markings and so on. In many cowries (Family: Cypraeidae) the area between where the two mantle lobes approach one another in the mid-dorsal line can be clearly recognised. This dorsal line may be white or only very slightly pigmented.

Little is known about the significance of shell coloration in molluscs. In a few cases, the appearance of the shell may match the surroundings – so that one can speak of camouflage. For example, a pattern of contrasting lines may help to break up the outlines of the shell and so make it more difficult to discern in its natural surroundings. In some cases the colour pattern lies more or less hidden beneath the periostracum.

FUNCTION OF THE SHELL

In many aquatic molluscs the shell protects against the attacks of enemies, particularly when it carries spines, tubercles or sharp lamellae. In terrestrial molluscs the shell protects against water loss leading to desiccation. In most cases the animal can withdraw completely or at least partly into the shell. In some gastropods (e.g. *Acanthina*, *Busycon*) and bivalves (e.g. wood-borers), the shell also serves as a tool, in others as on aid to locomotion, whether in crawling (e.g. Aporrhais) or in swimming (*Pecten*, *Lima*). In certain cephalopods (e.g. *Nautilus*, *Spirula*), the shell is used to maintain or adjust buoyancy.

CLASS: GASTROPODA

These are mainly asymmetrical animals with the typical mollusc division of the body into head, foot, visceral hump and mantle. They mostly have a spiral or cap-shaped shell (in some the shell is much reduced or even absent), and they usually have a radula (see below). The two classes are distinguished by their nervous system. In the Streptoneura (about 57,000 species), the visceral loop of the nervous system has become twisted into a figure of eight shape and the mantle cavity has one or two gills which lie in front of the heart (hence the name Prosobranchia or prosobranchs, meaning 'front gills'). In the second class, the Euthyneura (about 48,000 species) the visceral nerve loop is not twisted (de-torsion) and the mantle cavity has either a single gill lying behind the heart (hence the name Opisthobranchia or opisthobranchs, meaning 'rear gills'; about 13,000 species) or a lung (the Pulmonata or pulmonates with about 35,000 species).

These groups can only be understood in relation to the torsion of the visceral mass. Primitive gastropods have the mantle cavity at the rear of the body, but in later forms the visceral hump twists round (over the right side) so that the mantle cavity with its contained organs comes to lie towards the front of the animal. The gills now lie in front of the heart, so these gastropods are known as prosobranchs ('front gills'). Most recent marine gastropods belong to this group. Later when the shell, originally carried symmetrically on the centre of the back, moves over to the right, the organs on the right side of the mantle become more and more reduced. In the more primitive gastropods (families Pleurotomariidae, Scissurellidae, Haliotidae), there are still two gills (ctenidia) with their associated osphradia (sense organs) and two kidneys. Finally, the organs on the right side disappear completely. Corresponding with the two gills, the more primitive prosobranchs have a heart with two auricles; these are the Diotocardia. The more advanced prosobranchs have lost the right gill and the right auricle and these form the Monotocardia.

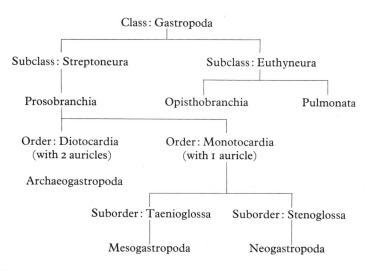

ORGANIZATION OF THE GASTROPOD BODY

The head, usually elongated and somewhere snout-like, has the mouth and one or two pairs of tentacles which often carry eyes at the tips or base. The foot, sometimes divided by a transverse furrow into a front part (propodium) and rear part (metapodium), is usually in the form of a flat, creeping sole (exceptions are gastropods of the families Strombidae and Vermetidae, and the group Pteropoda). In primitive prosobranchs the foot may have a fold of tissue running round it which carries numerous sensory cells. It often has tentacular processes in front and behind or lateral lobes (epipodia), which in some opisthobranchs fuse over the shell, in others are used for swimming. In most prosobranchs the foot has a cover, known as the operculum, which serves to close the shell aperture when the animal has withdrawn, but it may also have other functions (see below).

The mantle cavity of the gastropods that draw in water for respiration opens in the form of a slit. In the more highly developed prosobranchs, the slit becomes drawn out to form a tube of varying length, the siphon. This often lies protected in a groove of the shell, known as the siphonal canal. The visceral hump is spirally coiled.

The alimentary canal starts with a simple, muscular proboscis, which may become much elongated and retractile in the more highly evolved carnivorous prosobranchs.

The mouth leads to an enlarged pharynx which houses the radula, a ribbon of chitin bearing transverse rows of tiny teeth. As the teeth wear out they are replaced by new teeth further back on the ribbon. The number and form of these teeth are characteristic for the different prosobranch groups. The middle tooth of each row is known as the central or rachidial tooth. On either side of this there are the lateral teeth and beyond them the marginals. Thus:

a) in the rhipidoglossan radula there is a large central tooth, flanked on each side by five laterals and numerous closely packed marginals (Archaeogastropoda, with the exception of the Patellacea);

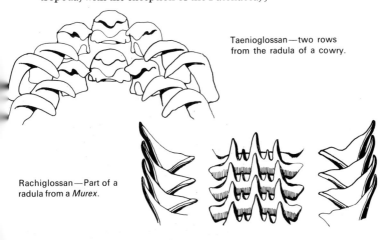

Taenioglossan—two rows from the radula of a cowry.

Rachiglossan—Part of a radula from a *Murex*.

b) in the docoglossan radula there is one usually small central tooth, flanked by 1-3 laterals and a few (3 at the most) hooked marginals, (Patellacea);

c) in the taenioglossan radula the central tooth is flanked on each side by one lateral and two marginal teeth (characteristic of the majority of the Mesogastropoda);

d) the ptenoglossan radula has no central tooth but a series of several uniform, pointed teeth (Epitoniacea);

e) the stenoglossan or rachiglossan radula has one central tooth and one lateral tooth on each side (most Neogastropoda);

f) in the toxoglossan radula each row has only two teeth of which only one is in use at a time. These teeth are very long and pointed, with venom channels and barbs, and are not firmly fixed to the basal plate. The teeth can therefore be individually transferred to the proboscis and ejected into the prey as a sting (Conacea).

The teeth of the radula become worn by use and they have to be constantly renewed from behind by posterior rows stored in the radula sac. The replacement rate varies with the age of the animal. Depending upon circumstances, complete replacement might take about 40 days.

The sense organs of gastropods are relatively simple. Tactile stimuli are perceived by the whole surface of the mantle and foot, and particularly by the tentacles. In addition, the tentacles are also thought to have an olfactory function. The osphradium is a sense organ located in the mantle cavity close to the gill; in the Archaeogastropoda and Mesogastropoda it consists of sense cells arranged in groups, in the Neogastropoda it is a complex organ with comb-like lamellae and hair cells that react to chemical stimuli. It has also been held that the osphradium is used to indicate the amount of suspended matter in the water. Eyes vary from a simple open visual pit (in Patellacea), to closed eyes with a lens, found on either side of the head and also on the tentacles. These can perceive light and darkness, as well as form. The sense of balance is served by organs known as statocysts. Each of these is a tiny cavity lined with sensory cells and filled with fluid containing calcareous particles.

The gastropods show the most varied forms of sexual differentiation from complete bisexuality to hermaphroditism. The prosobranchs are mostly bisexual, the opisthobranchs and pulmonates hermaphrodite. In between, there are forms (e.g. *Calyptraea*, *Crepidula*, *Crucibulum*) which change sex, young animals being male, fully grown ones female, or only a certain proportion of the males within a population may change to females (e.g. in *Patella vulgata*). In many of the higher prosobranchs, fertilisation is internal and the males have a penis, usually on the head behind the right tentacle, and in some cases this may be resorbed after the period of copulation. In other groups, the eggs and sperms are shed into the surrounding water where fertilisation takes place. With the exception of the few live-bearing species and of the pulmonates, gastropod development involves several larval stages (planktonic trochophore and veliger, and creeping stages). The simple, ciliated trochophore larva of some archaeogastropods is free-swimming. The veliger larva is so-called from the ciliated 'sail lobes' (velum). A veliger stage occurs in many prosobranchs and some opisthobranchs. Most pulmonates and opisthobranchs do not leave the egg capsule until they have reached the creeping stage.

DISTRIBUTION

Gastropods occur in the sea, in fresh waters and on land. In addition to water, or at least damp conditions, the other principal environmental factors affecting these molluscs are light, temperature and salinity. The prosobranchs and opisthobranchs are mostly marine (only a few prosobranch groups occur in fresh water) and they live primarily on the sea floor. Their geographical distribution extends from the tropics to the arctic and antarctic regions. Their vertical distribution extends from the spray zone of cliffs and reefs down to the deep sea. The greatest numbers of gastropod species occur on rocky, sandy and muddy bottoms in the littoral (seashore) and sublittoral. The number of species decreases in deeper water. A few specialised gastropods are pelagic, living in the upper waters of the sea. The pulmonates are mainly terrestrial, although some live in fresh water and a few along the sea coasts. The adjoining table shows the main gastropod groups found in the various zoogeographic areas of the world.

GEOGRAPHICAL DISTRIBUTION OF MARINE GASTROPODS

Area	Extent and dominant forms
Arctic	Circumpolar (*Ancistrolepis*, *Volutopsius*, *Sipho*, etc.)
North Atlantic boreal (sub-arctic)	Northern Norway, Iceland, southern Greenland, Hudson Bay, Labrador, Newfoundland, eastern coast U.S.A. to Cape Cod. (*Boreotrophon*, *Buccinum*, *Neptunea*, etc.)
Celtic	Baltic Sea, North Sea, Irish Sea, English Channel, Brittany (*Buccinum*, *Littorina*)
Mediterranean-Lusitanian	Mediterranean Sea and adjacent Atlantic (Biscay to Cape Verde), Canaries (*Cerithium*, *Galeodea*, *Murex*, etc.)
West African	Cape Verde to Walfisch Bay (*Cymbium*, *Marginella*, etc.)
South African	Cape Frio (S.W. coast) to Durban (*Bullia*, *Burnupena*, *Patella*, etc.)
Indo-Pacific	East African coast from Durban to Red Sea, Persian Gulf, Arabian Sea, Bay of Bengal, China Sea, Yellow Sea, tropical Pacific, including Hawaii (*Angaria*, *Conus*, *Cypraea*, *Lambis*, *Ovula*, *Strombus*, *Turbo*, etc.)
Japonic	Eastern coast of Korea, Sea of Japan, Japanese islands except Hokkaido (boreal) and Kiushio (Pacific) (*Babylonia*, *Latiaxis*, *Lischkeia*, *Siphonalia*, *Thatcheria*, etc.)

Area	Extent and dominant forms
Australian	Northern coast (tropical), western and eastern coasts (subtropical), southern coast (warm and cold temperate) (*Amoria, Phasianella, Scutus*, etc.)
New Zealand	Coasts of North Island (warm temperate), South Island, Stewart and Chatham Islands (cold temperate), Antipodes Island, Macquarie Island (subantarctic)
North Pacific boreal (sub-arctic)	Okhotsk Sea, Kamtchatka, Hokkaido, Bering Sea, Alaska, Aleutian Islands (*Boreotrophon*, etc.)
Oregon	Alexander Archipelago, Western coast U.S.A. to Point Conception (*Collisella, Tegula, Lottia*, etc.)
Californian	Point Conception to Lower California (Western coast) (*Haliotis, Forreria, Megathura, Norrisia*, etc.)
Panamic	Gulf of California, western coast central America to Ecuador (Punta Negra) (*Muricanthus, Oliva, Malea*, etc.)
Peruvian	Western coast South America from Punta Negra to Capo Taitao, southern Chile (*Concholepas, Talopena*, etc.)
Virginia-Carolina	Eastern coast U.S.A., Cape Cod to Florida and Texas (*Busycon, Fasciolaria, Melongena, Murex*, etc.)
Caribbean	Southern Florida, Bermuda, Antilles, Gulf of Mexico (except northern coast), Caribbean Sea, coast of Venezuela and Brazil to Salvador (*Cittarium, Fasciolaria, Melongena, Perotrochus, Purpura, Strombus*, etc.)
Patagonian	South American east coast from Salvador (Bahia) to Gulf of San Jorge (*Adelomelon, Agaronia, Zidona*, etc.)
Magellanic	Coasts of Patagonia and southern Chile, Tierra del Fuego, Falkland Islands, Crozet, Kerguelen (*Nacella, Trophon*, etc.)
Antarctic	South Shetlands, South Orkneys, South Georgia, South Sandwich Islands (*Margarella, Trophon, Submargarita*, etc.)

Habitat	Characteristics of habitat
Eulittoral	Extending from extreme high water (spray zone) to extreme low water. Rocky, sandy and muddy bottoms (coral reef surfaces in the tropics). Periods of exposure to sun, rain and wave action. Mainly hardy gastropods with good powers of attachment, or those that burrow in the substrate.
Continental Shelf	Extending from extreme low water to the edge of the Continental Slope, an area of shallow sea down to about 200m (66oft). Sufficient light for growth of green, brown and red algae down to about 60m (200ft). A variety of substrates (calcareous algae, coral sand, mud, etc.) Gastropods in the algal zone mostly vegetarian, those on other substrates mainly carnivorous.
Continental Slope	Extending from the edge of the Shelf to depths of about 3500-4000m (11,500ft-13,100ft). No effective light below about 400m (1300ft), hence a lack of plants. A reduced number of gastropod species, mostly with small, dull shells, and mainly carnivores or detritus feeders.
Deep-sea (abyssal)	Extending from 4000 to 6000m, or about 13,100-20,000ft (in the western Pacific to over 10,000m or 32,800ft). No light or plants, extreme water pressures, low temperatures, high carbon dioxide values. Few gastropods, mostly carnivorous or detritus feeding species with small, thin, white or colourless shells.

MORPHOLOGY OF THE SHELL

In some of the pulmonate and opisthobranch groups the shell is much reduced. Almost all the prosobranchs have a well developed shell. Special terms have been evolved to describe the differences in shell form and a knowledge of these is essential if one is to understand the descriptive text.

One can regard the original gastropod shell as a long tapering tube which has become coiled. If the walls of such a coiled tube touch one another along the axis of the spiral then they will form a spindle or columella, and in many shells this can be seen in the area of the aperture. The columella may be smooth, twisted, folded or even calloused. The spiral line where the coils touch externally is known as the suture. If the walls of the tube do not touch one another internally they will leave a space and this can be seen at the base of the shell in the form of an opening known as the umbilicus, which may be narrow, broad, slit-like or partly or completely covered.

The oldest part of the shell is the tip or apex. Growth of the shell starts with a small, usually roundish nucleus. The coils of the apex may be paucispiral – with a few (1-2) whorls – or multispiral (with 3 or more coils). In some species, the apex is later lost. At the opposite end to the apex, the base of the shell is in many species extended to form a siphonal canal to accommodate the respiratory siphon.

The opening through which the soft body of the mollusc emerges from the shell is known as the aperture. It may be circular, oval, angular or in the form of a narrow or broad slit. The aperture has an inner lip and an outer lip. The outer lip may be sharp-edged (simple), or thickened to form a lip which may internally be smooth, folded or toothed, and externally furnished with calluses, tubercles or spines. The inner lip has an upper or parietal area formed by the surface of the last coil, and a lower columellar area. Both parts of the inner lip may also be calloused.

In most gastropods the outer and inner lips are more or less clearly distinguishable from one another. The aperture is often extended to form a siphonal canal through which the respiratory siphon can be extended; this occurs in several of the more advanced Neogastropoda, e.g. in Muricidae, Buccinidae and others. This canal may be long, short, narrow, broad, straight, curved or (rarely) closed to form a tube. In some gastropods (*Bursa*, *Conus*),

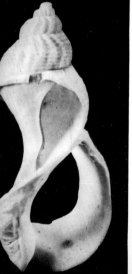

Left: columella in the broken shell of a Common Whelk, *Buccinum undatum* Linné, 1758.
Centre: umbilicus on the underside of *Natica* (*Naticarius*) *cruentata* Gmelin, 1791.
Right: columellar folds in *Amoria* (*Amorena*) *undulata* (Lamarck, 1804).

the upper end of the aperture has a groove which serves as an outlet for the water used in respiration and for the faeces. In certain of the less highly evolved groups (Pleurotomariidae, Scissurellidae), the outer lip of the aperture has a slit, the anal sinus, which becomes closed as the shell grows and

Spire forms; top left: evolute in *Pugilina* (*Hemifusus*) *colossea* (Lamarck, 1816); top centre: involute in *Hydatina albocincta* (v.d. Hoeven, 1839); top right: convolute in *Ovula costellata* (Lamarck, 1810); centre; devolute in *Vermicularia spirata* Philippi. 1836.
bottom left: circular in *Architectonica perspectiva* (Linné, 1758); bottom right: ear-shaped in *Haliotis corrugata* Wood, 1828.

remains recognisable on the older coils as a slit band. Some of the Turridae also have an anal sinus with the same function. In the Fissurellidae the anal sinus is in the form of a slit at the front edge of the shell or of a hole in front of the apex, while in the ormers (Haliotidae) the shell has a row of holes.

The distance between the apex and base of the shell is known as the shell height, while the distance between the outermost edge of the outer lip and the opposite side (the whorl with the largest diameter) is the shell breadth. In most cases the whorls form a spiral shell. The whorls lie either in one plane (planspiral) or rise steeply to form a conical or tower-like structure. The number of whorls varies from species to species but is usually more or less constant within a species. The total of whorls, with the exception of the last or body whorl, is known as the spire. The commonest type of shell is evolute, in which the whorls only touch one another on the inner side, where they form the columella. A shell is involute if the whorls enclose it so completely at the sides that the whorls at the upper end can only just be seen, e.g. in *Cypraea*, *Bulla*, *Cychlina* and others. A shell is convolute if the body whorl completely encloses the spire, e.g. in *Ovula*, *Trivia*, *Simnia*, and it is devolute if the coils form an open spiral without touching one another, e.g. in *Vermicularia*, *Caecum*, *Siliquaria*). Many shells are described in terms of well-known objects such as ears, cones, circles, barrels or horns.

With a few exceptions gastropod shells are dextrally coiled. This means that if the shell is held with the apex uppermost and the base furthest from the observer then the coils run in a clockwise direction. Sinistral coiling only occurs in a few species, e.g. *Busycon contrarium*, or as a rare abnormality in species that normally have dextrally coiled shells. If the coiling of a shell runs downwards from the apex (this is the commonest) the spire is known as orthostroph, if it runs upwards it is hypostroph. In some gastropods

Barrel-shaped in *Tonna galea* (Linné, 1758). Horn-shaped in *Neptunea despecta* (Linné, 1758).

 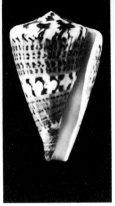 

(*Melampus, Acteon, Cychlina, Architectonica*) the coil direction changes during the course of development: the embryonic parts coil sinistrally, the later parts of the shell dextrally, giving a heterostroph spire. Alloiostroph means that the coils do not form a continuous spiral (*Vermetus, Caecum*).

Mention has already been made of the periodic nature of shell growth and the formation of various types of surface sculpture or ornament. The first part of the shell is the protoconch and this is usually smooth, but the later growth of the shell often shows extensive ornament resulting from the folding of the mantle edge and the timing of shell production. The longitudinal or axial ornament of a gastropod shell may comprise growth lines, folds, ribs, varices and lamellae. The spiral ornament includes a variety of ridges, tubercles or knobs, and other protuberances, as well as furrows and grooves. Both axial and

The general appearance of a spiral shell can be described in terms of the relation of length to breadth, and also by comparison with known objects, e.g. awl-shaped, screw-shaped, elongate, wedge-shaped, ovate, spherical, flat or disc-shaped. If the base is flat with the greatest depth below and tapering fairly uniformly then the shell is conical, but if it is broad above and pointed below it is obconical. Spindle shapes result from the presence of a siphonal canal. Above left: top-shaped (turbinate) in *Turbo petholatus* Linné, 1758; above centre: obconical in *Conus (Rhizoconus) capitaneus* Linné, 1758; above right: wedge-shaped in *Tectus dentatus* (Forskål, 1775); below left: conical in *Tectus (Rochia) niloticus* (Linné, 1767); below centre: coeloconoid in *Calliostoma (Maurea) tigris* (Gmelin, 1791); below right above: cyrtoconoid in *Gibbula (Steromphala) cineraria* (Linné, 1758); bottom right below: angular in *Gibbula magus* (Linné, 1758).

Left: screw-shaped in *Turritella terebra* (Linné, 1758); centre: spindle-shaped in *Fusinus salisburyi* Fulton, 1930; right: club-shaped in *Murex (Bolinus) cornutus* Linné, 1758.

spiral ornament may occur on the same shell, and if they are both equally prominent they will produce a net-like or reticulate pattern, sometimes with tubercles or spines at the intersections.

Many prosobranchs have a usually horny operculum (calcareous in some Archaeogastropoda, e.g. Turbinidae, Phasianellidae) which is attached towards the rear of the foot and serves to close the shell when the animal has withdrawn into it. The outline of the operculum usually corresponds to the aperture of the shell. It may be formed from a central or from an excentric nucleus. Horny opercula sometimes have lateral processes (apophyses) which help to grip the columella. In some species of *Strombus* the operculum, which is pointed and clawed, can be swung laterally and used as a weapon.

Subclass: Streptoneura (Prosobranchia)

ORDER: DIOTOCARDIA

Gastropods with primitive characters, 2 auricles in the heart (except Patellacea), 2 gills with a double row of filaments (Pleurotomariacea), or the right one may be lost in the Trochacea and Neritacea, which do, however, retain the 2 auricles. In the foot the nerve cells are not concentrated into ganglia. Foot usually with epipodium (carrying numerous sense cells). The shell is normally spirally coiled, but in some is simply conical in shape. Aperture is round. In primitive forms there is a slit at the outer edge of the

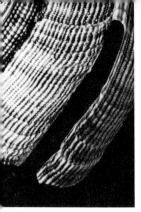

Left and centre: anal sinus in
Pleurotomaria and *Scissurella*.
Right: row of perforations in *Haliotis*.

Perotrochus atlanticus Rios and Matthews,
1968, a recently discovered species from
the coasts of Brazil, showing the anal sinus.

aperture (*Pleurotomaria, Scissurella*), or at the front edge of the shell in conical forms such as *Emarginula*. This slit allows the faeces to pass out and also acts as an outlet for water from the respiratory current. The same functions are served by a row of holes in ormers (*Haliotis*) and by a single apical hole in the keyhole limpets (*Fissurella*). The interior of the shell has a layer of mother-of-pearl, which in the less primitive forms may be partly or completely replaced by a porcelain-like layer (Acmaeidae). These gastropods feed mainly on plants (seaweeds and microscopic algae) which they rasp from the rocks with the radula. The radula is rhipidoglossan (Pleurotomariacea, Fissurellacea, Trochacea, Neritacea, Cocculinacea), or docoglossan (Patellacea).

SUPERFAMILY: PLEUROTOMARIACEA
See Plate 1

From the evolutionary standpoint this is the oldest group, and representatives occur as fossils as far back as the Cambrian age. Shell with numerous whorls, a mother-of-pearl layer, and with a slit band or a row of holes.

Family: Pleurotomariidae

Shell large and conical, the outer edge of the aperture with a slit which closes up during shell growth and on the older whorls can be recognised as a slit band.

31

Operculum horny. A few living species in the deep sea, in the western Atlantic, off southern Africa, Japan and the Moluccas. Genera: *Entemnotrochus* Fischer, 1885; *Mikadotrochus* Lindholm, 1927; *Perotrochus* Fischer, 1885. (The genus *Pleurotomaria* as described by Defrance, 1826 and numerous other genera are only known as fossils).

Family: Haliotidae (Ormers, Abalones)

Shell roundish-oval, with a flat spire. Body whorl wide with a peripheral row of holes which only remain open in the more recently deposited parts of the shell. Sensory tentacle-like processes protrude through these holes. Operculum absent. This family has about 100 species, widely distributed, but mainly in the western Pacific (Japan and Australia), and off California and southern Africa. They live in the lower littoral zones and in shallow water, attaching themselves firmly to rocks with the powerful suctorial foot. The flesh is edible and the shells are prized for their beauty. One genus: *Haliotis* Linné, 1758 (subgenera *Euhaliotis* Wenz, 1938; *Exohaliotis* Cotton and Godfrey, 1933; *Marinauris* Iredale, 1927; *Notohaliotis* Cotton & Godfrey, 1933; *Ovinotis* Cotton, 1943; *Padollus* Montfort, 1810; *Paua* Fleming, 1952; *Sanhaliotis* Iredale, 1929; *Schismotis* Gray, 1856; *Sulculus* H. & A. Adams, 1854).

Family: Scissurellidae

Shell very small (2-5mm), translucent white, with only a few whorls and usually with reticulate ornament. Umbilicus present. Interior with a thin mother-of-pearl layer. The outer or palatal lip has an open slit which closes over in the older whorls and becomes a slit band. Operculum horny. This family has worldwide distribution in deep water, even in the coldest seas. Genera: *Scissurella* d'Orbihny, 1823 = *Schismope* Jeffreys, 1856 (subgenus: *Anatoma* Woodward, 1859): *Incisura* Hedley, 1904 (subgenus: *Scissurona* Iredale, 1924); *Sinezona* Finlay, 1927.

SUPERFAMILY: FISSURELLACEA
See Plate 2

Shell conical (patelloid or limpet-like), bilaterally symmetrical, with an oval base and a front marginal slit (emargination) or a hole in front of or at the apex of the shell. This hole may be round, oval, elongate, like a keyhole or divided by a septum. Upper surface white or coloured, usually with reticulate ornament. Shell interior like porcelain, with one more or less distinct muscle impression, shaped like a horseshoe with the opening facing forwards. Operculum absent. Living in the lower tidal zones and upper sublittoral, mainly in warmer seas. These are vegetarian gastropods which become active at night when they browse algae from rocks.

Family: Fissurellidae (Keyhole limpets)

This family contains about 30 genera and over 500 species in three subfamilies. EMARGINULINAE: shell small, colourless, with a marginal slit at the front or a hole in the middle. Genera: *Emarginula* Lamarck, 1801 (subgenera: *Semperia*

Crosse, 1867; *Subzeidora* Iredale, 1924): *Clypidina* Gray, 1847 (subgenus: *Montfortula* Iredale, 1915): *Emarginella* Pilsbry, 1891; *Hemitoma* Swainson, 1840 (subgenera: *Montfortia* Recluz, 1843; *Montfortista* Iredale, 1929); *Notomella* Cotton, 1957; *Puncturella* Lowe, 1827 (subgenera: *Cranopsis* A. Adams, 1860; *Fissurisepta* Seguenza, 1863; *Rixa* Iredale, 1924); *Rimula* Defrance, 1927; *Scutus* Montfort, 1810 (subgenus: *Nannoscutum* Iredale, 1937): *Tugali* Gray, 1843 (subgenus: *Parmophoridea* Wenz, 1938); *Zeidora* A. Adams, 1860 (subgenus: *Nesta* H. Adams, 1870).

DIODORINAE: hole at shell apex, its internal callus truncated at the rear. Genera: *Diodora* Gray, 1821 (subgenera: *Austroglyphis* Cotton & Godfrey, 1934; *Elegidion* Iredale, 1924; *Megathura* Pilsbry, 1890; *Stromboli* Berry, 1954.

FISSURELLINAE: hole at shell apex, its internal callus not truncated. Shell usually more colourful than in the preceding group. Genera: *Fissurella* Bruguière, 1789 (subgenera: *Balboaina* Perez-Farfante, 1943; *Carcellesia* Perez-Farfante, 1952; *Clypidella* Swainson, 1840; *Cremides* H. & A. Adams, 1854); *Amblychilepas* Pilsbry, 1890; *Cosmetalepas* Iredale, 1924; *Fissurellidea* d'Orbigny, 1841 (subgenus: *Pupillaea* G. B. Sowerby, 1835): *Lucapina* G. B. Sowerby, 1835; *Lucapinella* Pilsbry, 1890; *Macroschisma* G. B. Sowerby, 1839 (subgenera: *Dolichoschisma* Iredale, 1940; *Forolepas* Iredale, 1940); *Megatebennus* Pilsbry, 1890.

SUPERFAMILY: PATELLACEA
See Plates 3 and 4

Shell small to large, conical, varying in height, with an oval base somewhat narrower in front and a forward-directed apex, often eroded by wave action. Shell surface smooth or with radial ribs, and showing concentric growth lines. Interior often brightly coloured with a horse-shaped muscle impression, open at the front. Radula docoglossan, differing from the rhipidoglossan type of other Archaeogastropoda in the much smaller number of teeth. No anal sinus at the edge of the shell. Primary gills have disappeared and are replaced by secondary structures in the form of a ring of gill filaments known as a gill

Anal openings (for the inflow and outflow of the respiratory current and for the removal of faeces) in *Scutus* (an indentation in the shell margin) (left), in *Emarginula* (a long notch, much enlarged) (centre), in *Fissurella* (top right) showing the underside of the perforation surrounded by a callus; in *Diodora* (bottom right), a similar perforation.

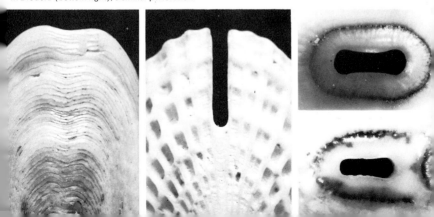

cordon. Operculum absent. These gastropods live in the upper and middle tidal zones, remaining firmly attached by day, moving out to browse algae by night, but always returning to the home site. These homes can often be found as shallow depressions in the rocks. In some places the edge of the shell may fit the unevenness of the substrate. The direction of the browsing paths changes each time the limpet moves out and when the algal growth is rich each sortie may only extend a few centimetres. Studies have shown that there is a direct relationship between the position of the home in the intertidal zone and the height of the shell. Individuals living low down on the shore have lower, shield-like shells, whereas those higher up where there are longer periods of desiccation have taller shells. Probably the individuals in the drier position require more storage space for water needed in respiration in order to survive the periods when the tide is out. Limpets live on all types of rocky shore, and there are several hundred species. The families differ in the structure of the radula and the form of the gills.

Family: Patellidae (True limpets)

With a complete circle of gill-like respiratory organs (gill cordon) round the mantle rim. Shell interior weakly to brightly iridescent. There are two subfamilies. PATELLINAE: *Patella* Linné, 1758 (subgenera: *Ancistromesus* Dall, 1871; *Cymbula* H. & A. Adams, 1854; *Olana* H. & A. Adams, 1854; *Patellastra* Monterosato, 1884; *Patellidea* Thiele, 1891; *Patellona* Thiele, 1891; *Penepatella* Iredale, 1929; *Scutellastra* H. & A. Adams, 1854 = *Patellanax* Iredale, 1924): *Helcion* Montfort, 1810 (subgenera: *Ansates* Sowerby, 1839; *Patinastra* Thiele, 1891; *Rhodopetala* Dall, 1921). NACELLINAE: shell interior often iridescent. Genera: *Nacella* Schumacher, 1817 (subgenus: *Patinigera* Dall, 1905); *Cellana* H. Adams, 1869.

Left: Deep scar left by *Patelloida nigrosulcata* (Reeve, 1855) on the shell of *Patella laticostata* (Blainville, 1825). Right: variations in shell height in *Patella vulgata* Linné, 1758.

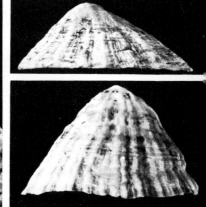

Family: Acmaeidae

Externally these are scarcely distinguishable from the Patellidae. The shell interior is porcelain-like, non-iridescent, and often coloured, with a strikingly patterned shell border. Genera: *Acmaea* Eschscholtz, 1833 (subgenera: *Actinoleuca* Oliver, 1926; *Asteracmea* Oliver, 1926; *Atalacmea* Iredale, 1915; *Chiazacmea* Oliver, 1926; *Collisella* Dall, 1871; *Collisellina* Dall, 1871; *Conacmea* Oliver, 1926; *Conoidacmea* Habe, 1944; *Kikukozara* Habe, 1944; *Naccula* Iredale, 1924; *Notoacmea* Iredale, 1915; *Parvacmea* Iredale, 1915; *Patelloida* Quoy & Gaimard, 1834; *Radiacmea* Iredale, 1915; *Subacmea* Oliver, 1926; *Tectura* Gray, 1847; *Thalassacmea* Oliver, 1926); *Lottia* Gray, 1833; *Pectinodonta* Dall, 1882; *Potamacmaea* Peile, 1922; *Scurria* Gray, 1847.

Family: Lepetidae

Small, eyeless limpets with thin, usually colourless shells with a smooth or slightly ribbed upper surface. They have no gills and respiration is by a mantle groove lined with cilia. Mainly from deep water or polar regions. Genera: *Lepeta* Gray, 1842 (subgenus *Cryptobranchia* Middendorff, 1851): *Pilidium* Forbes, 1849; *Propilidium* Forbes, 1849; *Punctolepeta* Habe, 1958.

SUPERFAMILY: COCCULINACEA

Small, usually eyeless deep-sea gastropods with a colourless, conical shell, the apex facing backwards, and a rhipidoglossan radula. Operculum absent. Hermaphrodite.

Family: Cocculinidae: genus *Cocculina* Dall, 1882

Family: Lepetellidae: genera: *Lepetella* Verrill, 1880; *Addisonia* (Dall, 1882; and others). Only a few known species.

SUPERFAMILY: TROCHACEA
See Plates 5-9

Shell conical and pointed to top-shaped, the interior (sometimes also the exterior) showing mother-of-pearl. Upper surface usually brightly coloured, aperture circular. Operculum spirally coiled: multispiral (Trochidae) or paucispiral (*Turbo, Astraea*, Phasianellidae). In some families the operculum is horny (Trochidae, Angariidae, Stomatellidae), in others it is calcareous (Turbinidae, Phasianellidae); sometimes the horny operculum has a calcareous surface.

The radula is of the rhipidoglossan type. Right gill reduced or lost. These gastropods are mainly vegetarian, feeding on algae and diatoms, but some browse on the polyps of hydrozoans. The group is distributed throughout the world, on the shore and also in deeper water. There are hundreds of species.

Family: Trochidae (Top shells)

Operculum horny, thin and circular with a central nucleus (the horny operculum distinguishes this family from the Turbinidae in which the operculum is calcareous). The subdivision into subfamilies is mainly based on details of radular structure. MARGARITINAE: from the evolutionary standpoint these are rather primitive forms with a relatively thin, conical to lens-shaped shell, usually with an umbilicus, and showing mother-of-pearl inside – sometimes also outside. Genera: *Margarites* Gray, 1847 (subgenera: *Bathymophila* Dall, 1881; *Cantharidoscops* Galkin, 1955; *Margaritopsis* Thiele, 1906; *Pupillaria* Dall, 1909); *Antimargarita* Powell, 1951; *Basilissa* Watson, 1879 (subgenus: *Ancistrobasis* Dall, 1889); *Euchelus* Philippi, 1847 (subgenera: *Antillachelus* Woodring, 1928; *Herpetopoma* Pilsbry, 1889; *Mirachelus* Woodring, 1928; *Vaceuchelus* Iredale, 1929); *Granata* Cotton, 1957; *Guttula* Schepman, 1908; *Hybochelus* Pilsbry, 1889; *Lischkeia* Fischer, 1879 (subgenus: *Calliotropis* Seguenza, 1903); *Margarella* Thiele, 1893 (subgenera: *Promargarita* Strebel, 1908; *Submargarita* Strebel, 1908); *Olivia* Cantraine, 1835; *Sequenzia* Jeffreys, 1876; *Tibatrochus* Nomura, 1940; *Tropidomarga* Powerll, 1951. ANGARIINAE (dolphin shells): shell relatively large, coiled rather like a turban and with an umbilicus. Spiral ornament with tubercles, curved spines and other processes. Aperture circular, with mother-of-pearl inside, operculum horny. A few species in the Indo-Pacific. Genus: *Angaria* Röding, 1798. MONODONTINAE: shell conical, thick-walled and smooth or with spiral ridges. Base of columella enlarged, simple or toothed, with one or more basal teeth. Usually without an umbilicus. Interior showing mother-of-pearl. Genera: *Monodonta* Lamarck, 1799 (subgenera: *Austrocochlea* Fischer, 1885; *Osilinus* Philippi, 1847); *Bankivia* Krauss, 1848 (subgenus *Leiopyrga* H. & A. Adams, 1863); *Bathybembix* Crosse, 1893 (subgenus: *Ginebis* Otuka, 1942); *Cantharidus* Montfort, 1810 (subgenera: *Iwakawatrochus* Kuroda & Habe, 1954; *Micrelenchus* Finlay, 1927; *Phasianotrochus* Fischer, 1885; *Plumbelenchus* Finlay, 1927); *Chrysostoma* Swainson, 1840; *Diloma* Philippi, 1845 (subgenera: *Anisodiloma* Finlay, 1927; *Cavodiloma* Finlay, 1927; *Chlorodiloma* Pilsbry, 1889; *Fractarmilla* Finlay, 1927; *Melagraphia* Gray, 1847; *Oxystele* Philippi, 1847; *Pictodiloma* Habe, 1946); *Jujubinus* Monterosato, 1884 (subgenus: *Strigosella* Sacco, 1896): *Tegula* Lesson, 1835 (subgenera: *Agathistoma* Olsson & Harbison, 1953; *Chlorostoma* Swainson, 1840; *Omphalius* Philippi, 1847; *Promartynia* Dall, 1909); *Thalotia* Gray, 1847 (subgenera: *Alcyna* A. Adams, 1860; *Calthalotia* Iredale, 1929; *Odontotrochus* Fischer, 1879; *Prothalotia* Thiele, 1930); *Turcica* A. Adams, 1854; *Turcicula* Dall, 1881. GIBBULINAE: shell usually roundish, conical, with convex whorls, the body whorl being large. Umbilicus present. Spiral ornament. Aperture usually with a smooth edge. Parietal lip often with a toothed thickening. Mother-of-pearl. Genera: *Gibbula* Risso, 1826 (subgenera: *Adriaria* Pallary, 1917; *Calliotrochus* Fischer, 1879; *Cantharidella* Pilsbry, 1889; *Colliculus* Monterosato, 1888; *Enida* A. Adams, *Eurytrochus* Fischer, 1879; *Forskalena* Iredale, 1918; *Hisseyagibbula* Kershaw, 1955; *Notogibbula* Iredale, 1924; *Phorcus* Risso, 1826; *Steromphala* Gray, 1847; *Tumulus* Monterosato, 1888); *Cittarium* Philippi, 1847; *Fossarina* A. Adams & Angas (subgenera: *Clydonochilus* Fischer, 1890; *Minopa* Iredale, 1924); *Gaza* Watson, 1879 (subgenus: *Callogaza* Dall, 1881); *Nanula* Thiele, 1924; *Norrisia* Bayle, 1880; *Phorculus* Gossmann, 1888; *Trochinella* Iredale, 1937. CALLIOSTOMATINAE: shell conical with an angular, rarely rounded base. Aperture squarish, with sharp edges. Umbilicus poorly developed or absent. Shell interior with mother-of-pearl. Genera: *Calliostoma* Swainson, 1840, with numerous species in almost all seas (subgenera: *Alertalex* Dall, 1956;

Ampullotrochus Monterosato, 1890; *Benthastelene* Iredale, 1936; *Eucasta* Dall, 1889; *Fautor* Iredale, 1924; *Laetifautor* Iredale, 1929; *Maurea* Oliver, 1926; *Otukaia* Ikebe, 1942; *?Putzeysia* Sulliotti 1889, synonym: *Gemmula* Seguenza, 1876 non Weinkauff, 1875; *Sinutor* Cotton & Godfrey, 1935; *Spikator* Cotton & Godfrey, 1935; *Tristichotrochus* Ikebe, 1942; *Ziziphinus* Gray, 1843); *Astele* Swainson, 1855 (subgenera: *Astelena* Iredale, 1924; *Callistele* Cotton & Godfrey, 1935; *Coralastele* Iredale, 1930; *Dentistyla* Dall, 1889; *Eurastele* Coen, 1946; *Mazastele* Iredale, 1936; *Omphalotukaia* Yoshida, 1948; *Pulchrastele* Iredale, 1929; *Scrobiculinus* Monterosato, 1889); *Falsimargarita* Powell, 1951; *Photinastoma* Powell, 1951; *Photinula* H. & A. Adams, 1854; *Venustatrochus* Powell, 1951. TROCHINAE: shell small to large, conical, without a true umbilicus. Aperture squarish with a sharp outer edge. Columella coiled, often toothed (*Trochus*), or more or less strongly folded and ending in a tubercle (*Tectus*). Parietal lip usually forming an angle with the basal edge. Mother-of-pearl. Genera: *Trochus* Linné, 1758 (subgenera: *Belangeria* Fischer, 1879; *Coelotrochus* Fischer, 1879; *Infundibulops* Pilsbry, 1889; *Infundibulum* Montfort, 1810; *Praecia* Gray, 1857; *Thorista* Iredale, 1915; *Thoristella* Iredale, 1915); *Clanculus* Montfort, 1810 (subgenera: *Camitia* H. & A. Adams, 1854); *Clanculopsis* Monterosato, 1879; *Euclanculus* Cotton & Godfrey, 1934; *Euriclanculus* Cotton & Godfrey, 1934; *Isoclanculus* Cotton & Godfrey, 1934; *Macroclanculus* Cotton & Godfrey, 1934; *Mesoclanculus* Cotton & Godfrey, 1934; *Microclanculus* Cotton & Godfrey, 1934; *?Panocochlea* Dall, 1908; *Paraclanculus* Finlay, 1927); *Tectus* Montfort, 1810 (subgenera: *Cardinalia* Gray, 1847; *Rochia* Gray, 1857). UMBONIINAE: shell rounded, conical to lens-shaped. Umbilicus often partly or completely covered by a callus, but open in some species. Mother-of-pearl. Genera: *Umbonium* Link, 1807 (subgenera: *Ethalia* H. & A. Adams, 1854; *Ethaliella* Pilsbry, 1905; *Suchium* Makiyama 1925; *Zethalia* Finlay, 1927); *Antisolarium* Finlay, 1927; *Callumbonella* Thiele, 1924; *Ethminolia* Iredale, 1924 (subgenus: *Sericominolia* Kuroda & Habe, 1954); *Isanda* H. & A. Adams, 1854

Aperture shape in the Trochidae. Top, from left to right: sharp outer lip in *Bathybembix*; thickened walls and an umbilicus in *Gibbula*; columella with teeth in *Clanculus*. Below, from left to right: with tooth in *Monodonta*; aperture distorted to a roundish rectangle in *Calliostoma*; columella with a strong spiral fold ending in a knob in *Tectus*.

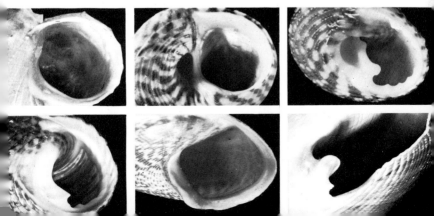

(subgenera: *Archiminolia* Iredale, 1929; *Conotalopia* Iredale, 1929; *Parminolia* Iredale, 1929; *Umbonella* A. Adams, 1863; *Vanitrochus* Iredale, 1929): *Monilea* Swainson, 1840 (subgenus: *Priotrochus* Fischer, 1879); *Rossiteria* Brazier, 1895; *Talopena* Iredale, 1918. SOLARIELLINAE: aperture more or less circular, umbilicus open. Radula with an exceptionally small number of lateral plates. Genera: *Solariella* Wood 1842 (subgenera: *Ethaliopsis* Schepman, 1908; *Machaeroplax* Friele, 1877; *Microgaza* Dall, 1881; *Micropiliscus* Dall, 1927; *Solaricida* Dall, 1919; *Spectamen* Iredale, 1924; *Suavotrochus* Dall, 1924; *Zetela* Finlay, 1927); *Cidarina* Dall, 1909; *?Lirularia* Dall, 1909; *Minolia* A. Adams, 1860; *?Zeminolia* Finlay, 1927. HALISTYLINAE: shell rather small, almost cylindrical, with tall spire and a rounded dome-shaped apex. No umbilicus. Whorls somewhat convex, smooth or with fine spiral ridges. Aperture small, circular. A single recent genus: *Halistylus* Dall, 1890, with only a few species, off the coast of Brazil.

Family: Stomatellidae (Wide mouths, False ears)

Shell usually small, with a low spire, as in ormers, but without the row of holes. Interior showing mother-of-pearl. The animal cannot withdraw completely into the shell. Distributed in the Indo-Pacific, on rocks in the intertidal zone and in deeper water. Genera: *Stomatella* Lamarck, 1816 (subgenus: *Gena* Gray, 1850); *Broderipia* Gray, 1847; *Pseudostomatella* Thiele, 1924 (subgenus: *Stomatolina* Iredale, 1937); *Roya* Iredale, 1912; *Stomatia* Helbling, 1779 (subgenera: *Microtis* H. & A. Adams, 1850; *?Miraconcha* Bergh, 1908); *Synaptocochlea* Pilsbry, 1890.

Family: Liotiidae

Shell small, top-shaped to flat disc-shaped, with mother-of-pearl interior, and a wide umbilicus. Operculum horny, spiral with calcareous overlay. Worldwide distribution, in depths of 50m and below. Genera: *Liotia* Gray, 1847; *Arene* H. & A. Adams, 1854 (subgenus: *Marevalvata* Olsson & Harbison, 1953); *Eccliseogyra* Dall, 1892; *Ilaira* H. & A. Adams, 1854; *Liotina* Fischer, 1885 (subgenera: *Austroliotia* Cotton, 1948; *Dentarene* Iredale, 1929; *Globarene* Iredale, 1929; *Liotinaria* Habe, 1955); *Macrarene* Hertlein & Strong, 1951.

Family: Skeneidae

Shell small (1-4mm), top-shaped to disc-shaped, without mother-of-pearl. Worldwide distribution from the intertidal zone down to 1000m. Genera: *Skenea* Fleming 1825; *Cirsonella* Angas, 1877; *Crossea* A. Adams, 1865; *Daronia* A. Adams, 1861; *Ganesa* Jeffreys 1883; *Tubiola* A. Adams, 1863; and others.

Family: Cyclostrematidae

In general these are very similar to the members of the preceding family, and indeed the two groups are often combined to form one family. Genera: *Cyclostrema* Marryat, 1818; *Brookula* Iredale, 1912; *Circulus* Jeffreys, 1865; *Parviturbo* Pilsbry & McGinty, 1945; and others.

Family: Turbinidae (Turban shells)

Shell rather large, solid, top-shaped and coiled, the outer surface sometimes smooth, but usually ornamented. Aperture with a smooth parietal edge and mother-of-pearl inside. Operculum calcareous, spiral, externally smooth or ornamented, white or coloured, with a central or excentric nucleus; these opercula are known colloquially as cat's eyes. The subfamilies are distinguished by the form of the operculum and radula. TURBININAE: shell more or less large, with convex whorls and a thick calcareous operculum with a central nucleus. Genera: *Turbo* Linné, 1758 (subgenera: *Batillus* Schumacher, 1817; *Callopoma* Gray, 1850; *Carswellena* Iredale, 1931; *Dinassovica* Iredale, 1937; *Euninella* Cotton, 1939; *Halopsephus* Rehder, 1943; *Lunatica* Röding, 1798; *Lunella* Röding, 1798; *Marmarostoma* Swainson, 1829; *Modelia* Gray, 1850; *Ninella* Gray, 1850; *Sarmaticus* Gray, 1847; *Subninella* Thiele, 1929; *Taeniaturbo* Woodring, 1928); *?Prisogaster* Morch, 1850. ASTRAEINAE (Star shells): shell conical to top-shaped, with a flat base, much ornament and numerous long processes. With or without an umbilicus. Operculum oval and calcareous. Worldwide distribution, but mainly in the Indo-Pacific and off the western coast of central America. Only one species, *Astraea rugosa* (Linné), in Europe. Genera: *Astraea* Röding, 1798 (subgenera: *Astralium* Link, 1807; *Bellastraea* Iredale, 1924; *Bolma* Risso, 1826; *Cookia* Lesson, 1832; *Distellifer* Iredale, 1937; *Lithopoma* Gray, 1850; *Micrastraea* Cotton, 1939; *Pagocalcar* Iredale, 1937; *Pomaulax* Gray, 1850; *Rugastella* Iredale, 1937; *Uvanilla* Gray, 1850; and others); *Galeoastraea* Kuroda & Habe, 1958 (subgenus: *Harisazaea* Habe, 1958); *Guildfordia* Gray, 1850. HOMALOPOMATINAE: shell small with distinct spiral ornament. Genera: *Homalopoma* Carpenter, 1864 (subgenera: *Argalista* Iredale, 1915; *Cantrainea* Jeffreys, 1883; *Collonista* Iredale, 1918; *Leptothyropsis* Woodring, 1928; *Phanerolepida* Dall, 1907); *Anadema* H. & A. Adams, 1854; *Charisma* Hedley, 1915 (subgenera: *Cavostella* Laseron, 1954; *Cavotera* Laseron, 1954); *Cirsochilus* Cossmann, 1888; *Leptocollonia* Powell, 1951; *Leptothyra* Pease, 1869; *Moelleria* Jeffreys, 1865.

Family: Phasianellidae (Pheasant shells)

Shell longish, conical, smooth and shiny or with fine spiral ridges. Colour and pattern very variable. Aperture almond-shaped, porcelain-white inside, without mother-of-pearl. Operculum thick and calcareous with the nucleus towards the edge. A widely distributed family, but with relatively few species, mainly in the Indo-Pacific. Only one genus (*Tricolia*) is represented in Europe. Genera: *Phasianella* Lamarck, 1804; *Gabrielona* Iredale, 1917; *Tricolia* Risso, 1826 (subgenera: *Eotricolia* Kuroda & Habe, 1954; *Hiloa* Pilsbry, 1917; *Pellax* Finlay, 1926).

SUPERFAMILY: NERITACEA
See Plate 9

With only one gill and one kidney. No mother-of-pearl.

Family: Neritidae (Nerites)

Shell spherical or hemispherical with few whorls, the body whorl being large. Spire low or flat, the outer surface smooth or with spiral ornament. Aperture semicircular, but restricted by a broad, flat extension of the columella, with more or less prominent teeth at the edge, and with its surface smooth, warty or wrinkled. Palatal lip often thickened, its interior with a varying number of teeth. Operculum calcareous, usually with rib-like reinforcement and a finger-like process (apophysis). The ability to store water in the shell enables these animals to withstand periods of desiccation, such as occur at low tide or if they are living in the spray zone. This family of vegetation gastropods contains several hundred species and in the tropics these take the place of winkles. The typical genus *Nerita* lives on rocks in the tidal zone. Other (e.g. *Neritina*, *Theodoxus*) have become adapted for life in brackish or fresh waters, while there are some (e.g. *Neritodryas*) which can periodically leave the water and browse on shore plants. NERITINAE: *Nerita* Linné, 1758 (subgenera: *Amphinerita* Martens, 1887; *Ritena* Gray, 1858; *Theliostyla* Morch, 1852): *Fluvinerita* Pilsbry, 1932; *Heminerita* Martens, 1887; *Neritina* Lamarck, 1816 (subgenera: *Clypeolum* Recluz, 1842; *Dostia* Gray, 1847; *Nereina* Cristofori & Jan, 1832 *Neripteron* Lesson, 1830; *Neritona* Martens, 1869; *Provittoida* Baker, 1923; *Pseudonerita* Baker 1923; *Vitta* Mörch, 1852; *Vittina* Baker, 1923; *Vittoida* Baker, 1923); *Neritodryas* Martens, 1869; *Puperita* Gray, 1858; *Septaria* Férussac, 1807 (subgenera: *Navicella* Lamarck, 1816; *Paraseptaria* Risbec, 1942; *Sandalium* Schumacher, 1817); *Theodoxus* Montfort, 1810 (subgenera: *Alinoclithon* Baker, 1923; *Clithon* Montfort, 1810; *Neritaea* Roth, 1855; *Neritoclithon* Baker, 1923; *Ninnia* Westerlund, 1903; *Pictoneritina* Iredale, 1936; *Vittoclithon* Baker, 1923). SMARAGDIINAE: shell small, oval, greenish or white. Genera: *Smaragdia* Issel, 1869 (subgenera: *Smaragdella* Baker, 1923; *Smaragdista* Iredale, 1936); *?Magadis* Melvill & Standen, 1899; *Pisulina* G. & H. Nevill, 1869. The shell is usually thick in the marine forms, thin in those from brackish and fresh waters.

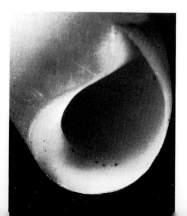

The aperture of the winkle *Littorina obtusata* (Linné, 1758), much enlarged.

Family: Phenacolepadidae

Shell small, smooth or with radial ornament and apex directed backwards. Interior with a horseshoe-shaped muscle impression (as in limpets). Numerous species in warmer seas. Genera: *Phenacolepas* Pilsbry, 1891; *Plesiothyreus* Cossmann, 1888.

ORDER: MONOTOCARDIA

In contrast to the Diotocardia, the Monotocardia have lost the organs of the right side of the body, namely the right gill, the right kidney and the right auricle. The nerve cells in the foot are mostly concentrated into ganglia. Shell form very variable, mainly spiral with a more or less tall spire, more rarely conical (e.g. in *Capulus*). No mother-of-pearl. Further subdivisions are based on differences in the structure of the radula.

Suborder: Taenioglossa

The taenioglossan radula can be derived from the rhipidoglossan (cf. the Archaeogastropoda or Diotocardia) by a great reduction in the number of teeth, leaving only a central tooth, flanked on each side by one lateral and 2 marginals. The ptenoglossan radula of the Epitoniacea also belongs here. More primitive forms have a roundish, entire edge to the aperture (e.g. Littorinacea), whereas in later forms the edge of the aperture has a slight indentation or a short siphonal canal (Cerithiidae, Triphoridae, Cypraeacea, Strombacea, Tonnacea). The operculum is horny.

SUPERFAMILY: LITTORINACEA
See Plate 10

Shell small to medium-sized, more or less roundish to tall, with the surface smooth or ornamented both spirally and axially, but without spines. Aperture ovate and entire (without indentations). Operculum horny and spirally coiled. These gastropods live mainly in the upper intertidal zones and in shallow water. Some families have become adapted for life in fresh waters or on land.

Three representatives of the superfamily Rissoacea. Left to right: *Acinopsis subcrenulata* (Schwartz, 1869), c. 5mm; *Rissoa guerini* Récluz, 1843, c. 5mm; *Truncatella subcylindrica* (Linné, 1767), c. 5mm. Mainly from the Mediterranean. All much enlarged.

Family: Littorinidae (Periwinkles)

Mostly living on the seashore among rocks and seaweed. In some species the shell thickness is correlated with the living conditions. Some winkles live so high up in the intertidal zone that they are only occasionally wetted by spray. Shell small, porcelain-like, without mother-of-pearl. The operculum provides an efficient closure, behind which the animal can retain sufficient water for respiration during periods of desiccation. They feed mainly on algae. The family has about 25 genera with over 100 living species. LITTORININAE: *Littorina* Ferussac, 1822 (subgenera: *Algamorda* Dall, 1918; *Austrolittorina* Rosewater, 1970; *Littoraria* Gray, 1834; *Littorinopsis* Morch, 1876; *Melarhaphe* Menke, 1828); *Laevilacunaria* Powell, 1951 (subgenus: *Pellilacunella* Powell, 1951); *Laevilitorina* Pfeffer, 1886 (subgenus: *Corneolitorina* Powell, 1951); *Masquariella* Finlay, 1926; *Nodilittorina* Martens, 1897 (subgenera: *Echinolittorina* Habe, 1956; *Granulilittorina* Habe & Kosuge, 1966); *Pellilitorina* Pfeffer, 1886; *Rissolittorina* Ponder, 1966. TECTARIINAE: *Tectarius* Valenciennes, 1832 (subgenus *Cenchritis* Martens, 1900). ECHININIAE: *Echininus* Clench & Abbott, 1942 (subgenus: *Tectininus* Clench & Abbot, 1942).

Family: Lacunidae

Mainly cold-water forms from northern seas (North Atlantic, Labrador, Bering Straits, Alaska, Japan). Shell small (6-10mm), thin-walled, colourless to yellowish, and smooth, with a slit-like umbilicus, living on tangleweeds (*Laminaria*). Genera: *Lacuna* Turton, 1827; *Stenotis* A. Adams, 1863; *Ersilia* Monterosato, 1872.

SUPERFAMILY: RISSOACEA

Very small gastropods (usually 2-5mm) varying in form and ornament. A microscope is necessary for their identification. The number of species is enormous, and there are over 300 species in European seas alone. As in the case of their closest relatives, the Littorinacea, there are marine, freshwater and terrestrial forms. These gastropods are not often noticed, partly because of their tiny size and partly because they live in dark places. *Truncatella* is commonly found under rocks or in damp sand above the spray zone on the seashore, *Alvania* and *Rissoa* in growths of algae in coastal waters, and *Barleeia* in felt-like algal mats in the intertidal zone.

Family: Assimineidae: *Assiminea* Fleming, 1828.

Family: Cingulopsidae: *Cingulopsis* Fretter & Graham, 1962.

Family: Hydrobiidae: *Hydrobia* Hartmann, 1821; *Peringia* Paladilhe, 1874; *Potamopyrgus* Stimpson, 1865.

Family Rissoellidae: *Rissoella* Gray, 1847.

Family: Rissoidae: *Rissoa* Desmarest, 1814; *Alvania* Risso, 1826; *Alvinia* Monterosato, 1884; *Amphithalamus* Carpenter, 1865; *Barleeia* Clark, 1855; *Cingula* Fleming, 1828; *Folinia* Crosse, 1868; *Goniostoma* Villa, 1841;

Merelina Iredale, 1915; *Putilla* A. Adams, 1867; *Rissoina* d'Orrbigny, *Turbona* Leach 1847; *Zebina* H. & A. Adams 1854; and others.

Family: **Skeneopsidae**: *Skeneopsis* Iredale, 1915.

Family: **Truncatellidae**: *Truncatella* Risso, 1826.

Family: **Tornidae**: *Tornus* Turton & Kingston, 1830; *Basilissopsis* Dautzenberg & H. Fischer, 1897; *Cochliolepis* Stimpson, 1858; *Vitrinella* C. B. Adams, 1850; *Pseudomalaxis* P. Fischer, 1885.

Family: **Trachysmidae**: *Trachysma* G. O. Sars, 1878; and others. See the literature references for the recent work on this group by Fritz Nordsieck.

SUPERFAMILY: ARCHITECTONICACEA
See Plate 11

Shell with relatively little contact between the surfaces of the whorls and a wide umbilicus. The embryonic shell is left-handed, but the adult is right-handed. The apex can be discerned through the open umbilicus. Whorls usually with spiral ornament. Operculum horny, its inner side with a conical or warty process. Due to the long larval period in the marine plankton some species are dispersed over long distances.

Family: Architectonicidae

Shell flat, conical with spiral ornament and a colour pattern following the spiral lines. Base flat. Umbilicus almost always with a thick marginal callus. Genera: *Architectonica* Röding, 1798, synonym: *Solarium* Lamarck, 1799; *Heliacus* d'Orbigny, 1842, synonym: *Torinia* Gray, 1847 (subgenera: *Architea* A. Costa, 1869; *Gyriscus* Tiberi, 1867); *Philippia* Gray, 1847 (subgenus: *Psilaxis* Woodring, 1928); and others.

SUPERFAMILY: TURRITELLACEA

Shell low to tall or long and tubular with a circular aperture and a horny operculum. Whorls more or less closely in contact with one another, arranged spirally (Turritellinae, Mathildidae, Modulidae), irregularly coiled (Vermiculariinae), with no regular arrangement (Vermetidae) or free (Caecidae).

Family: Turritellidae (Auger or Screw shells)

The family contains the true screw shells with regular whorls and the Vermiculariinae, in which the whorls begin with a fairly turritelloid apex, but then quickly change direction. Both groups live in coarse sand and feed on finely divided plant detritus, which they collect from the sea bottom. *Vermicularia* may also fix itself on to large rocks. TURRITELLINAE: *Turritella* Lamarck, 1799 (subgenera: *Archimediella* Sacco, 1895; *Ctenocolpus* Iredale, 1925; *Haustator* Montfort, 1810; *Maoricolpus* Finlay, 1927; *Torcula* Gray, 1847; *Zaria* Gray, 1847; *Zeacolpus* Finlay, 1927 and others); *Mesalia* Gray, 1847; *Protoma* Baird, 1870; *Turritellopsis* Sars, 1878; and others. VERMICULARIINAE: *Vermicularia* Lamarck, 1799; *Siliquaria* Bruguière, 1789.

43

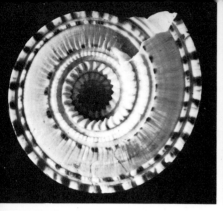

In the superfamily Architectonicacea the shell is advolute, the spiral being formed so that the whorls scarcely touch one another. Note the wide, open umbilicus.

Family: Caecidae

Shell very small, in the form of a curved tube, and requiring a microscope for identification. The first spiral coil is usually shed later on and the hole is then plugged by a septum. Operculum horny. Found in warm seas, including the Mediterranean. Genus: *Caecum* Fleming, 1813 (subgenera: *Brochina* Gray, 1857; *Elephantanellum* Bartsch, 1920; *Elephantulum* Carpenter, 1858; *Fartulum* Carpenter, 1857; *Micranellum* Bartsch, 1920; *Pseudoparastrophia* Distaso, 1905); *Meioceras* Carpenter, 1858; and others.

Family: Mathildidae

Shell (7-30mm) conical with a deep suture. Living in warm seas, including the Mediterranean, often on corals. Genera: *Mathilda* Semper, 1865; *Gegania* Jeffreys, 1884.

Family: Modulidae

Shell small, top-shaped, usually with tuberculate ornament, rounded whorls and an obliquely positioned circular aperture. Usually one tooth on the edge of the columella. Warm seas. Genus: *Modulus* Gray, 1842.

Family: Vermetidae (Worm shells)

Instead of starting with a spiral coil the shells of these gastropods begin with a tubular chamber. They live fixed to the substrate, often in colonies, and have a worldwide distribution. The systematics of the family are somewhat confused. Genera: *Vermetus* Daudin, 1800 (subgenus: *Thylaeodus* Morch, 1860); *Bivonia* Gray, 1842; *Spiroglyphus* Daudin, 1800, synonym: *Dendropoma* Morch, 1861; *Lemintina* Risso, 1826; *Petaloconchus* Lea, 1843 (subgenus: *Macrophragma* Carpenter, 1857); *Serpulorbis* Sassi, 1827 (*Aletes* Carpenter, 1857); *Tripsycha* Keen, 1961 (subgenus: *Eualetes* Keen, 1971).

Worm shells. Left: *Siliquaria ponderosa* (Mörch, 1860), Taiwan. Centre: *Siliquaria cumingi* (Mörch, 1860), Japan. Upper right: *Siliquaria squamata* Blainville, 1827, West Indies and, lower right: *Caecum floridanum* Stimpson, 1851, c. 3mm, Florida and West Indies.

SUPERFAMILY: CERITHIACEA
See Plate 12

Shell much coiled with a horny apex and usually a well developed siphonal canal at the lower edge of the aperture. Most species are marine, but some (Potamididae) live in the brackish waters of estuaries.

Family: Cerithiidae (Ceriths)

Shell small to relatively large, variously coloured and with distinct ornament. Lower edge of the aperture with all stages from a slight indentation to a well developed siphonal canal. These are all marine gastropods living on sandy substrates in the shallow waters of tropical seas, and poorly represented in European seas. They feed mainly on diatoms and plant detritus. CERITHIINAE: Shell firm, the aperture with a distinct indentation or a siphonal canal. Genera: *Cerithium* Bruguière, 1789 (subgenera; *Aluco* Martens, 1880; *Gourmya* Bayle, 1884; *Ochetoclava* Woodring 1928; *Proclava* Thiele, 1929; *Semivertagus* Cossmann, 1889; *Thericium* Monterosato 1890); *Argyropeza* Melvill & Standen, 1901; *Ataxocerithium* Tate, 1893; *Bittium* Leach, 1847 (subgenera: *Eubittium* Cotton 1937; *Semibittium* Cossmann, 1896; *Stylidium* Dall & Bartsch, 1907); *Clypeomorus* Jousseaume, 1888; *Colina* H. & A. Adams, 1854 (subgenus: *Ischnocerithium* Thiele, 1929); *Liocerithium* Tyron, 1887; *Rhinoclavis* Swainson, 1840; and others. CAMPANILINAE: shell large, with twisted columella. Genera: *Campanile* Bayle, 1884; *Hypotrochus* Cotton, 1932; *Plesiotrochus* Fischer, 1878. LITIOPINAE: very small, pelagic gastropods living on drifting algae. Genera: *Litiopa* Rang, 1829; *Austrolaba* Laseron, 1956; *Diala* A. Adams, 1861; and others.

Family: Cerithiopsidae

Shell small, with a slight indentation at the edge of the aperture and requiring a microscope for identification. Genera: *Cerithiopsis* Forbes & Hanley, 1849 (subgenera: *Dizoniopsis* Sacco, 1895; *Cerithiopsida* Bartsch, 1911; *Cerithiop-*

sidella Bartsch, 1911; *Cerithiopsilla* Thiele, 1912; *Laskeya* Iredale, 1918; and others); *Eumetula* Thiele, 1912; *Joculator* Hedley, 1909; *Laiocochlis* Dunker & Metzger, 1874; *Metaxia* Monterosato, 1884; *Seila* A. Adams, 1861; and others. Some authors include *Bittium* (see Cerithiinae) in this family.

Family: Diastomidae

Shell small with an ovate, slightly indented aperture. Genera: *Diastoma* Deshayes, 1850; *Alaba* H. & A. Adams, 1853; *Alabina* Dall, 1902; *Cerithidium* Monterosato, 1884; *Neodiastoma* Cotton, 1932; and others.

Family: Planaxidae

Shell easily confused with that of *Littorina*, but differing in having a slight indentation at the lower edge of the aperture. Usually with a marked periostracum. Warm coasts, in the intertidal zone. Genera: *Planaxis* Lamarck, 1822 (subgenera: *Hinea* Gray, 1847; *Holcostoma* H. & A. Adams, 1854; *Proplanaxis* Thiele, 1929; *Quoyia* Gray, 1839; *Supplanaxis* Thiele, 1929).

Family: Potamididae (Horn shells, Creepers)

Shells of varying size, more or less pointed and conical with axial or spiral ornament or both, and mainly brown. These gastropods differ from the Cerithiidae in having the outer lip somewhat expanded and the siphonal canal poorly developed and not twisted. Whereas the Cerithiidae live on sandy bottoms in sea water, the Potamididae live in mud in warm, brackish waters, often in large groups; they feed on detritus. *Pirenella* is the only genus represented in Europe. POTAMIDINAE: Genera: (*Potamides* Brongniart, 1810, only has fossil species); *Cerithidea* Swainson, 1840; *Pirenella* Gray, 1847; *Pyrazus* Montfort, 1810; *Royella* Iredale, 1912; *Telescopium* Montfort, 1810; *Terebralia* Swainson, 1840; *Tympanotonus* Schumacher, 1817. BATILLARIINAE: *Batillaria* Benson, 1842 (subgenera *Batillariella* Thiele, 1929; *Lampanella* Morch, 1876; *Velacumantus* Iredale, 1936; *Zeacumantus* Finlay, 1927); *Rhinocoryne* Martens, 1900; and others.

Family: Triphoridae

Shell small, slender, pointed and conical, usually with tuberculate spiral ridges, and normally coiled sinistrally (left-handed). Aperture circular, with a more or less curved canal which often becomes closed with age to form a tube. Genera: *Triphora* Blainville, 1828; *Notosinister* Finlay 1927; *Viriola* Jousseaume, 1884; and others.

SUPERFAMILY: EULIMACEA (AGLOSSA)
See Plate 12

Mesogastropods in which the radula is normally lacking and is replaced by a protrusible sucking proboscis; this is an adaptation to their predatory or parasitic mode of life. Shell small, smooth, pointed and conical, but often reduced in the parisitic forms.

Family: Eulimidae: *Eulima* Risso, 1826; *Balcis* Leach, 1847; *Leiostraca* H.

& A. Adams, 1853; *Niso* Risso, 1826; *Rostreulima* Cossmann, 1913; and others.

Family: Aclididae: primitive forms still retaining a ptenoglossan radula. **Genus:** *Aclis* Lovén, 1846.

Family: Stiliferidae: *Stilifer* Broderip, 1832; *Mucronalia* A. Adams, 1860; and others.

he giant *Campanile symbolicum* Iredale, 1917 nly occurs off the coast of south-western Aus- alia. It grows up to a length of 20cm, and its eavy, white shell, usually with the surface eroded, oks more like a fossil than the shell of a living astropod.

Top left: *Trichotropis cancellata* (Hinds, 1842), c. 25mm, off Alaska.
Bottom: *Fossarus ambiguus* (Linné, 1758), c. 2mm, Sicily.
Top right the shell of *Capulus hungaricus* (Linné, 1769) starts with a spirally coiled apex.

SUPERFAMILY: EPITONIACEA (Ptenoglossa)

Shell tall, pointed and conical (Epitoniidae) or roundish and conical (Janthinidae). As an adaptation to their predatory habits both groups have a ptenoglossan radula.

Family: Epitoniidae (Scalariidae) (Wentletraps)

Shell pointed and conical, the whorls more or less close to one another, with axial ribs (or lamellae). Aperture circular. The animals produce a violet secretion. Worldwide distribution, mainly in shallow waters (less than 15m), often among sea-anemones. Genera: *Epitonium* Röding, 1798, synonym: *Scalaria* Lamarck, 1801 (subgenera: *Clathrus* Oken, 1815; *Gyroscala* Boury, 1887; and others); *Acirsa* Mörch 1857; *Alora* H. Adams, 1861; *Amaea* H. & A. Adams, 1853 (subgenus: *Acrilla* H. Adams, 1860; and others); *Cirsotrema* Mörch, 1852; *Eglisia* Gray, 1847; *Opalia* H. & A. Adams, 1853; and others.

Family: Janthinidae

Shell thin, light, roundish, and violet or colourless. Living afloat in warmer seas and often found stranded in large numbers on the shore. Each animal forms a float out of air bubbles coated with a hard mucus to which it attaches itself by the foot. The float also carries the egg capsules (c. 500). The animal remains with its float throughout life, feeding on floating organisms, such as gastropod larvae and small jellyfishes. The adult cannot swim and it sinks and dies if the float is torn off. Genera: *Janthina* Röding, 1798; *Recluzia* Petit de la Saussaye, 1853.

SUPERFAMILY: HIPPONICACEA
See Plate 13

Shells spiral or cap-shaped. Radula taenioglossan. The systematics of this group require revision.

Family: Hipponicidae (Hoof shells)

Shells cap-shaped, varying in size, with apex directed to the rear. Radial ribs and occasionally spiral ridges. Interior smooth, with a horseshoe-shaped muscle impression opening forwards. The edge of the shell fits the substrate. These animals attach themselves to rocks, corals or the shells of other molluscs, and feed by filtering plankton from the surrounding water. Genus: *Hipponix* Defrance, 1819.

Family: Fossaridae

Shell very small, tall and top-shaped with only a few whorls, and a wide umbilicus. In warmer seas. Genus: *Fossarus* Philippi, 1841 and others.

Family: Vanikoridae

Shell similar to that of *Natica*, rather small, white and with an umbilicus. Genus: *Vanikoro* Quoy & Gaimard, 1832, with a few species in the tropical Pacific, feeding on detritus in sandy areas.

SUPERFAMILY: CALYPTRAEACEA
See Plates 13 and 14

Shell spiral or flat and top-shaped. In most cases the animals are protandrous hermaphrodites, that is all individuals are males when young, but later change into females. Radula taenioglossan.

Family: Calyptraeidae (Cup-and-saucer shells)

Shell flat, conical and more or less coiled with the apex nearly central. Inside there is a concave shelf-like structure which may occupy up to almost half the rear end of the shell. These are filter-feeding molluscs which live attached to rocks or shelled animals. Genera: *Calyptraea* Lamarck, 1799 (subgenus: *Trochita* Schumacher, 1817; and others); *Cheilea* Modeer, 1793; *Crepidula* Lamarck, 1799 (subgenus: *Maoricrypta* Finlay, 1927; and others): *Crepipatella* Lesson, 1830; *Crucibulum* Schumacher, 1817; and others.

Family: Capulidae (Cap shells)

Shell cap-shaped with the first whorl coiled backwards. Body whorl enlarged and funnel-shaped. Interior smooth and porcelain-like with or without a septum. Periostracum bristly. These are hermaphrodite gastropods which live attached to rocks or bivalve shells. Some species settle on the shells of scallops and use their long proboscis to steal the bivalves' algal food from its mouth. Genus: *Capulus* Montfort, 1810 (subgenus: *Krebsia* Morch, 1877). Distributed in all seas.

Family: Trichotropidae (Hairy shells)

Shell spiral with an ear-shaped expansion. Aperture usually somewhat curved and periostracum very bristly. Protandrous hermaphrodites from cold seas, mainly boreal and arctic. Genera: *Trichotropis* Broderip & Sowerby, 1829 (subgenera: *Ariadna* P. Fischer, 1864; *Iphinoe* H. & A. Adams, 1854; and others); *Neoconcha* Smith, 1907; *Torellia* Loven, 1867; and others.

Family: Xenophoridae (Carrier shells)

See the text accompanying Plate 14. It has been found that the animals pick up the foreign objects with parts of the foot and attach them to the shell with a secretion produced by the pedal gland. It is not clear why they do this. It is unlikely to be for camouflage as the animals live in deep water where there is no light. Some investigators believe it provides additional reinforcement to the shell, others that it serves to enlarge the shell base and thus prevent it sinking into the soft substrate. Genera: *Xenophora* Fischer von Waldheim, 1807, synonym: *Onustus* Gray, 1847; *Stellaria* Schmidt, 1832 (subgenus: *Tugurium* P. Fischer, 1876). In contrast to *Xenophora*, *Stellaria* has a deep umbilicus and usually carries no foreign objects.

SUPERFAMILY: STROMBACEA
See Plates 14-17

Shell biconical with a more or less tail spire and usually a long columella. The aperture and siphonal canal are correspondingly long. Aperture narrow, its outer edge enlarged and wing-like (*Strombus*), often with finger-like processes (*Aporrhais*, *Lambis*). Operculum horny. Mainly in tropical seas, only *Aporrhais* in Europe.

Family: Strombidae (True conchs)

Shell varying principally in size, spire height and the development of the outer lip. All have at the edge of the aperture what is known as a stromboid notch, through which the animal can protrude the stalked eye in order to observe its surroundings while feeding. The first whorls have radial ribs, later ones have roundish tuberculate varices, particularly on the shoulder. The spiral ornament is usually less pronounced. Operculum narrow, pointed and sickle-shaped, notched on one side and really too small to close the aperture. In practice, it is used as an aid to locomotion and as a defensive weapon (for protection against predatory crabs and fishes). The conchs occur mainly in the Indo-West-Pacific, with only a few species in tropical America. They feed on algae and plant detritus. Genera: *Strombus* Linné, 1758 (subgenera: *Canarium* Schumacher, 1817; *Conomurex* P. Fischer, 1884; *Dolomena* Iredale, 1931; *Doxander* Iredale, 1931; *Euprotomus* Gill, 1870; *Gibberulus* Jousseaume, 1888; *Labiostrombus* Oostingh, 1925; *Laevistrombus* Kira, 1955; *Lentigo* Jousseaume, 1886; *Tricornis* Jousseaume, 1886); *Lambis* Röding, 1798 (subgenera: *Harpago* Mörch, 1852; *Millepes* Mörch, 1852); *Rimella* Agassiz, 1840; *Terebellum* Röding, 1798; *Tibia* Röding, 1798, synonym: *Rostellaria* Lamarck, 1799).

Family: Aporrhaidae (Pelican's foot shells)

Shell fairly small with rows of axial tubercles which are continued at the edge of the aperture to form finger-like processes. Outer lip enlarged and wing-like. The family contains only a few species. Genera: *Aporrhais* Da Costa, 1778 off the Atlantic coasts of Europe and North Africa and in the Mediterranean; *Drepanocheilus* Meek 1864 (subgenus: *Arrhoges* Gabb, 1868) with only one recent species, *Drepanocheilus (Arrhoges) occidentalis* (Beck, 1836), off the Atlantic coast of North America.

Family: Struthiolariidae

Shell with fine spiral ridges and fairly prominent tubercles and ribs. Aperture edge thickened, without processes. Columellar callus broad. Only a few species. Genera: *Struthiolaria* Lamarck, 1816, off New Zealand and the east coast of Australia; *Perissodonta* Martens, 1883, with a single species *Perissodonta mirabilis* (E. Smith, 1875).

SUPERFAMILY: ATLANTACEA (= Heteropoda)

Shell small (1-10mm), thin or completely absent. Gastropods adapted for swimming, with several genera in tropical seas, in depths of 0-1300m. The shells are seldom washed ashore, so the animals have to be caught at sea in trawls.

Family: Atlantidae:

Shell small to medium-sized, large enough to accommodate the whole animal, flatly coiled and keeled. Genera: *Atlanta* Lesueur, 1817; *Oxygyrus* Benson, 1835.

Family: Carinariidae

Shell smaller than the animal and very fragile. Genera: *Carinaria* Lamarck, 1801; *Cardiapoda* d'Orbigny, 1836; *Pterosoma* Lesson, 1827.

Family: Pterotracheidae

Shell and mantle completely lacking. Genera: *Pterotrachea* Forskål, 1775; *Firoloida* Lesueur, 1817.

SUPERFAMILY: NATICACEA
See Plate 18

Shell almost spherical, often with a pronounced umbilicus, which may be open or closed. The animals use the foot for digging in soft sand, in search of

In *Lambis* (*Harpago*) *chiragra chiragra* (Linné, 1758), a spider conch from the Indian Ocean, the shells of the two sexes can be distinguished. The female shell (upper) is larger, with a larger tubercle at top right, and an erected fifth 'finger' whereas the male shell (lower) is smaller, the tubercles are all about the same size, and the fifth 'finger' lies flat.

bivalves and gastropods. They bore a hole in the shell of the prey and consume the contents. Recent investigations have cast doubt upon the idea that an acid is secreted to assist in the boring process.

Family: Naticidae (Necklace shells)

Shell spherical with a very slightly raised spire and a large body whorl. Found in all seas. The subfamilies are separated on differences in the form of the operculum. NATICINAE: shell medium-sized, roundish, with a rather flat spire, and colour flecks or a colour pattern. Umbilicus open, separated by a groove from the columellar callus. Operculum calcareous on the outside. Genera: *Natica* Scopoli, 1777, synonym: *Cochlis* Röding, 1798; *Nacca* Risso, 1826; *Notocochlis* Powell, 1933 (subgenera: *Lunaia* Berry, 1964; *Naticarius* Dumeril, 1806; *Stigmaulax* Mörch, 1852; *Tectonatica* Sacco, 1890, synonym: *Cryptonatica* Dall, 1892; *Euspira* Agassiz, 1838; *Payraudeautia* Bucquoy, Dautzenberg & Dollfus, 1883; and others. GLOBULARIINAE: shell large, spherical and solid, spire rather tall, whorls separated by a deep suture. Operculum rudimentary, umbilicus open or closed. A single recent genus *Globularia* Swainson, 1840. POLINICINAE: shell normally somewhat larger than in the Naticinae, ovate, usually uniformly coloured. Umbilicus present, but not separated from the columellar callus which often covers it. Operculum horny. Genera: *Polinices* Montfort, 1810 (subgenera: *Conuber* Finlay & Marwick, 1937; *Mammilla* Schumacher, 1817; *Neverita* Risso, 1826; *Glossaulax* Pilsbry, 1929; *Bulbus* Brown, 1839 (subgenus: *Amauropsis* Mörch,

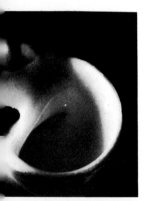

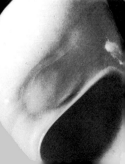

Differences in the base of the columella in the Naticidae. In sequence: umbilicus open in *Natica*, restricted in *Polinices* or *Conuber*, overlaid by a callus in *Neverita*, and completely covered in *Polinices*.

1857); *Friginatica* Hedley, 1916; *Frovina* Thiele, 1912; *Lunatia* Gray, 1847; *Sigaretotrema* Sacco, 1931; *Sigatica* Meyer & Aldrich, 1886; *Uberella* Finlay, 1928. SININAE: Shell thin and ear-shaped. Operculum horny, considerably smaller than the aperture. Genera: *Sinum* Röding, 1798, synonym: *Sigaretus* Lamarck, 1799 (subgenus: *Ectosinum* Iredale, 1931); *Eunaticina* Fischer, 1885; and others.

SUPERFAMILY: LAMELLARIACEA

Shell small, ear-shaped, very thin and smooth, without umbilicus, and in some species (Lamellariinae) completely or partly covered by the mantle. Radula taenioglossan, but without marginal teeth. These are predatory gastropods which feed on sessile sea-squirts (ascidians), on which they also lay their eggs. They form a transitional group between the Naticacea (of the *Sinum* type) and the Triviacea with which they share the same type of radula, nervous system, habits and larval form.

Family: Lamellariidae

Widely distributed gastropods, living under rocks in the intertidal zone, often in rock pools. Two subfamilies. LAMELLARIINAE: shell ear-shaped and covered by the mantle. Aperture wide. No operculum. Sexes separate. Genera: *Lamellaria* Montagu, 1815; *Marseniopsis* Bergh, 1886; *Mysticoncha* Allan, 1936. VELUTININAE: shell free or covered by the mantle, aperture roundish. Hermaphrodite. Genera: *Velutina* Fleming, 1821 (subgenera: *Velutella* Gray, 1847; *Limneria* H. & A. Adams, 1853); *Capulacmaea* Sars, 1859; *Marsenina* Gray, 1850: *Onchidiopsis* Bergh, 1853.

SUPERFAMILY: TRIVIACEA
See Plate 19

The gastropods in this group were formerly classified in the Cypraeacea (see below) and later, on account of many similarities, in the Lamellariacea. Like the Cypraeacea they have a toothed edge to the aperture. The shells have a varying amount of ornament. These are predatory molluscs which feed by boring into the bodies of ascidians and using their proboscis to suck up the contents. They are found in temperate and warm seas.

Family: Triviidae (Cowries)

Shell spherical or biconical, the aperture narrow, with both lips toothed. Two subfamilies. TRIVIINAE: shell roundish and often spotted, with spiral ridges. The aperture extends the full length of the shell and is parallel to its axis. Genera: *Trivia* Broderip, 1837 (subgenus: *Sulcotrivia* Schilder, 1933); *Cleotrivia* Iredale, 1930; *Niveria* Jousseaume, 1884 (subgenus: *Ellatrivia* Schilder, 1939); *Pseudotrivia* Schilder, 1936; *Pusula* Jousseaume, 1884; *Triviella* Jousseaume, 1884; *Trivirostra* Jousseaume, 1884 (subgenus: *Dolichupis* Iredale, 1936). ERATOINAE: shell biconical. No operculum. Aperture short and not parallel to the shell axis. Genera: *Erato* Risso, 1826 (subgenus *Eratopsis* Hoernes & Auinger, 1880); *Hesperato* Schilder, 1932; *Lachryma* Sowerby, 1832, synonym: *Proterato* Schilder, 1927.

The delicate shell of *Velutina* (*Limneria*) *undata* (Brown, 1839) dredged from a depth of 190m off the coast of Iceland. Original size c. 5mm.

SUPERFAMILY: CYPRAEACEA

Shell roundish, sometimes beaked, and usually coloured. Aperture long and slit-like with a front and rear canal. Apex usually concealed (convolute or involute whorls). Surface smooth, shiny and porcellanous. Outer lip thickened, turned inwards and almost always toothed or folded. Inner lip similarly shaped. Operculum absent, although present in the larval stage. These are popular shells with collectors on account of their beauty. Prices vary, and are very high for the rare species.

Family: Cypraeidae (Cowries)

Shells with variable colour and pattern and between 7 and 150mm long. The outer porcellanous layer and the colour pattern are deposited by the thin mantle lobes which extend over the shell from both sides. These two lobes come close to one another on the back of the shell. The family has about 190 species in the warm seas, and mainly in the Indo-Pacific (poorly represented in the Mediterranean, Caribbean and off the west coast of central America). The sexes are separate, and they feed on coral polyps, gorgonians, and animal detritus.

A special terminology has grown up to describe the different shell types, and a knowledge of this is essential for anyone studying the group. Thus, the shell shape may be pear-shaped, conical, ovate, spherical, spindle-shaped or almost cylindrical. The dorsal side of the shell may be much arched and the base slightly curved to flat. The spire may be projecting, drawn out to a point, or flat to navel-shaped (free or covered by a callus) or completely enclosed by the body whorl. The form and ornament of the sides may be described as rounded, angular, upturned, thickened, or engraved with little pits. The aperture may be straight or curved (particularly at the rear), with a canal at both ends. The siphonal canal is anterior, the other outlet posterior. The teeth on the outer lip (labial teeth) may continue in reduced form into the posterior canal. The front end of the inner or columellar lip is uniformly rounded or angular, its rear end more or less divergent. The teeth on the inner lip are the columellar teeth. The foremost tooth or terminal ridge differs from the others in shape and is separated from them by a gap. There may be one or more intermediate teeth inserted between the terminal ridge and the other teeth. Just behind the terminal ridge the inner lip is often expanded into a longish, concave depression, the fossula, whose inner edge is also toothed. Further towards the

Aperture shape in cowries. Left: the base of *Trivia* showing spiral ribs continuing as apertural teeth. Centre: *Jenneria* showing the teeth extending over the base and as far as the margin. Right: the smooth, shiny shell of *Erato*, showing the apex (above) and fine apertural teeth.

rear the columella often has a longitudinal furrow, the columellar sulcus. The shell ornament is basically spiral, and may have ribs (prolongations of the apertural teeth), tubercles or small pits. Coloration may be white, uniform, banded, spotted, blotched, with markings on the side, back or at both ends, occasionally with a dark marking below the tip of the spire and a dorsal marking. The dorsal line running along the back of the shell marks the line where the two halves of the mantle meet. The shell pattern is often composed of several layers, for earlier details of coloration can be discerned through later deposits of shell material. Young shells are strikingly thinner and lighter, with a longer, somewhat smooth body whorl, a short but still clearly visible apex, a wide open aperture and a sharp outer lip with a smooth interior, and the pattern tends to consist of spiral bands. In the shell of an almost mature animal the aperture is narrower and there are teeth on both lips. The shell is then

Regularly recurring colour patterns in cowries. Clockwise: the dorsal stripe (where the two mantle lobes covering the shell meet in the mid-dorsal line); a darker transverse band on a paler shell; a dorsal spot, usually with an irregular outline; two views to show terminal dark patches (usually on both ends of the shell).

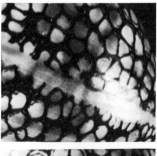 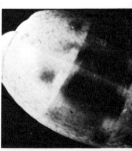

Shell development in cowries. Left: a young shell, with aperture still wide open, outer lip scarcely toothed, shell thin and light. Centre: as it grows the aperture becomes increasingly narrower, more shell material is deposited and the teeth on the outer lip are more prominent. Right: an almost fully grown shell with narrow aperture and prominent teeth.

stronger and heavier and the colour pattern has started to develop. Fully grown shells are heavy and solid, with a narrow aperture, usually well developed teeth and a very shiny enamel-like outer layer. Periostracum completely lacking. Radula taenioglossan.

Over the years this family has been intensively investigated by various workers. The nomenclature is by no means clear. A classification of the family put forward by Schilder in 1938-41 named over 400 species with several subspecies and races. More recent studies, however, have shown that the suggested differences in shell characters are not always reliable. There may be considerable variation within the geographic range of a given species and so the exact identification of some species becomes very difficult. More conservative workers are turning back to the old Linnaean genus *Cypraea*. Others would make use of subgenera to cover the more important differences. In spite of this controversy a review of the most important generic names that have been used is given below, because cowry shells are frequently to be found under these names in identification lists. It is possible to choose between three different systems of nomenclature:

a) to retain the older system,
b) simplify this, or
c) simply to give the species binomial names.

Thus, a shell of the Arabian Cowry could be designated in one of three ways:

Mauritia (Arabica) arabica (Linné, 1758);
Cypraea (Mauritia) arabica Linné, 1758;
Cypraea arabica Linné, 1758.

All these forms are in use alongside one another. Using system c) and arranging the species alphabetically gives one no idea of relationships within the genus. CYPRAEINAE: shell medium-sized to fairly large, ovate to cylindrical, with an attractive pattern; the teeth and the spaces between them may also be coloured. Back of shell smooth, sides rounded, underside flat, spire pointed to flat, occasionally with terminal markings. Genera: *Cypraea* Linné, 1758; *Callistocypraea* Schilder, 1927; *Chelycypraea* Schilder, 1927; *Luria*

Inner lip of cowries, showing (left) an oblique columellar furrow, (centre) a fossula and (right) a terminal tooth.

Jousseaume, 1884 (subgenus: *Basilitrona* Iredale, 1930); *Lyncina* Troschel, 1863; *Macrocypraea* Schilder, 1930; *Mauritia* Troschel, 1863 (subgenera: *Arabica* Jousseaume, 1884; *Leporicypraea* Iredale, 1930); *Talparia* Troschel, 1863 (subgenus: *Arestorides* Iredale, 1930); *Trona* Jousseaume, 1884. CYPRAEORBINAE: the oldest and most primitive group, mainly fossil, but with a few living relict forms. Genera: *Siphocypraea* Heilprin, 1887; *Zoila* Jousseaume, 1884. ERRONEINAE (CYPRAEOVULINAE): shell medium-sized to large usually pear-shaped to cylindrical, frequently with greenish ground coloration and brownish markings, including terminal spots. Spire often sunken. Genera: *Erronea* Troschel, 1863 (subgenera: *Adusta* Jousseaume, 1884; *Melicerona* Iredale, 1930); *Blasicrura* Iredale, 1930 (subgenera: *Bistolida* Cossmann, 1920; *Talostolida* Iredale, 1931); *Cribraria* Jousseaume, 1884 (subgenus: *Ovatipsa* Iredale, 1931); *Cypraeovula* Gray, 1824 (subgenus: *Luponia* Broderip, 1837); *Notadusta* Schilder, 1935; *Notocypraea* Schilder, 1927 (subgenus: *Guttacypraea* Iredale, 1935); *Palmadusta* Iredale, 1930 (subgenus: *Purpuradusta* Schilder, 1930); *Schilderia* Tomlin, 1930; *Umbilia* Jousseaume, 1884; *Zonaria* Jousseaume, 1884 (subgenera: *Neobernaya* Schilder, 1927; *Pseudozonaria* Schilder, 1927). PUSTULARIINAE (NARIINAE): shell rather small, back smooth or granular and often with a dorsal furrow. Usually yellow-brown with dark or pale spots. Terminal markings poorly developed. Underside flat, often with radial ridges. Spire short, without a dark marking. Genera: *Pustularia* Swainson, 1840 (subgenus: *Ipsa* Jousseaume, 1884); *Annepona* Iredale, 1935; *Erosaria* Troschel, 1863 (subgenus: *Ravitrona* Iredale, 1930; *Monetaria* Troschel, 1863 (subgenus: *Ornamentaria* Schilder, 1936); *Naria* Broderip, 1837; *Paulonaria* Iredale, 1930; *Propustularia* Schilder 1927; *Staphylaea* Jousseaume, 1884 (subgenus: *Nuclearia* Jousseaume, 1884).

Family: Ovulidae (Egg shells)

Shell pear-shaped to spindle-shaped, elongated at the ends, often with an umbilicus. Teeth poorly developed. Differentiated from the Cypraeidae by a few anatomical features and by certain differences in the shell, such as the absence of a pattern of coloured markings and the reduction of the enamel-like, outer layer, which is thin or lacking. Distributed mainly in tropical seas, where they prey on gorgonians, madreporarian corals and alcyonarians.

57

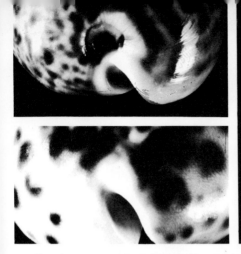
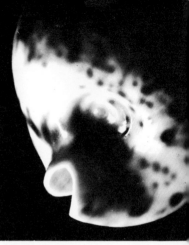

The spiral structure of the shell can still be seen in young cowries. The apex (top left) is still visible in young stages, but becomes increasingly overlaid (bottom left) as growth continues. Right: in *Umbilia hesitata* (Iredale, 1916) from Australia the spire is deeply sunken.

OVULINAE: shell pear-shaped, with short, protruding teeth on the lips and a well developed terminal ridge. Fossula smooth and broad. No columellar teeth. Found in all warm seas, in cavities in coral reefs, or under soft corals and gorgonians. Genera: *Ovula* Bruguière, 1789; *Calpurnus* Montfort, 1810 (subgenus: *Procalpurnus*, Thiele, 1929); *Primovula* Thiele, 1925 (subgenera: *Dentiovula* Habe, 1961; *Diminovula* Iredale, 1930, synonym: *Margovula* Schilder, 1939; *Pseudosimnia* Schilder, 1927); *Prionovolva* Iredale, 1930. SIMNIINAE: shell spindle-shaped, with elongated ends. Lip teeth reduced or lacking. Columella smooth, without terminal ridge. Fossula narrow or lacking. Living on gorgonians and alcyonarians, sometimes taking on the colour of the host coral. Genera: *Simnia* Risso, 1826, synonym: *Neosimnia* Fischer, 1884; *Cyphoma* Röding, 1798; *Volva* Röding, 1798 (subgenus: *Phenacovolva* Iredale, 1930). EOCYPRAEINAE: shell pear-shaped to ovate, rather smooth, with transverse ribs or granules. Aperture narrow, its lips toothed and the columella well developed. Living under corals. Numerous fossil species, but only two recent genera: *Cyproterina* Gregorio, 1880 (subgenus: *Jenneria* Jousseaume, 1884); *Pseudocypraea* Schilder, 1927.

Family: Pediculariidae

Shell small, cap-like and irregularly shaped, the aperture wide with sharp edges. Back with spiral ridges, the apex protruding or sunken. Living on corals, the outline and colour of the shell matching the host coral. Mainly fossil, only one recent genus: *Pedicularia* Swainson, 1840, with 10 species.

SUPERFAMILY: TONNACEA
See Plates 23-25

Shell large to very large, convex, with a more or less low spire and a large body whorl. Aperture with siphonal canal. Operculum longish and semi-circular or absent. Living in warm seas at various depths. These gastropods have a long

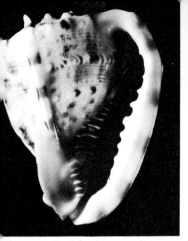

Young shells of *Cassis cornuta* do not yet show the typical characters of the adults (see Plate 24/1). The parietal shield is lacking, and the circular shoulder carries a ring of regularly arranged tubercles, all about the same size.

proboscis and they prey on echinoderms, crustaceans and other small marine invertebrates. They use an acid-containing salivary secretion to soften and bore into the calcareous exoskeleton of the prey and at the same time to paralyse it. While examining a *Tonna galea* (Linné, 1758) in Sicily in 1854 the naturalist Troschel observed that when stimulated the animal ejected its saliva for a distance of 0·5m on to a marble flooring slab which then started to foam vigorously. Later investigations have shown that in addition to the Tonnidae, the Cassidae, Cymatiidae and Bursidae are also able to discharge free acid, probably aspartic acid and 2-5% sulphuric acid, and possibly also a neurotoxin with paralysing properties. In this way they paralyse the prey and destroy part of the exoskeleton so that it no longer offers any resistance to the radula. The attack by a *Cassis* on a sea-urchin starts with a careful investigation of the prey. The gastropod's foot then holds the spines down while its proboscis searches the surface for a suitable place in which to discharge the acid secretion. In contrast to the Conacea which paralyse their prey by giving a subcutaneous injection, the Tonnacea secrete their paralysing agent externally, on to a limited area of tissue. The secretion may also be discharged in defence. The radula is of the taenioglossan type. The animal cuts out large pieces from the prey and swallows them.

Family: Tonnidae (Tun shells)

Shell rather large, roundish-ovate, relatively thin and light, with a low spire and a large body whorl. The ornament is spiral, without varices. The edge of the outer lip is scarcely thickened. Aperture with a deep siphonal canal at its lower end. No operculum. Living in fairly deep water. Genera: *Tonna* Brünnich, 1772; *Eudolium* Dall, 1889; *Malea* Valenciennes, 1833; *Parvitonna* Iredale, 1931.

Family: Cassidae (Helmet shells)

In contrast to the Tonnidae, the shell is solid and heavy, with additional

Aperture shape. Left: aperture with siphonal canal (below) in *Cymatium*. Centre: *Bursa* with siphonal (inhalant) canal (below) and exhalant canal (above). Right: *Colubraria obscura* (Reeve, 1844) from south-east Florida, West Indies and coasts of Brazil.

ornament (usually tuberculate varices), a relatively narrow aperture, a thickened outer lip and a short curved siphonal canal. Columella enlarged to give a prominent parietal shield. Some sexual dimorphism, e.g. in male *Cassis cornuta* the shoulder tubercles are fewer and longer than in the female, and in the male *Phalium* the shell is shorter than in the female. Helmet shells living on sandy bottoms in shallow water, mainly in warm seas. Genera: *Cassis* Scopoli, 1777 (subgenus: *Hypocassis* Iredale, 1927); *Casmaria* H. & A. Adams, 1853; *Cypraecassis* Stutchbury, 1837 (subgenus: *Levenia* Gray, 1847); *Dalium* Dall, 1889; *Galeodea* Link, 1807, synonym: *Cassidaria* Lamarck, 1812; *Morionella* Dall, 1909; *Morum* Röding, 1798 (subgenera: *Cancellomorum* Emerson & Old, 1963; *Oniscidia* Swainson, 1840); *Phalium* Link, 1807 (subgenera: *Echinophoria* Sacco, 1890; *Semicassis* Morch, 1852; *Tylocassis* Woodring, 1928; *Xenophalium* Iredale, 1927); *Sconsia* Gray, 1847; *Taieria* Finlay & Marwick, 1937.

Family: Oocorythidae

Shell fairly large, roundish-ovate, with spiral ornament. A few species in deep water. Genus: *Oocorys* P. Fischer, 1884; *Oocorys sulcata* lives off the Azores in depths down to 1000m.

Family: Ficidae (Fig shells)

Shell thin and light, but surprisingly solid, with elegant curves, in outline resembling a large fig. Spire fairly flat, aperture large and wide, gradually tapering to the long siphonal canal. Surface with fine spiral and axial ornament. No operculum. These gastropods have a long siphon. In life the two lateral mantle lobes extend over the shell. Only a few species in tropical seas (off East Africa, Indo-West-Pacific, Atlantic and Pacific coasts of central America, but not in the Mediterranean). Genus: *Ficus* Röding, 1798.

SUPERFAMILY: CYMATIACEA
See Plate 26

Shell variously shaped, with an oval aperture and a more or less long, well developed siphonal canal. Aperture closed above (Cymatiidae) or with a second canal opposite the siphonal canal for the exhalant respiratory current (Bursidae). Shell with much ornament. The group is characterised by the equally spaced varices (evidently for stabilising the shell). Operculum oval. These are predatory gastropods, feeding mainly on large echinoderms, worms, smaller gastropods and bivalves which, as in the Tonnacea, they paralyse with an acid secretion. Some species swallow their prey whole. Found in tropical seas, below the intertidal zone and in deeper water, mainly in the vicinity of coral reefs and on sand. The following families were formerly classified among the Tonnacea. Whether the new superfamily Cymatiacea will find favour with malacologists remains to be seen.

Family: Cymatiidae (Tritons)

Shell variously shaped, with strong spiral ornament, large tuberculate varices, and often a thick bristly periostracum. Outer lip thickened, inner lip toothed. Columellar callus folded. Aperture with its upper edge closed, thus clearly differing from the Bursidae which have an upper canal. Some species are distributed by free-swimming larvae. The family has been recently revised (Kilias, 1973), and this has resulted in the disappearance of certain names used in the current literature, such as *Monoplex* Perry, 1811 and *Turritriton* Dall, 1904. This revision also dealt with the problem of the generic names *Gyrineum* Link, 1807 and *Apollon* Montfort, 1810. As a result the designation *Gyrineum* was established as the valid name (for a cymatiid and not a bursid form), while *Apollon* became a synonym. ARGOBUCCININAE: whorls rounded, seldom angular. Varices roundish to lamellar, fairly regularly spaced (one varix to each half whorl). Genera: *Argobuccinum* Herrmannsen, 1846 (subgenera: *Fusitriton* Cossmann, 1903; *Mayena* Iredale, 1917; *Priene* H. & A. Adams, 1858; *Ranella* Lamarck, 1816); *Gyrineum* Link, 1807, synonym: *Apollon* Montfort, 1810 (subgenus *Biplex* Perry, 1811). CYMATIINAE: whorls roundish to very angular, varices flat to very protruding, widely spaced (one varix to 2–3 whorls). Genera: *Cymatium* Röding, 1798 (subgenera: *Cabestana* Röding, 1798, synonym: *Turritriton* Dall, 1904; *Linatella* Gray, 1857; *Ranularia* Schumacher, 1817; *Septa* Perry, 1810, synonym: *Monoplex* Perry, 1811); *Charonia* Gistel, 1848 (subgenera: *Cymatiella* Iredale, 1924; *Negyrina* Iredale, 1929); *Distorsio* Röding, 1798 (subgenus: *Rhysema* Clench & Turner, 1957).

Family: Bursidae (Frog shells)

Shell in many ways similar to that of the Cymatiidae, but with a second (exhalant) canal at the upper end of the aperture. Siphonal canal short. A relatively small family. Genus: *Bursa* Röding, 1798, synonym: *Ranella* Lamarck, 1916).

61

Family: Colubrariidae (False or Dwarf tritons)

Shell small, long and slender with prominent varices, finely tuberculate spiral ornament and a short curved siphonal canal. Aperture with a broad columellar callus. These animals creep about on rocks, and sometimes occur in shallow water. Genera: *Colubraria* Schumacher, 1817; *Antemetula* Rehder, 1943 (subgenus: *Colubrarina* Kuroda & Habe, 1971); *Kanamarua* Kuroda, 1951; *Nivitriton* Iredale, 1929; and others.

Suborder: Stenoglossa (Neogastropoda)

Highly developed gastropods with a more or less long siphon, a retractile proboscis and a well developed osphradium. The siphon lies protected in a correspondingly long siphonal canal. The radula is narrow (rachiglossan) or stiletto-like (toxoglossan). In the rachiglossan radula each transverse row has only one tooth on each side of the central tooth plate, but these may have three or more points, according to the genus and species. In the toxoglossan radula the central plate has completely disappeared, and the two lateral plates have become elongated, barbed and folded to form a channel, as in *Conus*. They are connected to venom glands and used to inject venom. Stenoglossan gastropods are almost exclusively predators and carrion-feeders. The sexes are separate.

 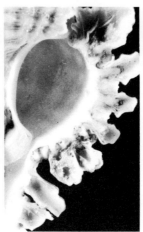 

In shells of the Muricidae there are relatively few basic types of varix. Thus (left) spines, usually formed by varices closing over, lobes (centre), and leaf-like lamellae (right).

SUPERFAMILY: MURICACEA
See Plates 27-32

Shell spiral, roundish-ovate to long and spindle-shaped with prominent ornament. Aperture oval, with a longish siphonal canal. Mantle with the hypobranchial gland producing a purple pigment. Operculum with a terminal or marginal nucleus. Radula rachiglossan, but reduced in the Coralliophilidae, in conformity with their habit of living in and on corals.

Family: Muricidae (Rock shells)

In these gastropods the hypobranchial gland produces a pale secretion which, on exposure to sunlight, changes first to yellow-green, then to a deep violet colour. Owing to its fastness this pigment, known as Tyrian purple, was much valued from Roman times right up to the Middle Ages as a dye for imperial and ecclesiastical robes.

The family has about 1000 widely distributed species living mainly in tropical seas, on rocky shores, coral reefs, or on stony, muddy or sandy bottoms; these habitats also have barnacles and small bivalves on which the Muricidae feed. Some forms drill holes in the prey, e.g. *Eupleura*, *Ocenebra* and *Urosalpinx*, and cause damage in oyster beds. Others have a conical tooth on the lip of the shell which is inserted between the shells of the bivalves on which they prey.

Shell spiral, varying in size and form, often convex with a short apex, and usually with prominent varices. Depending upon the form of the mantle edge these may be tuberculate, folded, leaf-like or spiny. As in many other gastropods shell growth is not continuous but takes place periodically. The edge of the aperture is first enlarged and then as growth in this area ceases the mantle starts to deposit the varices. Finally, the edge of the aperture starts to grow again. As the body whorl grows round towards an old varix the latter becomes re-absorbed. The distance between the varices and thus the number of varices per whorl is constant within each species. The siphonal canal may be short or very long, and open or partly closed. The shells of the Typhinae have tubular processes protruding from the angular shoulder of the whorls.

The identification of muricid shells is often difficult even for the specialist. The surface is seldom completely clean. Very often the fine spines, folds and sculptural details lie hidden among massive algal growths and they may easily be broken off during cleaning. In addition, even within a single species, the form and extent of the ornamental details may vary according to the conditions in which the animal has been living. The shell of an animal that has grown up in sheltered waters may develop richer and more delicate ornament than one which has been continuously subjected to the buffeting of waves. Some genera and subgenera of the Muricidae are also not very well defined. They may be based on small differences in the form of the shell, which may lead to a multiplicity of names, many of which are quite unnecessary. In recent years the systematics of the family have been revised in various ways, so that the status of some genera and subgenera may vary according to the system being followed. This family has usually been subdivided into six subfamilies (Muricinae, Ocenebrinae, Trophoninae, Typhinae, Thaidinae, Rapaninae). However, for various reasons there is a view that the Thaidinae should be established as a family in their own right (the Thaididae) and that the Rapaninae should be regarded as one of its subfamilies. The following survey is based on the investigations of the American scientist Emily H. Vokes (1964, 1971). MURICINAE: shell medium-sized to large, variously shaped with well developed varices. Genera: *Murex* Linné, 1758, synonyms: *Acupurpura* Jousseaume, 1880 and *Tubicauda* Jousseaume, 1880 (subgenera: *Bolinus* Pusch, 1837; *Haustellum* Schumacher, 1817); *Aspella* Mörch, 1877 (subgenera: *Dermomurex* Monterosato, 1890; *Gracilimurex* Thiele, 1929; *Takia* Kuroda, 1953; *Trialatella* Berry, 1964); *Calotrophon* Hertlein & Strong, 1951

(subgenus: *Attiliosa* Emerson, 1968); *Chicoreus* Montfort, 1810, synonym: *Euphyllon* Jousseaume, 1880 (subgenera: *Phyllonotus* Swainson, 1833; *Siratus* Jousseaume, 1880): *Favartia* Jousseaume, 1880 (subgenus: *Caribiella* Perrilliat Montoya, 1871); *Hexaplex* Perry, 1810, synonyms: *Bassiella* Wenz, 1941, *Muricanthus* Swainson, 1840 and *Trunculariopsis* Cossmann, 1921; *Homalocantha* Mörch, 1852; *Maxwellia* Baily, 1950; *Murexiella* Clench & Perez Farfante, 1945 (subgenus: *Subpterynotus* Olsson & Harbison, 1953); *Murexsul* Iredale, 1915; *Muricopsis* Bucquoy, Dautzenberg & Dollfus, 1882; *Poirieria* Jousseaume, 1880 (subgenus: *Paziella* Jousseaume, 1880); *Pterynotus* Swainson, 1833, synonym: *Marchia* Jousseaume, 1880 (subgenera: *Naquetia* Jousseaume, 1880; *Pterochelus* Jousseaume, 1880; *Purpurellus* Jousseaume, 1880). OCENEBRINAE: shell small to medium-sized with conspicuous spiral and axial ornament, and a siphonal canal which in some forms is closed to form a tube. Varices, when present, are irregular. Some cold-water forms, e.g. *Ocenebra*, *Urosalpinx*. Genera: *Ocenebra* Gray, 1847,

In some species of Muricidae the surface ornament varies according to the local environmental conditions. Above: two shells of *Truncular iopsis trunculus* (Linné, 1758). Right: two shells of *Murex brandaris* Linné, 1758. Both species (from the Mediterranean) showing tuberculate and spiny forms.

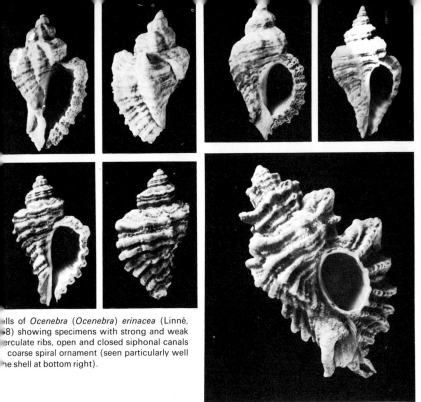

...lls of *Ocenebra* (*Ocenebra*) *erinacea* (Linné, ...8) showing specimens with strong and weak ...erculate ribs, open and closed siphonal canals ...coarse spiral ornament (seen particularly well ...he shell at bottom right).

synonym: *Tritonalia* Fleming, 1828 (subgenera: *Hadriania* Bucquoy, Dautzenberg and Dollfus, 1882; *Ocenebrina* Jousseaume, 1880); *Jaton* Pusch 1837 (subgenera: *Ceratostoma* Herrmannsen, 1846; *Pterorytis* Conrad, 1863); *Pteropurpura* Jousseaume, 1880, synonym: *Centrifuga* Grant & Gale, 1931, 1931 (subgenera: *Calcitrapessa* Berry, 1959; *Ocinebrellus* Jousseaume, 1880; *Poropteron* Jousseaume, 1880). The inclusion of the following genera in the subfamily Ocenebrinae has been questioned in recent years: *Eupleura* H. & A. Adams, 1853; *Hanetia* Jousseaume, 1880; *Urosalpinx* Stimpson, 1865; *Vitularia* Swainson, 1840, synonym: *Transtrafer* Iredale, 1929 (subgenus: *Crassilabrum* Jousseaume, 1880). TROPHONINAE: shell relatively thin, with spiral or reticulate ornament, and varices, which are rather thin and leaf-like, often with spines on the shoulder. Genera: *Trophon* Montfort, 1810 (subgenera: *Acanthotrophon* Hertlein & Strong, 1951; *Austrotrophon* Dall, 1902; *Axymene* Finlay, 1927; *Comptella* Finlay, 1927; *Xymene* Iredale, 1915; *Zacatrophon* Hertlain & Strong, 1951; *Zeatrophon* Finlay, 1927); *Actinotrophon* Dall, 1902; *Bedeva* Iredale, 1924; *Boreotrophon* Fischer, 1884; *Trophonopsis* Bucquoy, Dautzenberg & Dollfus, 1882 (subgenus *Pagodula* Monterosato, 1884); and others. TYPHINAE: shell small, with more or less distinct varices and tubular points on the angular shoulder. Genera: *Typhis* Montfort, 1810 (subgenera: *Haustellotyphis* Jousseaume, 1880; *Siphonochelus* Jousseaume, 1880; *Typhina* Jousseaume, 1880; *Typhinellus* Jousseaume,

Typical shells (left to right) of *Paratrophon, Vitularia, Eupleura* and *Urosalpinx*. Species: *Paratrophon patens* (Hombron & Jacquinot, 1854), 17mm, New Zealand; *Vitularia miliaris* (Gmelin, 1791), 30mm, Solomon Islands; *Eupleura caudata sulcidentata* Dall, 1890, 17mm, southern Florida; *Urosalpinx tampaensis* (Conrad, 1846), 20mm, also Florida.

1880; *Typhisopsis* Jousseaume, 1880); *Cinclidotyphis* Du Shane, 1969; *Distichotyphis* Keen & Campbell, 1964; *Pterotyphis* Jousseaume, 1880 (subgenus: *Tripterotyphis* Pilsbry & Lowe, 1932); and others.

Family: Thaididae (Dog whelks)

As a result of an Opinion issued by the International Commission for Zoological Nomenclature (Opinion No. 886, 1969) this family name replaces the older names Purpuridae and Thaisidae. The shells do not vary so much in form as those of the previous subfamily Muricinae. They are small-to-medium size, solid, more or less roundish-ovate to spindle-shaped, without varices, but with variable tuberculate or spiny spiral ornament, and usually with only a short siphonal canal. The animals are active predators that creep about on rocks, feeding on barnacles and bivalves, often in the intertidal zone. THAIDINAE: Body whorl large, spire relatively short, aperture wide and in contrast to the Drupinae (see below) with less callus deposited. Teeth only on the outer lip. Genera: *Thais* Röding, 1798 (subgenera: *Mancinella* Link, 1807; *Stramonita* Schumacher, 1817; *Thaisella* Clench, 1947; *Tribulus* H. & A.

Left: *Vitularia (Transtrafer) longmani* (Iredale, 1929); centre and right: *Typhis (Typhinellus) sowerbyi* Broderip, 1837, 10mm, Mediterranean, showing the tubular outgrowths between the varices that are characteristic of the genus *Typhis*.

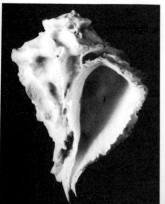

From left to right: *Acanthina tyrianthina* Berry, 1957, 30mm, West Mexico, showing the stout tooth on the outer lip, characteristic of the genus *Acanthina*, which is used in opening bivalves. (A similar tooth is seen well in Plate 31/1); *Acanthina spirata* Blainville, 1832, 25mm, Newport Bay, California (the small tooth is not visible in this photograph); *Morula (Cronia) avellana* (Reeve, 1846), 25mm, western Australia; *Haustrum (Lepsiella) scobina* Quoy & Gaimard, 1833, 20mm, New Zealand.

Adams, 1853; *Vasula* Mörch, 1860); *Acanthina* Fischer von Waldheim, 1807; *Agnewia* Tenison-Woods, 1878; *Concholepas* Lamarck, 1801; *Cymia* Mörch, 1860; *Haustrum* Perry, 1811 (subgenus: *Lepsiella* Iredale, 1912): *Lepsithais* Finlay, 1928; *Nassa* Röding, 1798; *Neothais* Iredale, 1912; *Nucella* Röding, 1798; *Pinaxia* H. & A. Adams, 1853; *Purpura* Bruguière, 1789; *Vexilla* Swainson, 1840; and others. DRUPINAE: shell small to medium-sized with teeth on both lips. Genera: *Drupa* Röding, 1798 (subgenera: *Drupina* Dall, 1923; *Ricinella* Schumacher, 1817); *Drupella* Thiele, 1925; *Maculotriton* Dall, 1904; *Morula* Schumacher, 1817 (subgenera: *Azumamorula* Emerson, 1968; *Cronia* H. & A. Adams, 1853; *Trachypollia* Woodring, 1928; *Risomurex* Olsson & McGinty, 1958. RAPANINAE: shell medium-sized, convex, with a rather short spire, a wide aperture and a short, fairly broad siphonal canal. Genera: *Rapana* Schumacher, 1817; *Chorus* Gray, 1847; *Forreria* Jousseaume, 1880; *Neorapana* Cooke, 1918; *Xanthochorus* P. Fischer, 1888.

Shell forms in *Thais, Nassa* and *Concholepas*. Species (left to right): *Thais (Mancinella) bufo* (Lamarck, 1822), 55mm, Queensland; *Nassa serta* (Bruguière, 1789), 40mm, Taiwan; *Concholepas concholepas* (Bruguière, 1792), 60mm, Chile.

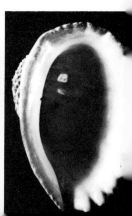

The genus *Forreria* has several fossil forms, but only a few living species, two of which live off the coast of California. The shell of *Forreria belcheri* (Hinds, 1843) has ten coarse-ribbed varices which carry fairly long spines at the shoulders. The shell shown is 90mm tall and was found on a sandy bottom in a depth of 20m off San Diego. The species *Forreria catalensis* Oldroyd is considerably smaller (up to 60mm), and has seven leaf-like varices and a longer siphonal canal.

Family: Coralliophilidae

A relatively small family, formerly known as the Magilidae, and differing from the Muricidae in their specialised adaptations for living in or on coral stocks. They have no radula. The family contains the turnip shells (e.g. *Rapa*) and coral shells (e.g. *Coralliophila*). The genus *Coralliophila* has been so much subdivided that it is almost impossible to give a specific name to some specimens, and in some cases it may even be difficult to assign a specimen to a genus. There is obviously need for a thorough revision of the group. Modern investigators try to restrict the designation *Latiaxis* to forms with the structural characters originally laid down for the type, i.e. *L. mawae*, namely, spire almost flat, shoulder keeled and lobed, spiral ornament fine, umbilicus wide with a large lobed margin and to regard specimens deviating from this (e.g. with a tall spire, coarse scaly sculpture) as belonging to *Coralliophila* in the wider sense. Genera: *Coralliophila* H. & A. Adams, 1853 (subgenera: *Fusomurex* Coen, 1922; *Genkaimurex* Kuroda, 1953; *Hirtomurex* Coen, 1922; *Lataxiena* Jousseaume, 1888; *Latimurex* Coen, 1922; *Lepadomurex* Coen, 1922; *Liniaxis* Laseron, 1955; *Mipus* Gregoria, 1885; *Orania* Pallary, 1900: *Pseudomurex* Monterosato, 1872); *Coralliobia* H. & A. Adams, 1853); *Coralliofusus* Kuroda, 1953; *Latiaxis* Swainson, 1840 (subgenera: *Babelomurex* Coen, 1922; *Tolema* Iredale, 1929): *Magilopsis* Sowerby, 1818; *Magilus* Montfort, 1810; *Quoyula* Iredale, 1912; *Rapa* Bruguière, 1792.

Family: Columbariidae (Pagoda shells)

Shell spindle-shaped with keeled whorls and a long siphonal canal. This family was established in 1928 for the single genus *Columbarium* Martens, 1881 which had previously been included in the Muricidae. The genus comprises about 15 species at depths of 100-1000m off Japan, Australia, South Africa and the West Indies. The New Zealand genus *Coluzea* Allan, 1929 should be regarded merely as a subgenus of *Columbarium*.

SUPERFAMILY: BUCCINACEA
See Plates 33-37

Shell small to medium-sized, ovate or spindle-shaped with a tall spire and smooth or ornamented whorls, without spires. The siphonal canal may be short or fairly long, depending upon the family and genus. Operculum with terminal or marginal nucleus. These gastropods have a long proboscis, but they do not bore, and with a few exceptions (e.g. *Columbella*) prey on other animals or feed on carrion. *Busycon* can open closed bivalves by inserting the edge of its shell.

Family: Buccinidae (Whelks)

Shell ovate to spindle-shaped smooth or ornamented, with a short or long siphonal canal. Columella usually smooth, sometimes wrinkled, without folds. With or without a periostracum. Living as predators or carrion-feeders. The family should possibly be subdivided into several subfamilies but in the absence of detailed anatomical investigations this is not yet possible. Genera: *Buccinum* Linné, 1758 (subgenus: *Madiella* Wenz, 1838); *Aeneator* Finlay, 1927; *Afrocominella* Iredale, 1918; *Ancistrolepis* Dall, 1894 (subgenera: *Clinopegma* Grant & Gale, 1931; *Japelion* Dall, 1916), *Antistreptus* Dall, 1902 (subgenus: *Anomacme* Strebel, 1905); *Austrofusus* Kobelt, 1881; *Babylonia* Schlüter, 1838; *Bailya* Smith 1944; *Bayerius* Olsson, 1971; *Beringius* Dall, 1886; *Buccinulum* Deshayes, 1830 (subgenera: *Euthrena* Iredale, 1918; *Euthrenopsis* Powell, 1929; *Euthria* Gray, 1850; *Evarnula* Finlay, 1927; *Nodopelagia* Hedley, 1915; *Tasmeuthria* Iredale, 1925); *Burnupena* Iredale,

Ancistrolepis (*Clinopegma*) *magna* Dall, 1895, a whelk from the ice-cold waters of the Bering Sea, having a thin shell with a periostracum. Exact locality: 58° 12' N, 171° 23' W, depth 100m.

69

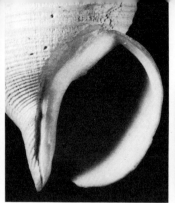
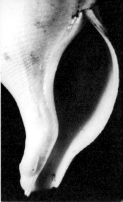

Apertures in *Neptunea*, *Buccinum* and *Sipho*. Species (left to right): *Neptunea kuroshio* Oyama, 1958, 80mm, Japan (aperture large, wide, oval; canal slightly curved, truncated at the top); *Buccinum leucostoma* Lischke, 1872, 80mm, Japan (aperture short, semicircular; canal very short, broad, truncated at the end); *Sipho gracilis* (Da Costa, 1778), 80mm, North Sea (aperture small, narrow; canal curved backwards and somewhat twisted).

1918; *Cantharus* Röding, 1798 (subgenera: *Gemophos* Olsson & Harbison, 1953; *Muricantharus* Olsson, 1971; *Pollia* Sowerby, 1834; *Pseudosalpinx* Olsson & Harbison, 1953); *Chauvetia* Monterosato, 1884; *Chlanidota* Martens, 1878 (subgenera: *Bathydomus* Thiele, 1912; *Notoficula* Thiele, 1917; *Pfefferia* Strebel, 1908); *Cominella* Gray 1850 (subgenera: *Acominia* Finlay, 1926; *Cominista* Finlay, 1926; *Cominula* Finlay, 1926; *Eucominia* Finlay, 1926; *Zephos* Finlay, 1926); *Ellicea* Finlay, 1928; *Engina* Gray, 1839; *Engoniophos* Woodring, 1928; *Eosipho* Thiele, 1929; *Exilioidea* Grant & Gale, 1931; *Glypteuthria* Strebel, 1905; *Hindsia* A. Adams, 1851; *Iredalula* Finlay, 1926; *Kelletia* Fischer, 1884; *Liomesus* Stimpson, 1865; *Macron* H. & A. Adams, 1853; *Metula* H. & A. Adams, 1853; *Mohnia* Friele, 1879; *Neobuccinum* Smith, 1879; *Neptunea* Röding, 1798; *Northia* Gray, 1847; *Pareuthria* Strebel, 1905; *Penion* Fischer, 1884, synonym: *Austrosipho* Cossmann, 1906; *Phos* Montfort, 1810 (subgenera: *Antillophos* Woodring, 1928; *Cymatophos* Pilsbry & Olsson, 1941; *Fax* Iredale, 1925; *Metaphos*

Left to right: *Cominella adspersa* (Bruguière, 1789), 50mm, New Zealand; *Trajana perideris* (Dall, 1910), 25mm, western Mexico; *Buccinulum multilineum* Powell, 1929, 35mm, New Zealand; *Pisania pusio* (Linné, 1758), 35mm, Florida.

Olsson, 1964; *Strombinophos* Pilsbry & Olsson, 1941); *Pisania* Bivona, 1832 (subgenera: *Caducifer* Dall 1904; *Ecmanis* Gistel, 1848; *Japeuthria* Iredale, 1918; *Jeannea* Iredale, 1912; *Prodotia* Dall, 1924); *Pisanianura* Rovereto, 1899; *Plicifusus* Dall, 1902 (subgenera: *Helicofusus* Dall, 1916; *Latifusus* Dall, 1916; *Microfusus* Dall, 1916; *Retifusus* Dall, 1916); *Prosipho* Thiele, 1912; *Pyrulofusus* Mörch, 1869; *Savatieria* Rochebrune & Mabille, 1885; *Searlesia* Harmer, 1915; *Sipho* Bruguière, 1792, synonym: *Colus* Röding, 1798 (subgenera: *Anomalisipho* Dautzenberg & Fischer, 1912; *Aulacofusus* Dall, 1918; *Latisipho* Dall, 1916; *Limatofusus* Dall, 1918; *Siphonellona* Wenz, 1938); *Siphonalia* A. Adams, 1863; *Siphonorbis* Mörch, 1869; *Solenosteira* Dall, 1890; *Sulcosinus* Dall, 1894; *Thalassoplanes* Dall, 1908; *Trajana* Gardner, 1948; *Triumphis* Gray, 1857 (subgenus: *Nicema* Woodring, 1964); *Truncaria* A. Adams & Reeve, 1848; *Turrisipho* Dautzenberg & Fischer, 1912; *Volutharpa* Fischer, 1856; *Volutopsius* Mörch, 1857; and others.

Family: Columbellidae (Dove shells)

Shell relatively small, smooth or ornamented, often with a striking pattern. Aperture narrow, usually open below (siphonal canal) and running out to a point above. Outer lip and columella usually toothed. This family, formerly known as the Pyrenidae, has about 400 species, varying considerably in shape, colour and ornament. They live on the shore and in deeper water in warm seas, and feed on algae and detritus. Genera: *Columbella* Lamarck, 1799; *Aesopus* Gould, 1860 (subgenus: *Ithiaesopus* Olsson & Harbison, 1953); *Anachis* H. & A. Adams, 1853 (subgenera: *Antizafra* Finlay, 1927; *Costoanachis* Sacco, 1890; *Glyptanachis* Pilsbry & Lowe, 1932; *Macrozafra* Finlay, 1927; *Parvanachis* Radwin, 1968; *Zafra* A. Adams, 1860; *Zafrona* Iredale, 1916); *Amphissa* H. & A. Adams, 1853 (subgenus: *Cosmioconcha* Dall, 1913); *Bifurcium* P. Fischer, 1884; *Decipifus* Olsson & McGinty, 1958; *Graphicomassa* Iredale, 1929; *Mazatlania* Dall, 1900; *Microcithara* P. Fischer, 1884; *Mitrella* Risso, 1826 (subgenera: *Alcira* H. Adams, 1860; *Antimitrella* Powell, 1937; *Columbellopsis* Bucquoy, Dautzenberg & Dollfus, 1882; *Paratilia* Thiele, 1924; *Paxula* Finlay, 1907; *Pyreneola* Iredale, 1918; *Zemitrella* Finlay, 1927); *Nassarina* Dall, 1889 (subgenera: *Cigclirina* Woodring, 1928; *Radwinia* Shasky, 1970; *Steironepion* Pilsbry & Lowe, 1932; *Zanassarina* Pilsbry & Lowe, 1932); *Nitidella* Swainson, 1840; *Parametaria* Dall, 1916; *Psarostola* Rehder, 1943; *Pyrene* Röding, 1798 (subgenus: *Euplica* Dall, 1889); *Ruthia* Shasky, 1970; *Strombina* Mörch, 1852; *Zetekia* Dall, 1918; and others.

Family: Fasciolariidae (Tulip, Band or Spindle shells)

Shell more or less spindle-shaped, whorls usually with spiral ridges and axial ribs, more rarely smooth. Aperture with a longish siphonal canal, often curved somewhat to the left. Columella with or without foles. Operculum horny with a terminal nucleus. These are carnivorous gastropods, living in tropical seas. FASCIOLARIINAE: aperture with a more or less curved siphonal canal, columella with folds. From shallow water (5-60m) or on coral reefs. Genera: *Fasciolaria* Lamarck, 1799 (subgenera: *Cinctura* Hollister, 1957; *Tarantinaea* Monterosato, 1917; *Pleuroploca* Fischer, 1884; *Cyrtulus* Hinds, 1843; *Latirus*

The shell of *Fusinus* (*Fusinus*) *irregularis* (Grabau, 1904) is often offered as *F. dupetitthouarsi* (see Plate 35/7), but it has a relatively longer and more curved siphonal canal with a reddish end. They both come from Lower California.

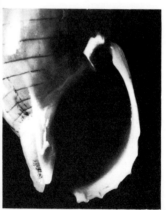

Anticlockwise: *Alectrion, Nassarius* and *Niotha* showing differences in the development of the columellar callus (parietal shield), in the folds at the top of the aperture and in the roundish exhalant canals. *Alectrion* also has saw-teeth on the outer lip.

Montfort, 1810 (subgenera: *Dolicholatirus* Bellardi, 1884; *Fractolatirus* Iredale, 1936; *Fusilatirus* McGinty, 1955; *Latirulus* Cossmann, 1901; *Polygona* Schumacher, 1817); *Leucozonia* Gray, 1847 (subgenus: *Latirolagena* G. F. Harris, 1897); *Opeatostoma* Berry, 1958; *Peristernia* Mörch, 1852; *Saginafusus* Iredale, 1931; *Taron* Hutton, 1884. FUSININAE: aperture usually with a very long, straight or only slightly curved siphonal canal. Columella without folds. From shallow to deep water (20-3000m). Deep-water forms have white shells. Genera: *Fusinus* Rafinesque, 1815, synonym: *Fusus* Bruguière, 1789 (subgenera: *Aptyxis* Troschel, 1868; *Barbarofusus* Grabau & Shimer, 1909; *Gracilipurpura* Jousseaume, 1880; *Kryptos* Dautzenberg & Fischer, 1896; *Microcolus* Cotton & Godfrey, 1932; *Propefusus* Iredale, 1924; *Simplicifusus* Kira, 1962); *Buccinofusus* Conrad, 1867; *Granulifusus* Kuroda & Habe, 1952; and others.

Family: Nassariidae (Dog whelks)

Shell solid, ovate to spherical, small to medium-sized, with spiral or axial sculpture, or both. Aperture roundish-ovate, usually with a callus in the lower part. Outer lip with a toothed inner edge. Columella often with a broad parietal shield. Siphonal canal very short or deep and somewhat curved. Operculum roundish-triangular or claw-shaped, frequently with a jagged edge. These gastropods have an extraordinary ability to detect the presence of prey or carrion in the water. The European *Nassarius reticulatus* (netted dog whelk), for example, lies buried in the bottom waiting for prey with its proboscis stretched out on the sand in the direction of the water current. When the water is moving the animal can detect prey at a distance of up to 30m. It will then creep up-current towards it. At low tide their tracks can be detected in the sand, usually ending in a small mound, which marks the position of the animal itself. The family is mainly distributed in tropical waters from the shore down to depths of 1000m. Identification of individual shells is often difficult, because they vary considerably according to the living conditions (age, food supply, fluctuations in the water salinity). The parietal shield is only fully developed in adult specimens. The following survey of genera and subgenera follows the revision by the New Zealand zoologist W. O. Cernohorsky (1972). Genera: *Nassarius* Dumeril, 1806 (subgenera: *Aciculina* H. & A. Adams, 1853; *Alectrion* Montfort, 1810; *Arcularia* Link, 1807; *Hinia* Leach in Gray, 1847, synonym: *Hima* Leach in Gray, 1852; *Ilyanassa* Stimpson, 1865; *Niotha* H. & A. Adams, 1853; *Pallacera* Woodring, 1964; *Phrontis* H. & A. Adams, 1853; *Plicarcularia* Thiele, 1929; *Telasco* H. & A. Adams, 1853: *Uzita* H. & A. Adams, 1853; *Zaphon* H. & A. Adams, 1853; *Zeuxis* H. & A. Adams, 1853); *Adinopsis* Odhner, 1922; *Amyclina* Iredale, 1918; *Bullia* Gray, 1833, synonym: *Dorsanum* Gray, 1847; *Cyllene* Gray, 1838; *Cyclope* Risso, 1826 (subgenus: *Panormella* Monterosato, 1917); *Demoulia* Gray, 1838; *Hannonia* Pallary, 1914; *Hebra* H. & A. Adams, 1853, synonym: *Scabronassa* Peile, 1939; *Naytia* H. & A. Adams, 1853; *Naytiopsis* Thiele, 1929; *Profundinassa* Thiele, 1929; *Pygmaeonassa* Annandale, 1924; *Sphaeronassa* Locard, 1886.

Above left: the elegant
Busycon coarctatum
(Sowerby, 1825) from the
Gulf of Mexico is one of the
rarest collectors' pieces.

Volema pyrum (Gmelin,
1791) on the left, in comparison with its tuberculate
subspecies *Volema pyrum
nodosa* (Lamarck, 1822).
Both 50mm, from East
Africa.

74

Family: Melongenidae (Crown Conchs)

Formerly known as the Galeodidae. Shell large to very large, varying considerably in form and ornament. Operculum thick and claw-shaped. These are predatory or carrion-feeding gastropods from shallow waters in the tropics. The family has only a few genera and species, usually restricted to definite regions. Thus, *Melongena* off tropical America, *Pugilina* off Africa and in the Indo-Pacific, *Syrinx* off Australia. *Melongena* has hitherto been regarded as a full genus but has recently been placed as a subgenus of *Volema*, and the same applies to *Pugilina*. The North American genus *Busycon* has shells with dextral coiling (e.g. *B. canaliculatum*, Plate 37, No. 12) and sinistral coiling (e.g. *B. contrarium* Plate 37, No. 11). The species *B. coarctatum* Sowerby, 1825 was until a few years ago only known from a few museum specimens, with labels that gave no proper locality. About 1950 its area of distribution was re-discovered off the Yucatan Peninsula. Genera: *Volema* Röding, 1798 (subgenera: *Hemifusus* Swainson, 1840, synonym: *Semifusus* Agassiz, 1846; *Melongena* Schumacher, 1817, synonym: *Galeodea* Röding, 1798; *Pugilina* Schumacher, 1817, synonym: *Volegalea* Iredale, 1938); *Busycon* Röding, 1798; *Syrinx* Röding, 1798, synonym: *Megalatractus* Fischer, 1884.

SUPERFAMILY: VOLUTACEA
See Plates 38-44

Shell cylindrical to spindle-shaped, frequently smooth, sometimes with axial ribs and spiral ornament. Aperture often very narrow, but may be wide, with a siphonal canal of varying length. Columella usually with folds. Operculum normally absent, but present in a few groups, with an almost terminal nucleus. Radula rachiglossan. These are predatory gastropods with a protrusible proboscis which feed on molluscs and other small marine animals. The superfamily contains a large number of species, with several groups that are easily distinguishable by their appearance.

Family: Volutidae (Volute shells)

Shell medium-sized to very large, spindle-shaped to ovate. Aperture longish, truncated and emarginate below. Usually without an operculum. So far some 200 species have been described of which about 30 are known only from 2 or 3 specimens. The family is best represented in warm seas, and mainly off Australia, the east and west coasts of Africa, the West Indies, and particularly the Indo-Pacific, which is the centre of distribution. These shells are much prized by collectors on account of their form and range of colours. The genus *Amoria* is typical of Australia, *Scaphella* of the eastern coast of America, *Cymbium* of west Africa, and *Ampulla* of north Africa, Portugal and southern Spain. The Pacific coast of central America is relatively poor in volutes (a few species of *Lyria* in shallow water and of *Adelomelon, Calliotectum* and *Tractolira* in depths of 700-3000m). There are also species adapted for colder temperatures, off New Zealand, South Australia, South Africa and in the Arctic and Antarctic. The dull greyish *Arctomelon stearnsi* Dall, 1872, for example, lives under drift ice in the Bering Sea. The larval stage is stationary and not free-swimming and as a result many volute species are restricted to a very small range. Unlike the cowries, none of the volutes have a range covering more or less the whole of Indo-Pacific. In practice they can only increase their range by creeping. Local differences in form (sometimes designated as subspecies) are possibly due to inbreeding. The animals dig in sand or muddy sand, using the large, often very colourful foot and, in keeping with their predatory habits, they can move faster than most other marine gastropods. A couple of species live in the intertidal zone or in very shallow water, but the majority live in depths of 10-100m, and a few are known only from dredge hauls taken at depths of 100-3000m. In recent years Australian trawlers have brought up large numbers of such deep-water forms from off the Australian coast. VOLUTINAE: *Voluta* Linné, 1758. ATHLETINAE: *Ternivoluta* von Martens, 1897; *Volutocorbis* Dall, 1890; CALLIOTECTINAE: *Calliotectum* Dall, 1890; *Fusivoluta* von Martens, 1902; *Neptuneopsis* Sowerby, 1898; *Teramachia* Kuroda, 1931. CYMBIINAE: *Cymbium* Röding, 1798; *Callipara* Gray, 1847; *Cymbiola* Swainson, 1831 (subgenera: *Aulica* Gray, 1847; *Aulicina* Rovereto, 1899; *Cymbiolena* Iredale, 1929); *Cymbiolacca* Iredale, 1929; *Melo* Broderip & Sowerby, 1826 (subgenus: *Melocorona* Pilsbry & Olsson, 1954); *Sigaluta* Rehder, 1967. FULGORARIINAE: *Fulgoraria* Schumacher, 1817 (subgenera: *Kurodina* Rehder, 1969; *Musashia* Hayashi, 1960; *Psephaea* Crosse, 1871; *Saotomea* Habe, 1943; *Volutipysma* Rehder, 1969); *Ericusa* H. & A. Adams, 1858 (subgenus: *Mesericusa* Iredale, 1929); *Festilyria* Pilsbry & Olsson, 1954; *Guivillea* Watson, 1886; *Harpavoluta* Thiele, 1912; *Iredalina* Finlay, 1926; *Livonia* Gray, 1855. LYRIINAE: *Lyria* Gray, 1847 (subgenera: *Enaeta* H. & A. Adams, 1853; *Harpeola* Dall, 1907; *Lyreneta* Iredale, 1937). ODONTOCYMBIOLINAE: *Odontocymbiola* Clench & Turner, 1964; *Miomelon* Dall, 1907; *Tractolira* Dall, 1896; *Volutoconus* Crosse, 1871; SCAPHELLINAE: *Scaphella* Swainson, 1832 (subgenera: *Aurinia* H. & A. Adams, 1853; *Clenchina* Pilsbry & Olsson, 1853); *Amoria* Gray, 1855 (subgenera: *Amorena* Iredale, 1929; *Relegamoria* Iredale, 1936; *Zebramoria* Iredale, 1929); *Ampulla* Röding, 1798, synonym: *Halia* Risso, 1826; *Cymbiolista* Iredale, 1929); *Nannamoria* Iredale, 1929; *Notopeplum* Finlay, 1927; *Notovoluta* Cotton, 1946; *Paramoria* McMichael, 1960; *Volutifusus* Conrad, 1863. ZIDONINAE: *Zidona* H. & A. Adams, 1853; *Adelomelon* Dall, 1906 (subgenera: *Pachycymbiola* von Ihering, 1907; *Weaveria* Clench & Turner, 1964); *Alcithoe* H. & A. Adams, 1853 (subgenus: *Leporemax* Iredale, 1937); *Arctomelon* Dall, 1915; *Cottonia* Iredale, 1934; *Harpulina* Dall, 1906; *Pachymelon* Marwick, 1926 (subgenus: *Palomelon* Finlay, 1926); *Provocator* Watson, 1882; *Teremelon* Marwick, 1926.

Many species of *Cymbium* come from off the west coast of Africa. The specimen of *Cymbium glans* shown here is 25cm tall and comes from a depth of 10m off the coast of Senegal (Dakar). The animal secretes a lacquer-like layer over the brown periostracum, in which small sand granules often become embedded. Other West African species are *Cymbium cucumis* Röding, 1798, *C. marmoratum* Link, 1807 and *C. pachys* (Pallary, 1930) as well as those shown in Plate 38: *C. cymbium* (Linné, 1758); *C. olla* (Linné, 1758) and *C. pepo* (Lightfoot, 1786).

Both shells belong to the genus *Melo*. In the subgenus *Melo* (*Melo*) the apex becomes increasingly covered by the growth of the shell whorls, whereas in the subgenus *Melo* (*Melocrona*) (right) the apex becomes encircled by a crown-like spiny spiral.

Many genera and species show a characteristic embryonic apex, which is often only properly visible under a strong lens, and this is particularly so in the Volutidae. Thus the apex may be (from left to right) stumpy (e.g. *Volutoconus*), globular (e.g. *Cymbium*), spherical (e.g. *Fulgoraria*) or nipple-shaped (e.g. *Alcithoe*).

Family: Harpidae (Harp shells)

Shell strikingly shaped, with a short spire and a larger body whorl, more or less strongly ribbed, with a bright colour pattern. The family has only 14 living (and 27 fossil) species, distributed in all tropical and subtropical seas, except the western Atlantic, on sandy bottoms in depths of 40-200m. In so far as the process has been observed these animals feed on small crabs which they enclose in a covering of sticky saliva and sand before consuming them. This evidently causes the crabs to fall into a kind of stupor. When stimulated harp shells produce considerable amounts of saliva and it is possible that as in the Tonnacea this contains a neurotoxin with paralysing properties. They have the ability to cast off the rear part of the foot in order to escape from an enemy. Genera: *Harpa* Röding, 1798; *Austroharpa* Finlay, 1931 (subgenus: *Palamharpa* Iredale, 1931).

Development of the apex in the Harpidae. After a small, rather smooth embryonic whorl the ornament of the shell quickly becomes quite characteristic. Species (left to right): *Harpa crenata* Swainson, 1822; *Harpa ventricosa* Lamarck, 1816; *Harpa major* Röding, 1798.

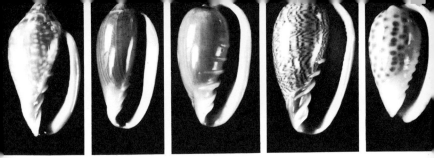

Shells of the Marginellidae show the typically thickened outer lip and the variation in length of the aperture. Examples) (left to right): *Marginella* (raised spire, end of aperture reaching the upper quarter of the shell); *Prunum* (flat, wedge-shaped spire and long, narrow aperture); *Closia* (flat, somewhat sunken spire, outer lip very long); *Cryptospira* (hidden spire, aperture as long as the shell); *Persicula* (aperture thickened above, ending at the apex with an exhalant canal).

The Pacific coast of central America has the heaviest and the largest of the Olividae. *Oliva incrassata* (Lightfoot, 1786) lives near low water on the outer side of sandy reefs from Lower California to Peru. Young individuals do not have the conspicuous shoulder angle of the adults. With a length of 65cm and a width of 40cm a fully grown shell weights 60g, and is nearly three times as heavy as the other species.

Oliva porphyria is one of the few shells from the west coast of America described by Linné in 1758, so this large, beautiful and rather rare shell had already been brought to Europe by travellers and sailors. It is distributed from the Gulf of California to Panama. It is frequently confused with the very rare *Conus gloriamaris* Chemnitz, 1777, to which it has a slight resemblance in colour and pattern.

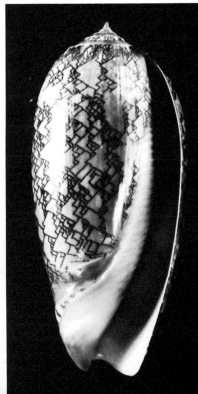

In the brown *Vasum rhinoceros* (Gmelin, 1791), from the waters off Zanzibar, East Africa, the shells may have pointed, spiny folds or stumpy tubercles. The lines of colour on the surface may run spirally and axially. There is also a yellow form, see Plate 44/1.

Family: Marginellidae (Margin shells)

Shell, with a few exceptions, rather small, very colourful, smooth and shiny, rarely with weak ornament. Spire conical. Aperture usually very narrow, without operculum. Lip edges thickened (hence 'margin' shells). The family contains about 600 species of predatory gastropods distributed in all warm seas, but particularly off the western coast of Africa. Two of the subfamilies (Marginellinae and Cystiscinae) are based on differences in the structure of the radula, the third (Marginelloninae) is restricted to a few species differing considerably in size. The nomenclature is not very satisfactory. The following survey is based on a revision by the American zoologist E. Coan (1965).

MARGINELLINAE: *Marginella* Lamarck, 1799 (subgenera: *Alaginella* Laseron, 1957; *Austroginella* Laseron, 1957; *Carinaginella* Laseron, 1957; *Denticuloglabella* Sacco, 1890; *Gibberula* Swainson, 1840, synonym: *Eratoidea* Winkauff, 1879; *Protoginella* Laseron, 1957) *Balanetta* Jousseaume, 1875 (subgenus: *Ovaginella* Laseron, 1957); *Bullata* Jousseaume, 1875 (subgenera: *Closia* Gray, 1857; *Cryptospira* Hinds, 1844); *Canalispira* Jousseaume, 1875; *Dentimargo* Cossmann, 1899; *Glabella* Swainson, 1840; *Hyalina* Schumacher, 1817; *Mesoginella* Laseron, 1957 (subgenera: *Plicaginella* Laseron, 1957; *Spiroginella* Laseron, 1957; *Urniginella* Laseron, 1957); *Persicula* Schumacher, 1817, synonym: *Rabicea* Gray, 1857); *Prunum* Hermannsen, 1852, synonyms: *Egouena* Jousseaume, 1875, *Egociena* Cotton, 1949 and *Leptegouana* Woodring, 1928; *Serrata* Jousseaume, 1875 (subgenera: *Baroginella* Laseron, 1957; *Conuginella*, Laseron, 1957; *Exiginella* Laseron, 1957; *Hydroginella* Laseron, 1957; *Vetaginella* Laseron, 1957); *Volvarina* Hinds, 1844 (subgenera: *Diluculum* Barnard, 1962; *Haloginella* Laseron, 1957; *Neptoginella* Laseron, 1957; *Phyloginella* Laseron, 1957; *Sinuginella* Laseron, 1957); *Volvarinella* Habe, 1951; CYSTISCINAE: *Cystiscus* Stimpson, 1865, synonym: *Euliginella* Laseron, 1957; *Crithe* Gould, 1860 (subgenus: *Epiginella* Laseron, 1957); *Cypraeolina* Cerulli-Irelli, 1911; *Deviginella* Laseron, 1957; *Extra* Jousseaume, 1894; *Granula* Jousseaume, 1875; *Granulina* Jousseaume, 1888: *Kogomea* Habe, 1951; *Marginellopsis* Bavay, 1911; *Triginella* Laseron, 1957. MARGINELLONINAE: *Marginellona* Martens, 1903; *Afrivoluta* Tomlin, 1947.

Family: Olividae (Olive shells)

Shell cylindrical to spindle-shaped, smooth and shiny, usually colourful and variously patterned, often covered by an enamel-like layer deposited by the mantle lobes (this is comparable with the similar layer in cowries). Spire fairly low. Aperture long, its upper end often with a swollen exhalant canal, its lower end usually somewhat concave. With or without an operculum. These gastropods are distributed in warm seas, living mostly in the shore region and feeding on small crabs and other invertebrates, as well as carrion. They spend the day hidden under the sand and become active at night, moving about just beneath the surface of the sand. OLIVINAE: *Oliva* Bruguière, 1789 (subgenera: *Carmione* Gray, 1858; *Galeola* Gray; *Neocylindrus* P. Fischer, 1883; *Omogymna* Martens, 1897; *Parvoliva* Thiele, 1929; *Strephona* Mörch, 1852; *Strephonella* Dall, 1909); *Agaronia* Gray, 1839; *Ancilla* Lamarck, 1799 (subgenera: *Alocospira* Cossmann, 1899; *Ancillista* Iredale, 1936; *Ancillus* Montfort, 1810; *Baryspira* P. Fischer, 1883; *Chiloptygma* H. & A. Adams, 1853; *Eburna* Lamarck, 1801; *Gracilispira* Olsson, 1956; *Pinguispira* Finlay, 1927; *Sparella* Gray, 1857; *Turrancilla* Martens, 1903); *Belloliva* Peile, 1922 (subgenera: *Gemmoliva* Iredale, 1924; *Olivellopsis* Thiele, 1929); *Jaspidella* Olsson, 1956; *Olivancillaria* d'Orbigny, 1839 (subgenus: *Micana* Gray, 1858; and others); *Olivella* Swainson, 1831 (subgenus: *Callianax* H. & A. Adams, 1853; and others). PSEUDOLIVINAE: shell roundish to pear-shaped, with a spiral groove which ends in a small tooth at the outer edge of the aperture. A few species off Australia, southern and western Africa. Genera: *Pseudoliva* Swainson, 1840: *Fulmentum* P. Fischer, 1884; *Melapium* H. & A. Adams, 1853; *Sylvanocochlis* Melvill, 1903; *Zemira* H. & A. Adams, 1858.

Family: Vasidae (Vase shells)

Shell fairly large, solid and heavy, spirally ornamented with spines or tubercles. This is a small family with only about 30 species, but widely distributed in warm seas. Little is known of their biology. They live in shallow water (sandy, stony, sometimes with algal growths), and feed on bivalve

Volutomitra groenlandica (Beck, 1842) from far northern seas is the type species of the genus *Volutomitra*. The actual height of the specimen shown here is 25mm. It is brown and came from a depth of 200m in Grindavíkurdjúp, Iceland.

   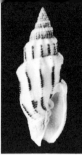 

Examples of shell form in the Mitridae (left to right): *Pterygia* (c.f. Plate 45/20), ovate with low spire and long aperture; *Imbricaria*, wedge-shaped, with extended apex and long, narrow aperture; 2 species of *Vexillum* (c.f. Plate 45/10 and 45/19), spindle-shaped, whorls ribbed or folded, aperture varying in length; *Strigatella* (c.f. Plate 45/14), globose with aperture restricted to the lower half of the shell.

molluscs, possibly also on marine worms. The division of the family into two subfamilies is based on the structure of the radula and the columellar folds. The subfamily Turbinellinae was formerly known as the Xancinae (chank shells, from the Hindi word *Cankh*, a shell). The type genus was first named *Xancus* by Röding, 1798, then *Turbinella* by Lamarck, 1799. After various nomenclatorial arguments the International Commission for Zoological Nomenclature decided in 1957 that the genus should be known as *Turbinella*.
VASINAE: *Vasum* Röding, 1798 (subgenera: *Altivasum* Hedley, 1914; *Globivasum* Abbott, 1950; *Siphovasum* Rehder & Abbott, 1951); *Tudicla* Röding, 1798; *Tudicula* H. & A. Adams, 1863; *Afer* Conrad, 1858; *Metzgeria* Norman, 1879; *Piestochilus* Meek, 1864; *Ptychatractus* Stimpson, 1865.
TURBINELLINAE: *Turbinella* Lamarck, 1799, synonym: *Xancus* Röding, 1798.

In the Terebridae the pale and dark spiral bands on the surface of the shell are remarkably constant even in varying local conditions and they are a valuable aid to species identification.
Left to right: *Terebra subulata* (Linné, 1767), with 3 rows of dark markings on the body whorl; *Terebra areolata* (Link, 1807), with 4 rows; *Terebra strigata* Sowerby, 1825, with tiger pattern; *Terebra maculata* (Linné, 1758), with 2 rows of marking, those in the upper row larger.

Family: Volutomitridae

Shell 4-45mm, resembling that of the Mitridae, but the radula is of the volutid type. About 24 living (66 fossil) species, living in sand and mud at depths of 10-2000m in all cold and temperate seas. Genera: *Volutomitra* H. & A. Adams, 1853 (subgenera: *Latiromitra* Locard, 1897; *Paradmete* Strebel, 1908); *Microvoluta* Angas, 1877; *Peculator* Iredale, 1924; *Waimatea* Finlay, 1927.

SUPERFAMILY: MITRACEA
See Plates 45 and 46

A transitional group between the Volutacea with a rachiglossan radula and the Conacea with a toxoglossan radula.

Family: Mitridae

Shells mostly spindle-shaped, with a spire of varying height, a narrow aperture pointed at the top, with a short canal at the bottom, and with 3-4 prominent columellar folds. Radula rachiglossan. Some species have a venom gland, used to kill the prey. Widely distributed in warm seas, particularly in the Indo-Pacific (about 400 of the 600 known species); a few in the Mediterranean. The animals burrow in the sand. About 85% live on the shore, the remainder in depths down to 1400m. MITRINAE: *Mitra* Lamarck, 1798, synonyms: *Atrimitra* Dall, 1918 and *Fuscomitra* Pallary, 1900 (subgenera *Nebularia* Swainson, 1840; *Strigatella* Swainson, 1840); *Charitodoron* Tomlin, 1932. CYLINDROMITRINAE: *Pterygia* Röding, 1798. IMBRICARIINAE: *Imbricaria* Schumacher, 1817; *Cancilla* Swainson, 1840 (subgenus: *Domiporta* Cernohorsky, 1970): *Neocancilla* Cernohorsky, 1966; *Scabricola* Swainson, 1840 (subgenus: *Swainsonia* H. & A. Adams, 1853); *Subcancilla* Olsson & Harbison, 1953; *Ziba* H. & A. Adams, 1853. VEXILLINAE: *Vexillum* Röding, 1798 (subgenera: *Costellaria* Swainson, 1840; *Pusia* Swainson, 1840); *Austromitra* Finlay, 1927; *Thala* H. & A. Adams, 1853; *Zierliana* Gray, 1847.

Family: Cancellariidae (Nutmeg shells)

Shell small with the axial ribs and the narrow spiral striae forming a kind of network. Aperture ovate, often rounded-triangular, with an exhalant canal above, the inner lip toothed or folded. Columella with 2-4 folds. No operculum. Siphonal canal somewhat beak-like but poorly developed. With or without an umbilicus. Distributed in warm seas, in fairly deep water, and mainly off the western coasts of tropical America. Little is known of their feeding habits, but from the structure of the radula they may take shell-less micro-organisms from the sea floor. Genera: *Cancellaria* Lamarck, 1799 (subgenera: *Agatrix* Petit, 1967; *Bivetia* Jousseaume, 1887; *Bivetiella* Wenz, 1943: *Bivetopsia* Jousseaume, 1887; *Euclia* H. & A. Adams, 1854; *Hertleinia* Marks, 1949; *Merica* H. & A. Adams, 1854; *Ovilia* Jousseaume, 1887; *Pyruclia* Olsson, 1932); *Cancellaphera* Iredale, 1930; *Admete* Krøyer, 1842 (subgenus: *Zeadmete* Finlay, 1927); *Aphera* H. & A. Adams, 1854 (subgenera: *Massyla* H. & A. Adams, 1854; *Sydaphera* Iredale, 1929); *Bonellitia* Jousseaume, 1887; *Narona* H. & A. Adams, 1854 (subgenera: *Anapepta*

Finlay, 1930; *Brocchinia* Jousseaume, 1887; *Craw-fordina* Dall, 1918; *Inglisella* Finlay, 1924; *Mericella* Thiele, 1929; *Progabbia* Dall, 1918; *Solatia* Jousseaume, 1887; *Sveltella* Cossmann, 1889; *Sveltia* Jousseaume, 1887; *Tribia* Jousseaume, 1887); *Oamaruia* Finlay, 1924; *Pepta* Iredale, 1925; *Perplicaria* Dall, 1890; *Trigonostoma* Blainville, 1827 (subgenera: *Arizelostoma* Iredale, 1936; *Extractrix* Korobkow, 1955; *Olssonella* Petit, 1970; *Scalptia* Jousseaume, 1887; *Ventrilia* Jousseaume, 1887): *Waipaoa* Marwick, 1931.

Right: *Terebra triseriata* (Gray, 1834) from the Indo-Pacific is the gastropod with the largest number of whorls. With a length of 10cm and a diameter of 7mm the shell has c. 50 whorls.

Conus (*Lithoconus*) *prometheus* Hwass in Bruguière, 1792, a large cone shell from the northern part of the West African coast. This specimen, 13cm tall, came from Lanzarote in the Canary Islands.

SUPERFAMILY: CONACEA (Toxoglossa)

See Plates 46-50

Shell very variable in form. Radula with stiletto-like teeth, connected with a venom gland, the venom being used to kill the prey.

Family: Conidae (Cone shells)

Shell heavy, conical, of various sizes, with a flat spire, a sharp-edged outer lip and a periostracum. Aperture long and fairly narrow, corresponding with the shape of the operculum. Columella without folds. Distributed in all warm, particularly tropical seas, mainly in fairly deep water, under rocks or in reef crevices. The animal has a long, fleshy proboscis which can be extended far beyond the edge of the shell. The venom apparatus consists of a venom gland connected by a duct with the radula sac which contains the hollow and barbed teeth. A single poison-filled tooth is transferred from the radula sac to the proboscis which ejects it into the prey, in whose tissues it remains. If the proboscis misses its aim the tooth is shed. Normally the animal uses this apparatus for paralysing its prey, but it can also use it as a weapon if aroused. The sting of one of these gastropods can cause paralysis and even death in man. The most dangerous species are *Conus aulicus*, *C. geographus*, *C. marmoreus*, *C. striatus*, *C. textile* and *C. tulipa*. On account of the beautiful shape and colours of the shells this family is very popular with collectors. The most highly prized species is the rather rare *Conus gloriamaris* of which only 25 specimens have so far been found. Genera: *Conus* Linné, 1758 (subgenera: *Asprella* Schaufuss, 1869; *Chelyconus* Mörch, 1852; *Cleobula* Iredale, 1930; *Conasprella* Thiele, 1929; *Cylinder* Montfort, 1810; *Darioconus* Iredale, 1930; *Dauciconus* Cotton, 1945; *Endemoconus* Iredale, 1931; *Floraconus* Iredale, 1930; *Gastridium* Modeer, 1793; *Hermes* Montfort, 1810; *Lautoconus* Monterosato, 1923; *Leporiconus* Iredale, 1930; *Leptoconus* Swainson, 1840; *Lithoconus* Mörch, 1852; *Parviconus* Cotton & Godfrey, 1932; *Phasmoconus* Mörch, 1852; *Pionoconus* Mörch, 1852; *Puncticulis* Swainson, 1840; *Pyruconus*

In the last major families of the Neogastropoda we again come across shells with a slit or indentation at the upper end of the aperture (for the passage of used respiratory water and excrement). This is not homologous with the similar structure in *Pleurotomaria* (see p. 34). Left: anal sinus in the form of a curved indentation at the upper end of the aperture in a cone shell. Centre and right: notch and sinus in *Daphnella* and *Turris*.

Olsson, 1967; *Regiconus* Iredale, 1930; *Rhizoconus* Mörch, 1852; *Rhombus* Montfort, 1810; *Stephanoconus* Mörch, 1852; *Strioconus* Thiele, 1929; *Textilia* Swainson, 1840; *Tuliparia* Swainson, 1840; *Virgiconus* Cotton, 1945; *Virroconus* Iredale, 1930; *Ximeniconus* Emerson & Old, 1962); *Hemiconus* Cossmann, 1889; *Mamiconus* Cotton & Godfrey, 1932.

Family: Terebridae (Auger shells)

Shell tall and pointed, with numerous whorls, a small aperture, a sharp outer lip and a short siphonal canal. Operculum horny. Species of the genus *Terebra* lack the radula, whereas those in the genera *Duplicaria* and *Hastula* have a pair of slender, curved teeth, and *Impages* has a venom apparatus similar to that of the cone shells. These gastropods mostly live in fine sand in tropical seas. Little is known of their feeding habits. Genera: *Terebra* Bruguière, 1789 (subgenera: *Abretiella* Bartsch, 1923; *Decorihastula* Oyama, 1961; *Clathroterebra* Oyama, 1961; *Noditerebra* Cossmann, 1896; *Oxymeris* Dall, 1903; *Perirhoe* Dall, 1908, synonym: *Dimidacus* Iredale, 1929; *Strioterebrum* Sacco, 1891; *Subula* Schumacher, 1817; *Triplostephanus* Dall, 1908); *Duplicaria* Dall, 1908, synonym: *Duplomeriza* Dall, 1919); *Hastula* H. & A. Adams, 1853, synonym: *Punctoterebra* Bartsch, 1923); *Impages* Smith, 1873.

Family: Turridae (Turrids or Turrets)

Shell very small to relatively large, spindle-shaped, with a slit-like anal sinus in the edge of the outer lip. Whorls angular or rounded, with axial or spiral ornament. Siphonal canal long and slender or short and compact. Columella smooth or folded. Operculum horny. Many species have a venom apparatus, as in the cone shells, but in others the radula is rachiglossan. All groups have a venom gland. This is a large family with hundreds of species distributed in all seas. In the 19th century the few species then known were placed in the genus *Pleurotoma* Lamarck, 1799. On the grounds of priority this genus had to give place to *Turris* Röding, 1798. As increasing numbers of species became known the group was divided up into a vast number of genera. In fact, something like six hundred have been designated. The German systematist Thiele (1929) established 3 subfamilies and the New Zealander A. W. B. Powell (1966) had 9, but modern American workers are proposing no fewer than 12 subfamilies, based primarily on differences in the shell and the structure of the radula. Subdivision on this scale can only be discussed in a specialist monograph. Here the survey must be restricted to relatively few of the main genera. TURRINAE: *Turris* Röding, 1798; *Antiplanes* Dall, 1902; *Cryptogemma* Dall, 1918; *Fusiturris* Thiele, 1929; *Gemmula* Weinkauff, 1875 (subgenus: *Unedogemmula* McNeil, 1960); *Lophiotoma* Casey, 1904 (subgenus: *Lophioturris* Powell, 1964); *Polystira* Woodring, 1928; *Taranis* Jeffreys, 1870; *Xenuroturris* Iredale, 1929; and others. BORSONIINAE: *Borsonia* Bellardi, 1939; *Borsonella* Dall, 1908; *Bathytoma* Harris & Burrows, 1891 (subgenus: *Micantapex* Iredale, 1936); and others. CLAVATULINAE: *Clavatula* Lamarck, 1801; *Clionella* Gray, 1847; and others. CLAVINAE: *Clavus* Montfort, 1810; *Brachytoma* Swainson, 1840; *Drillia* Gray 1838; *Clathrodrillia* Dall, 1918 (subgenus: *Imaclava* Bartsch, 1944); *Inquisitor* Hedley, 1918; *Kylix* Dall, 1919; *Spirotropis* Sars, 1878; and others. CONORBIINAE: *Conorbis* Swainson, 1840; *Benthofascis* Iredale, 1936; and others. DAPHNELLINAE: *Daphnella* Hinds, 1844; *Philbertia* Monterosato, 1884; *Pleurotomella* Verrill, 1873; *Raphitoma* Bellarti, 1848; and others. MANGELIINAE (CLATHURELLINAE): *Mangelia* Risso, 1826; *Agathotoma* Cossmann, 1899; *Bela* Gray, 1847; *Bellaspira* Conrad, 1868; *Clathromangelia* Monterosato, 1884; *Clathurella* Carpenter, 1857; *Cytharella* Montserosato, 1875; *Eucithara* Fischer, 1883; *Glyphostoma* Gabb, 1872; *Lienardia* Jousseaume, 1884; *Oenopota* Mörch, 1852; and others. THATCHERIINAE: *Thatcheria* Angas, 1877. TURRICULINAE: *Turricula* Schumacher, 1817; *Aforia* Dall, 1889; *Ancystrosyrinx* Dall, 1881; *Cochlespira* Conrad, 1865; *Comitas Finlay,* 1926; *Hormospira* Berry, 1958; *Knefastia* Dall, 1919; *Leucosyrinx* Dall, 1889; *Steiraxis* Dall, 1895; *Vexitomina* Powell, 1942; and others. The classification proposed by Powell is based principally on shell characters. On the other hand, the more recent scheme proposed by American workers is based on differences in the structure of the radula.

Subclass: Euthyneura

Gastropods with the mantle cavity and gills on the right side (Opisthobranchia) or with the mantle cavity modified to form a lung (Pulmonata). With a few exceptions (Acteonidae), the visceral nerve loop is untwisted (de-torsion). The radula is rather uniform with a varying number of teeth and the shell is spiral or cap-shaped, in many species partly reduced or even lacking. The animals are hermaphrodite. Some authors regard the Opisthobranchia and Pulmonata as separate subclasses with the Prosobranchia forming the third subclass of Gastropoda.

OPISTHOBRANCHIA

In this group the mantle cavity has come to lie on the right side, and the gills are behind the heart. In most Cephalaspidea and Anaspidea the gills are feathery, in the other groups folded. In the Pleurobranchidae the mantle cavity is shallow and it contains a large gill on the right side. In the Nudibranchia or sea slugs there are no true gills, and respiration is by newly developed structures on the back, known as cerata. If even these are lacking, respiration takes place through the skin. The head is usually not very clearly separated from the body. The tentacles near the mouth serve as tactile organs and behind them are the often complex rhinophores, which are olfactory organs. The central part of the foot is used in creeping, and the sides may be developed as expansions or epipodia of varying sizes, and in some groups, they are used in swimming (Gastropteridae, Thecosomata, Gymnosomata). There is a general tendency for the shell to be reduced, in fact it is often thin and overgrown by the mantle. Only in the more primitive groups can the animals withdraw completely into its shell. These animals live mainly on the shore or in shallow water, usually in quiet bays, but occasionally at greater depths. The following survey deals only with the shelled opisthobranchs, and does not cover those which lack a shell (Gymnosomata, Nudibranchia, etc.).

ORDER: ENTOMOTAENIATA
See Plate 51

Shell slender and turret-like to ovate and conical with pronounced columellar folds. This is a mainly fossil group.

Family: Pyramidellidae

Shell (with some exceptions, see Plate 51 1-3) only a few millimetres long. No radula, but a long sucking proboscis with a stiletto-like tip (for piercing the prey). These animals live as ectoparasites on a variety of hosts (polychaete worms, sponges, sea-squirts, molluscs) or as predators roaming the bottom sediments. Nordsieck (1972, see bibliography) has produced a new revision of the European species. Genera: *Pyramidella* Lamarck, 1799; *Kleinella* A. Adams, 1860; *Odostomia* Fleming, 1813; and others.

ORDER: CEPHALASPIDEA

Shell usually free, sometimes enclosed by the mantle. Operculum present only in the Acteonidae. These gastropods have a characteristic expansion of the head (cephalic shield), formed by thickening of the body wall in the head region, which helps the animal to burrow in sand. The foot is used in creeping, and may or may not have lateral lobes (epipodia). The latter are only used for swimming in the Gastropteridae. These gastropods are predators living in bottom sediments.

SUPERFAMILY: ACTEONACEA
See Plate 51

Shell external, more or less solid, with a visible apex. A group of relatively unspecialised species, some with the visceral nerve loop still twisted.

Family: Acteonidae

Shell medium-sized, ovate to spindle-shaped, the spire usually short and conical, or even sunken. Aperture longish, narrow above, broad below. Columella twisted, usually with one fold. Foot with an operculum. Genera: *Acteon* Montfort, 1810; *Pupa* Röding, 1798; and others.

Family: Ringiculidae

Shell small, roundish, with a short, conical spire. Living in warm seas. Genus: *Ringicula* Deshayes, 1838; and others.

Family: Hydatinidae

Shell thin, medium-sized, roundish-ovate, with a sunken spire. Living in warm seas. Genera: *Hydatina* Schumacher, 1817; *Aplustrum* Schumacher; and others.

SUPERFAMILY: BULLACEA
See Plate 51

Shell bladder-like. Spire deeply sunken, in most cases not visible. Aperture as long as the shell. Living in warm seas.

Family: Bullidae

Shell medium-sized, fairly solid, usually with coloured markings. Genus: *Bulla* Linné, 1758; and others.

Family: Atyidae

Shell thin, ovate, small to medium-sized, with a sunken spire and a large body whorl. Genera: *Atys* Montfort, 1810; *Cylichnium* Dall, 1908; *Haminoea* Turton & Kingston, 1830; and others.

Family: Retusidae

Shell very small, with a sunken or slightly raised spire. Genus: *Retusa* Brown, 1827; and others.

SUPERFAMILY: DIAPHANACEA

Shell small, ovate to pear-shaped, thin and translucent, with a wide aperture and few body whorls. Spire slightly raised or somewhat sunken.

Family: Diaphanidae

From cold seas in the Arctic and Antarctic, and from the deep sea. Genus: *Diaphana* Brown, 1827; and others.

Family: Notodiaphanidae

Shell very small, ovate, with an umbilicus and a sunken spire. Indo-Pacific. Genus: *Notodiaphana*, Thiele, 1917.

Left to right: *Ringicula auriculata* (Ménard, 1811), 5mm, Mediterranean; *Philine aperta* (Linné, 1769), up to 20mm, European coasts; (top) *Clio pyramidata* Linné, 1767, c. 15mm; and (bottom) *Diacria trispinosa* Lesueur, 1821, c. 11mm, the last two species with a worldwide pelagic distribution.

Left to right: *Ellobium aurisjudae* (Linné, 1758), up to 60mm, western Pacific; *Amphibola crenata* (Gmelin, 1791), up to 40mm, New Zealand; *Pythia scarabaeus* (Linné, 1758), up to 50mm, western Pacific (synonyms: *P. castaneus* Lesson, 1831; *P. helicina* Röding, 1798; *P. pantherina* A. Adams, 1851).

SUPERFAMILY: PHILINACEA

Shell small to medium-sized, ear-shaped or cylindrical, free or enclosed by the mantle. Spire more or less completely sunken. Mainly in warm seas.

Family: Philinidae

Shell ovate, thin and translucent, colourless. Body whorl much expanded. Genus: *Philine* Ascanius, 1772; and others.

Family: Aglajidae

Shell small, wide open, consisting of conchyolin, and overgrown by the mantle. Genus: *Aglaja* Renier, 1807; and others.

Family: Scaphandridae

Shell small to medium-sized, longish-ovate to cylindrical. Spire usually sunken. Living mainly in warm seas. *Scaphander* Montfort, 1810 lives on scaphopods; *Cylichna* Lovén, 1846; and others.

ORDER: SACCOGLOSSA

Shell rather small, thin, colourless and spiral with small whorls and a more or less wide aperture, but sometimes lacking. Exceptionally, the shell may be in two pieces. The radula has one series of strong teeth, and those that become worn out do not drop off but are collected in a special sac. The foot may or may not have lateral lobes (epipodia) and in the shell-less forms the back carries respiratory appendages (cerata). These are plant-sucking gastropods found exclusively among algal growths in warm and tropical seas. Using the single row of teeth, they rasp algae and feed by sucking up the contents.

Family: Cylindrobullidae

Shell small, cylindrical with a sunken spire. Genus: *Cylindrobulla* Fischer, 1857.

Family: Juliidae

Shell small and consisting of two parts, the left one having a small apical spire. Formerly regarded as belonging to the Bivalvia. Genera: *Julia* Gould, 1862; *Berthelinia* Crosse, 1875.

Family: Oxynoidae

Shell small, thin and translucent, ovate. Genus: *Oxynoe* Rafinesque, 1819; and others.

Family: Volvatellidae

Shell small, pear-shaped with a sunken spire. Genus: *Volvatella* Pease, 1860.

ORDER: ANASPIDEA (Aplysiacea)

Shell small and much reduced, usually covered by the mantle, or it may be completely lacking. The animals have no cephalic shield, but the head is prominent with two pairs of tentacles. The animals swim with the help of epipodia. Living mostly in warm coastal areas, and feeding on algae.

Family Aplysiidae (Sea-hares)

Shell small, overgrown by the mantle, but the animal is relatively very large (up to 20cm long). Genus: *Aplysia* Linné, 1767; and others.

Family: Akeridae

Shell free, moderately large, thin and translucent. Genus: *Akera* (Müller, 1776).

Family: Dolabellidae

Shell medium-sized, flat, and strongly calcified. Genus: *Dolabella* Lamarck, 1801.

Family: Dolabriferidae

Shell small, reduced or absent. Genus: *Dolabrifera* Gray, 1847; and others.

ORDER: NOTASPIDEA

Shell external and cap-shaped, or overgrown and ear-shaped; absent in some forms. The mantle cavity contains one large gill on the right side of the body. The head has two pairs of tentacles. Mainly found in warm seas.

Family: Pleurobranchidae

Shell small, shaped like that of an ormer, overgrown, often reduced. Genus: *Pleurobranchus* Cuvier, 1804; and others.

Family: Tylodinidae

Shell free, cap-shaped, with an uncalcified edge. Genus: *Tylodina* Rafinesque, 1819; and others.

Family: Umbraculidae

Shell cap-shaped with an almost central apex, the inside with a fluted muscle impression. Genus: *Umbraculum* Schumacher, 1817.

ORDER: THECOSOMATA

Shell reduced or soften absent and replaced by a secondary structure, the pseudoconch. Foot extending round the dorsal side of the head to form two lateral fins which give the animal a butterfly-like appearance. These animals living pelagically in tropical and polar seas, often in large swarms and feed on microplankton.

Family: Cavoliniidae

Shell not spiral, but funnel-shaped, with bilateral symmetry. Genera: *Cavolinia* Abildgaard, 1791; *Clio* Linné, 1767; *Diacria* Gray, 1847; and others.

Family: Cymbuliidae

With a pseudoconch. Genus: *Cymbulia* Peron & Lesueur, 1810; and others.

Family: Peraclidae

Shell spiral, sinistrally coiled. Found in warm seas, at considerable depths. Genus: *Peracle* Forbes, 1844.

Family: Procymbulidae

Found in deep water. Genus: *Procymbulia* Meisenheimer, 1905.

Family: Spiratellidae

Shell spiral with a rather flat spire. Genus: *Spiratella* Blainville, 1817; and others.

PULMONATA

Family: Parallelodontidae
See Plate 51

A network of vessels in the roof of the mantle cavity functions as a lung. The opening of the mantle cavity is reduced to a pore on the side of the body.

Pulmonates mostly live on land or in fresh water. There are a few species in coastal regions.

Family: Amphibolidae

Shell spiral, roundish with a few whorls. Genus: *Amphibola* Schumacher, 1817.

Family: Ellobiidae

Shell ovate to spindle-shaped. Aperture narrowed by teeth. Genera: *Ellobium* Röding, 1798; *Melampus* Montfort, 1810; *Pythia* Röding, 1798; and others.

Family: Siphonariidae

Shell limpet-like. These are marine animals with aquatic respiration. Genus: *Siphonaria* Sowerby, 1823; and others.

Family: Trimusculidae

Shell circular, dish-shaped. Genus: *Trimusculus* Schmidt, 1818, synonym: *Gadinia* Gray, 1824.

CLASS: BIVALVIA (Bivalves)

Exclusively aquatic molluscs with a mainly bilateral symmetry, a laterally compressed body, and bivalve shell which is generally large enough to contain the whole animal. Heart with two auricles. Nervous system without any striking pecularities. Respiration by gills. The mouth leads by way of a short oesophagus to the stomach and there is no radula. Bivalves are mostly filter-feeders, with separate sexes, and are rarely hermaphrodite. Fertilisation takes place in the open water or in the mantle cavity.

Organisation of the Bivalve Body

Only a few bivalves (mainly young ones) move by slowly creeping over the surface of the substrate. Most species burrow into sand or mud with the help of the expansile foot. Others are completely sessile, being attached to a firm underlay by byssus threads (*Mytilus*) or glued by one of the two shell valves (*Ostrea*). A few bore into timber or soft rock (*Petricola, Pholas*). Some swim by expelling water held within the shell in a powerful jet through a slit in the rear edge (*Solemya, Ensis, Solen*). *Pecten* and *Lima* swim by clapping their shells like a pair of bellows and thus forcing water out. In keeping with their filter-feeding habits they do not require great mobility or methods of defence, and the head is reduced to the mouth opening and its immediate surrounding area. The gills serve for respiration and for filtering minute particles of food from the surrounding water.

The soft body is enclosed on both sides by the two large mantle lobes, and these also secrete the two valves of the shell. In some species the mantle edges are free with folds for shell building and for the perception of sensory stimuli; in *Pecten* and *Spondylus* the mantle edge has a series of eye-spots. A third fold regulates the inflow of water for respiration and the outflow of water from the mantle cavity during swimming (in *Pecten* and *Lima*). In most bivalves, however, the adjacent parts of the mantle edge fuse with one another, leaving two openings at the rear for the inhalant and exhalant water used in respiration, and a ventral, pedal opening for the foot. In burrowing and boring species the edges of the inhalant and exhalant openings are elongated to form an inhalant siphon and an exhalant siphon. Both siphons may fuse to form a retractile double tube. When extended this is often longer than the bivalve itself.

Depending upon whether it is used for creeping, burrowing or for attachment by byssus threads, the ventrally positioned foot assumes a variety of shapes, and can be described as axe-like, tongue-like or worm-like. Only in a few forms (*Nucula*, *Glycymeris*, *Tellina*, *Venus*) does the foot form a true creeping organ, and in most forms it functions primarily in burrowing. In sessile and swimming species, it is more or less reduced.

The gills lie in the mantle cavity which extends along each side of the animal. Some bivalves extend their long, tentacular, mantle lobes from the shells and pick up from the bottom any protozoans, algae, eggs, larvae and small invertebrates, as well as detritus that they can reach. The food is led to the mouth in a ciliated groove in the mantle cavity. However, most bivalves filter their food almost exclusively from the respiratory current. This current is created by the beating of the cilia in the mantle cavity and it draws in tiny food particles which are caught on the outer side of the gills and from there transported to the mouth in strands of sticky mucus. At the same time the exhalant current carries away with it the excretions of the kidney and anus. In the Filibranchia, each gill has two rows of long filaments which hang down into

Hinge dentition: top row, left to right: toxodont (teeth in rows, transverse or oblique to the hinge plate) in *Glycymeris gigantea* (Reeve, 1843); heterodont (few cardinal teeth and ridge-like lateral teeth) in *Acanthocardia* (*Rudicardium*) *tuberculata* (Linné, 1758); desmodont (with a shell process, the chondrophore, formed by fusion of the cardinal teeth) in *Mya* (*Arenomya*) *arenaria* Linné, 1758 (left valve); bottom row, left to right: isodont (two large peg-like teeth fitting into grooves in the opposite shell) in *Spondylus* (*Spondylus*) *americanus* Hermann, 1781; hemidapedont (a few cardinal teeth on a poorly developed hinge) in *Tellina* (*Cyclotellina*) *remies* Linné, 1758; anomalodesmatic (toothless, with weak ridges parallel to the margin) in *Myadora* (*Myadora*) *striata* (Quoy & Gaimard, 1835).

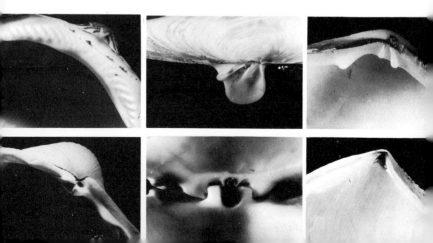

the mantle cavity on each side of the foot from a common base on the dorsal side of the animal, and before reaching the shell edge they are doubled back on one another, forming a U-shape. In the Pseudolamellibranchia, the gill filaments are also reflected, but the reflected part may be united with the mantle towards the outside, and with the base of the foot towards the inside. In the Eulamellibranchia, the gill filaments are connected with one another by bridges of tissue through which blood flows. In some forms living only in deep water (*Lyonsiella, Poromya, Cuspidaria*), the mantle cavity is subdivided into an upper and a lower chamber by a horizontal septum pierced by numerous slits. Water flows through this septum which rises and falls four to six times a minute, like a diaphragm. As these animals lie on their backs in the mud the food particles are deposited on the septum and are moved along it to the mouth (Septibranchia).

Closure of the valves is effected by the adductor muscles. Many species have two adductor muscles (Dimyaria), one anterior and the other posterior. Some of the Pholadidae even have a third adductor muscle lying ventrally. Only rarely are both adductor muscles equally developed (Isomyaria, e.g. in *Glycymeris*). The anterior adductor muscle may also be completely absent (Monomyaria, e.g. in Limidae, Ostreidae, Pectinidae, Pteriidae and others). In such cases the posterior muscle moves to the centre of the shell. In an empty shell the attachment points of the adductor muscles can be seen as muscle impressions or scars on the inside of the valve.

In many forms (e.g. *Arca, Mytilus, Pecten, Pinna*) the pedal glands secrete filamentous byssus threads which are used to attach the animal to rocks and other solid objects. The secretion from the gland is formed into threads by a groove in the foot, and then fixed to the underlay by the tip of the foot. The animal can later release itself, either by completely breaking off the hardened byssus, as in *Pinctada*, or by tearing off the threads individually, as in *Mytilus*. In former times, the byssus threads of *Pinna* were used as a kind of silk.

The Shell

The shell of a bivalve mollusc, like that of a gastropod is made up of several layers and it consists of two valves which are joined together on the dorsal side by a ligament. They vary considerably in shape and may be more or less compressed or convex, roundish, ovate, elliptical, wedge-shaped, beak-shaped, or sheath-like. The anterior and posterior ends often differ from one another, the former being sometimes roundish, the latter pointed, or

Hinge dentition (*contd.*): left to right: schizodont ('split-toothed', the (lower) left valve with split central teeth into which the teeth of the (upper) right valve fit), in *Neotrigonia margaritacea* (Lamarck, 1804); dysodont (poorly toothed, practically without teeth) in *Ostrea edulis* Linné, 1758; pachydont (a few thick teeth) in *Chama lazarus* Linné, 1758.

occasionally truncated. The valves are usually symmetrical and formed so that their edges meet and firmly close off the mantle cavity. There are, however, shells which gape and those in which one valve overlaps the other. Sometimes the two valves differ in convexity, usually as a result of always lying on one side, as in the scallops (Pectinidae), or because one valve is attached to the substrate, as in the Chamidae, Ostreidae and Spondylidae. The lower shell is more convex, the upper one flatter. In the Tellinidae and Semelidae, the posterior part of the shell may be curved to one side.

The ligament joining the two valves is made up of two parts, the external ligament proper and the internal cartilage. The ligament is not elastic but the cartilage is very elastic and slightly iridescent. When the adductor muscles relax, the elastic cartilage pulls the valves apart.

The growth of each valve starts at the umbo (plural: umbones), which lies dorsally and usually at or near the middle of the valve. In most cases the umbones lie quite close to one another, but occasionally, as in *Arca*, there may be quite a broad expanse of shell between them. Usually, the umbones lie so close that they divide this area into an anterior lunule and a posterior escutcheon. However, an escutcheon is only rarely present.

The dorsal edge of each valve is usually modified to form the hinge which has teeth or ridges that fit into comparable structures on the other valve. The arrangement of these hinge teeth has a special terminology, thus:

a) in taxodont dentition there is a series of alternating teeth and sockets along the hinge line, below the umbones;
b) in desmodont dentition there is one short, spoon-shaped process formed by the fusion of two cardinal teeth (Myidae, Mactridae);
c) in pachyodont dentition there are a few conical teeth and corresponding grooves on the opposite valve (Chamidae);
d) in dysodont or edentulous dentition the hinge structure is feeble and there are no teeth (*Mytilus*, *Ostrea*);
e) in schizodont dentition the left valve has one central or cardinal tooth, which is often forked, and the right valve has too wedge-shaped teeth;
f) in isodont dentition there are two pairs of teeth and sockets which interlock (e.g. in *Spondylus*);
g) in anomalodesmatic dentition the hinge is poorly developed, with or without small tooth ridges (*Laternula*, *Lyonsia*, *Myadora*, *Pandora*).

The inside of the shell is usually white, but in some forms it has coloured markings or shows mother-of-pearl. It also shows the pallial (or mantle) line and the muscle impressions where the adductor muscles were attached to the shell. The pallial line runs ventrally and roughly parallel to the edge of the shell. In bivalves in which the siphon can be withdrawn into the shell the pallial line is often much indented to form the pallial sinus. The outside of the shell may be smooth or ornamented, the concentric growth rings, radial ribs, sometimes also knobs and spines. Some bivalve shells are strikingly coloured, others white – often with a periostracum.

Classification

A number of different names have been used for the class as a whole, including Acephala, Pelecypoda and Lamellibranchiata but these have in one way or another proved unsatisfactory, and it is now customary to use the name

Bivalvia originally proposed by Linné.

In recent years three main systems of classifying the Bivalvia have been proposed:

a) by J. Thiele (in *Handbuch der systematischen Weichtierkunde*, Vol. 2, Berlin, 1935);
b) by A. Franc (in Grassé's *Traité de Zoologie*, 5/II, Paris, 1960) and
c) by N. D. Newell, 1965 (in R. C. Moore's *Treatise on Invertebrate Paleontology*, Part N, Mollusca 6, The University of Kansas and the Geological Society of America, 1969).

The first two were based primarily on differences in the hinge dentition, closure musculature and gill structure. Newell's system proposes a rather larger number of subdivisions and is the one used in the present system. However, as the following table shows it is possible to interrelate the three systems.

Thiele, 1935	Franc, 1960		Newell, 1965	
Taxodonta	*Protobranchia*	Nuculidae Nuculanidae Malletiidae	*Palaeotaxodonta*	Nuculoida
		Solemyidae	*Cryptodonta*	Solemyoida
				Praecardioida (fossil)
	Filibranchia	Taxodonta	*Pteriomorphia*	Arcoida
Anisomyaria		Anisomyaria		Mytiloida
				Pterioida
Eulamellibranchia — Schizodonta	*Eulamellibranchia*	Schizodonta	*Palaeoheterodonta*	Trigonioida
				Unionioida
				Modiomorphoida (fossil)
		Rudistes	*Heterodonta*	Hippuritoida (fossil)
Heterodonta		Heterodonta		Veneroida
Adapedonta		Adapedonta		Myoida
Anomalodesmata		Anomalodesmacea	*Anomalodesmata*	Pholadomyoida
		Septibranchia		

Subclass: Palaeotaxodonta
ORDER: NUCULOIDA

Shell with equal valves, the inside with mother-of-pearl or porcellanous, with two similar adductor muscle impressions. Dentition taxodont.

SUPERFAMILY: NUCULACEA
See Plate 52

Shell not very large, roundish-triangular, usually with the anterior part long and somewhat arched above. Umbo positioned rather far to the rear. No pallial sinus (no siphons). Mother-of-pearl inside. Foot with a sole which can be compressed for entry into the substrate and then expanded to provide the animal with anchorage. Food consisting of microorganisms and detritus is procured by the richly ciliated labial palps.

Family: Nuculidae (Nut clams)

A cosmopolitan family of bivalves which live just below the surface of the sediment, through which they plough, using the powerful foot. Genera: *Nucula* Lamarck, 1799 (subgenera: *Lamellinucula* Schenck, 1944; *Leionucula* Quenstedt, 1930); *Acila* H. & A. Adams, 1858; *Brevinucula* Thiele, 1934; *Pronucula* Hedley, 1902; and others.

SUPERFAMILY: NUCULANACEA
See Plate 52

Shell elongated posteriorly, with or without resilium, usually with a pallial sinus (with siphons). No mother-of-pearl inside.

Family: Malletiidae

Shell roundish or longish, ligament external. Mainly in deep water. Genera: *Malletia* Des Moulins, 1832; *Neilo* A. Adams, 1852; *Pseudoglomus* Dall, 1898; *Tindaria* Bellardi, 1875; and others.

Family: Nuculanidae (Ledidae)

Shell ovate, longish, with the rear end beak-like. In deep water. Genera: *Nuculana* Link, 1807, synonym: *Leda* Schumacher, 1817 (subgenera: *Jupiteria* Bellardi, 1875; *Ledella* Verrill & Bush, 1897; *Lembulus* Risso, 1826; *Saccella* Woodring, 1925); *Adrana* H. & A. Adams, 1858; *Phaseolus* Monterosato, 1875, synonym: *Silicula* Jeffreys, 1879; *Portlandia* Mörch, 1857 (subgenus: *Yoldiella* Verrill & Bush, 1897); *Pristigloma* Dall, 1900; *Sarepta* A. Adams, 1860; *Yoldia* Möller, 1842; and others.

Subclass: Cryptodonta
ORDER: SOLEMYOIDA

Shell gaping, with an internal ligament (resilium). Hinge without teeth. No byssus. Anterior muscle impression larger than posterior.

SUPERFAMILY: SOLEMYACEA

Shell thin, elongated, with rounded ends. Umbo rather far to the rear. Shell very shiny with a marginal fringe of periostracum. Living in depths down to 3000m.

Family: Solemyidae (Awning clams)

Genera: *Solemya* Lamarck, 1818 (subgenera: *Petrasma* Dall, 1908; *Solemyarina* Iredale, 1931); *Acharax* Dall, 1908; and others. The only European species is *Solemya togata* in the Mediterranean.

Subclass: Pteriomorpha
ORDER: ARCOIDA

Shell often attached to solid objects by byssus threads. Hinge with taxodont dentition. No pallial sinus (no siphons), no mother-of-pearl. Gill filaments loosely connected to one another by ciliary junctions.

SUPERFAMILY: ARCACEA
See Plate 52

Shell with equal valves, trapezoid, often ribbed. Two muscle impressions, about equal in size. Periostracum often bristly.

Family: Arcidae (Ark shells)

Shell trapezoid to oval, with a broad dorsal surface. About 200 species, mostly tropical. ARCINAE: shell edge straight, byssus threads emerging through a slit in the edge of the lower valve. Attached to rocks and in cliff crevices. Genera: *Arca* Linné, 1758; *Barbatia* Gray, 1842; *Litharca* Gray, 1892; *Trisidos* Röding, 1798; and others. ANADARINAE: shell trapezoid to roundish-triangular, hinge area curved. No slit for byssus threads. Genera: *Anadara* Gray, 1847 (subgenus: *Lunarca* Gray, 1857); *Bathyarca* Kobelt, 1891; *Bentharca* Verrill & Bush, 1898; *Larkinia* Reinhart, 1935; *Samacar* Iredale, 1936; *Scapharca* Gray, 1847; (subgenus: *Cunearca* Dall, 1898); *Scaphula* Benson, 1834; *Senilia* Gray, 1842.

Family: Parallelodontidae

Hinge teeth oblique and horizontal. A single recent genus: *Porterius* Clark, 1925.

Family: Cucullaeidae

Shell trapezoid, the left valve somewhat overlapping. Dorsal edge straight, with short central (cardinal) and longer very oblique lateral teeth. Genus: *Cucullaea* Lamarck, 1801.

Family: Noetiidae

Shell with equal valves. No slit for the byssus threads. Cosmopolitan. Genera: *Noetia* Gray, 1857; and others.

SUPERFAMILY: LIMOPSACEA
See Plate 52

Shell round to obliquely ovate, usually with a fibrous periostracum.

Family: Limopsidae

Ligament short, with resilium. Anterior muscle impression smaller than posterior. Cosmopolitan. Genera: *Limopsis* Sassi, 1827; *Empleconia* Dall, 1908; *Lissarca* Smith, 1877; and others.

Family: Glycymeridae

Shell round and solid, with the umbo in the centre. Hinge line curved, with a few large teeth. Two muscle impressions equal in size. Living mainly in warm seas. Genera: *Glycymeris* Da Costa, 1778; *Axinactis* Mörch, 1861 (subgenus: *Glycymerella* Woodring, 1925); *Felicia* Mabille & Rochebrune, 1889; and others.

Family: Manzanellidae (Nucinellidae)

Shell very small (similar to *Nucula*) inside without mother-of-pearl. Living in warm seas. Genera: *Nucinella* Wood, 1851; *Huxleyia* A. Adams, 1860, synonym: *Cyrilla* A. Adams, 1860; and others.

Family: Philobryidae

Shell small, roundish, the valves equal in size, umbo raised, hinge with a few large vertical teeth, ligament internal. Byssus thin, emerging between the front edges of the valves. Mainly in southern seas. Genus: *Philobrya* Carpenter, 1872; and others.

ORDER: MYTILOIDA

Shell with equal valves, dysodont. Muscle impressions differing in size. Ligament external. No siphons. Living free or attached by a byssus.

SUPERFAMILY: MYTILACEA
See Plate 53

Shell longish or round, umbo at or near the front end. Mother-of-pearl inside. Hinge generally toothless, sometimes with a few small teeth.

Family: Mytilidae (Mussels)

Cosmopolitan, on the shore and in deeper water. MYTILINAE: shell medium-sized, longish, pointed at the front, broad and rounded at the rear. Umbo at the front end. With concentric stripes and a brown periostracum through which the bluish surface of the shell can often be seen. Living fixed by the byssus to rocks, piles and empty shells, often in large banks. Genera: *Mytilus* Linné, 1758; *Aulacomya* Mörch, 1853; *Brachidontes* Swainson, 1840 (subgenus: *Hormomya* Mörch, 1853); *Ischadium* Jukes-Browne, 1905; *Mytella* Soot-Ryen, 1955; *Mytilaster* Monterosato, 1883; *Perna* Retzius, 1788; *Septifer* Récluz, 1848; and others. CRENELLINAE: shell small, rounded with fine reticulate ornament. Not sessile. Genera: *Crenella* Brown, 1827; *Arcuatula* Jousseaume, 1919, synonym: *Lamya* Soot-Ryen, 1958; *Arvella* Bartsch, 1960; *Gregariella* Monterosato, 1883; *Lioberus* Dall, 1898; *Musculus* Röding, 1798, (subgenus: *Ryenella* Fleming, 1959); *Solamen* Iredale, 1924; and others. LITHOPHAGINAE: shell elongated, cylindrical, umbo near the front end, hinge area smooth, ligament long and sunken. With the help of an acid secretion the animals excavate soft calcareous rocks, making holes in which the shell fits exactly. Genera: *Lithophaga* Röding, 1798; *Adula* H. & A. Adams, 1857; and others. MODIOLINAE: umbo somewhat behind the front end. Not sessile. Genera: *Modiolus* Lamarck, 1799; *Amygdalum* Megerle v Muhlfeld, 1811; *Botula* Mörch, 1853; *Idasola* Iredale, 1915; *Stavelia* Gray, 1858; and others.

SUPERFAMILY: PINNACEA
See Plate 53

Shell medium-sized to large, wedge-shaped and gaping, with an internal layer of mother-of-pearl. Umbo near the front end. Hinge without teeth. Ventral edge with a narrow slit at the front for the byssus. Anterior muscle impression relatively small, posterior impression large and approximately in the centre of the shell.

Family: Pinnidae (Pen shells, Fan Mussels)

Shell positioned vertically with the pointed end embedded in sand or mud and anchored by the byssus to rocks, shells, etc. Living in the shallow waters of quiet bays, in warm seas. Genera: *Pinna* Linné, 1758 (subgenus: *Cyrtopinna* Mörch, 1853); *Atrina* Gray 1842; *Streptopinna* v. Martens, 1880.

ORDER: PTERIOIDA

Shell generally with two unequal valves, the inside porcelain-like or with mother-of-pearl, and the hinge without teeth (dysodont). Anterior adductor muscle impression small or absent. Pallial line without a sinus (no siphons). Free-living or sessile.

Suborder: Pteriina

Adults attached to a firm underlay by a byssus emerging through a notch in the right valve or by a calcareous secretion.

SUPERFAMILY: PTERIACEA
See Plate 53

Shell variously shaped, the valves more or less unequal, ligament external, the anterior adductor muscle reduced. Right valve usually with a byssus notch. Sessile.

Family: Pteriidae (Pearl oysters)

Hinge straight, elongated to the rear, with one or two toothlike thickenings below the umbo. Ligament fairly long and rather sunken. Inside with brilliant mother-of-pearl, the adductor muscle in the centre. Living in warm seas. Genera: *Pteria* Scopoli, 1777; *Arcavicula* Cox, 1964; *Electroma* Stoliczka, 1871 (subgenus *Pterelectroma* Iredale, 1939); *Pinctada* Röding 1798; synonym: *Meleagrina* Lamarck, 1819.

Family: Isognomonidae

Shell taller than long, with unequal valves, and mother-of-pearl inside. Hinge with several ligament grooves. Byssus emerging through a notch. Living in warm seas. Genera: *Isognomon* Lightfoot, 1786 (subgenus: *Isogonum* Röding, 1798); *Crenatula* Lamarck, 1803.

Family: Pulvinidae

Shell medium-sized, roundish-triangular, hinge without teeth, but with several longish ligament grooves. Genus: *Foramelina* Hedley, 1914.

Family: Malleidae (Hammer oysters)

Shell with almost equal valves, the edges often gaping. Hinge long with pronounced lateral extensions. Ligament in the form of a large knob in a triangular groove. Warm seas. Genera: *Malleus* Lamarck, 1799 (subgenus: *Malvufundus* De Gregorio, 1885); *Vulsella* Röding, 1798.

SUPERFAMILY: PECTINACEA
See Plates 54-56

Shell with more or less unequal valves, fixed by byssus or calcareous secretion. Outline of shell circular, with radial ribs and folds, with ear-like lateral extensions. Hinge without teeth, but with ridges and grooves, or isodont (Spondylidae). Ligament with a central knob. One central adductor muscle impression. Inside of shell procellanous.

Family: Pectinidae (Scallops)

Shell varying in size, usually with unequal valves, which show a varying amount of convexity. Often with bright coloration. 'Ears' varying in size, the anterior ear of the right valve with a byssus notch. Mantle edge free, with eye-spots and tentacles. Some species can swim. *Lentipecten* group: shell small, round, gaping in front and behind. Genus: *Adamussium* Thiele, 1934.

Amusium group: shell disc-shaped, smooth or finely ornamented externally, and with radial ribs internally. Genera: *Amusium* Röding, 1798; *Propeamussium* De Gregorio, 1884 (subgenus: *Parvamussium* Sacco, 1897). *Camptonectes* group: *only fossil forms, except that Camptonectes* Agassiz, 1864 may be included here, see Plate 54/6. *Eburneopecten* group: shell small, thin. Genera: *Cyclopecten* Verrill, 1897 (subgenera: *Chlamydella* Iredale, 1929; *Pectinella* Verrill, 1897); *Hemipecten* Adams & Reeve, 1849; *Palliolum* Monterosato, 1884 (subgenera: *Delectopecten* Stewart, 1930; *Hyalopecten* Verrill, 1897); *Pseudamussium* Mörch, 1853. *Chlamys* group: both valves convex, the left usually more than the right. Byssus emerging through a large notch in the anterior 'ear' of the right valve. Radial ornament fine to coarse. Genus: *Chlamys* Röding, 1798 subgenera: *Aequipecten* Fischer, 1886; *Annachlamys* Iredale, 1939; *Argopecten* Monterosato, 1899; *Cryptopecten* Dall, Bartsch & Rehder, 1938, synonym: *Gloripallium* Iredale, 1939; *Equichlamys* Iredale, 1929; *Flexopecten* Sacco, 1897, synonym: *Glabropecten* Sacco, 1897; *Juxtamusium* Iredale, 1939; *Leptopecten* Verrill, 1897; *Manupecten* Monterosato, 1889; *Nodipecten* Dall, 1898; *Pacipecten* Ilsson, 1961; *Placopecten* Verrill, 1897; *Swiftopecten* Hertlein, 1936). *Hinnites* group; when young the shell lies free, later the right valve becomes attached by a calcareous secretion near the umbo, and it then develops an irregular form. Genera: *Hinnites* Defrance, 1821; *Pedum* Lamarck, 1799. *Decatopecten* group: right valve more convex than the left. Usually with few ribs. Hinge short. Genera: *Decatopecten* Rüppel 1839 (subgenus: *Sinectenolium* Eames & Cox, 1956); *Semipallium* Jousseaume, 1928 (subgenera: *Excellichlamys* Iredale, 1939; *Mirapecten* Dall, Bartsch & Rehder, 1938). *Pecten* group: right valve very convex, left valve less so, flat or concave. Radial ribs usually rather broad. Genera: *Pecten* Müller, 1776 (subgenera: *Euvola* Dall, 1898; *Flabellipecten* Sacco, 1897; *Minnivola* Iredale, 1939; *Opeenheimopecten* von Teppner, 1922; *Patinopecten* Dall, 1898).

Family: Plicatulidae

Shell small to medium-sized, with unequal valves, a triangular outline, and smooth or with rays. 'Ears' absent. Hinge with two conspicuous teeth on each side. One adductor muscle and the mantle edge free, without eye-spots. Right valve attached at the umbo. Warm seas. Genus: *Plicatula* Lamarck, 1801.

Family: Spondylidae (Thorny oysters)

Shell with unequal valves, with long spins on the ribs and widely spaced umbos of unequal size. Attached to rocks and other objects by the anterior edge of the right valve. Left (upper) valve with conspicuous 'ears'. Hinge with two large teeth on each side (isodont). Mantle edge free, with eye-spots. Warm seas. Genus: *Spondylus* Linné, 1758 (subgenera: *Corallospondylus* Monterosato, 1917; *Eltopera* Iredale, 1939).

Family: Dimyidae

Shell small, with unequal valves, the right one attached. Hinge area with 'ears'.

Two adductor muscle impressions, mantle edge without eye-spots. Warm seas. Genus: *Dimya* Rouault, 1850.

SUPERFAMILY: ANOMIACEA
See Plate 57

Shell with unequal valves, attached throughout life or only when young (*Placuna*). Anchored by a calcified byssus plug which emerges through a hole in the right valve. The structure of the two valves often differs, the left showing mother-of-pearl, the right prismatic externally. Hinge toothless. One adductor muscle.

Family: Anomiidae (Jingle shells, Saddle oysters)

Shell thin and translucent, roundish, more or less compressed with unequal valves, often saddle-shaped. *Placuna* is disc-shaped and when adult lives unattached. Genera: *Anomia* Linné, 1758 (subgenus: *Patro* Gray, 1850); *Enigmonia* Iredale, 1918; *Isomonia* Dautzenberg & Fischer, 1897; *Placuna* Lightfoot, 1786; *Placunanomia* Broderip, 1832; *Pododesmus* Philippi, 1837 (subgenera: *Heteranomia* Winckworth, 1922; *Monia* Gray, 1850; *Tedinia* Gray, 1853).

SUPERFAMILY: LIMACEA
See Plate 56

Shell with unequal, rhomboidal valves, which are ornamented with rough, scaly ribs. Hinge area smooth or with fine teeth, and with short 'ears'. Mantle edges with tentacles, with eye-spots only in a few species. One adductor muscle. These animals can swim. Some species build nests on the bottom out of pebbles and shell fragments which protect the occupant from attack. The materials of the nest are bound together with byssal secretion. The animal is often reddish, and luminescent in the dark.

Family: Limidae (File shells)

Genera: *Lima* Bruguière, 1797, synonym: *Mantellum* Röding, 1798; *Acesta* H. & A. Adams, 1858 (subgenus: *Plicacesta* Vokes, 1963); *Ctenoides* Mörch, 1853; *Divarilima* Powell, 1958; *Limaria* Link, 1807 (subgenera: *Limaria* sensu stricto, synonym: *Promantellum* Iredale, 1939; *Limatulella* Sacco, 1898; *Stabilima* Iredale, 1939); *Limatula* Wood, 1839; *Limea* Bronn, 1831, synonym: *Limaea* Gray, 1847 (subgenera: *Escalima* Iredale, 1929; *Gemellima* Iredale, 1929; *Isolimea* Iredale, 1929; *Notolimea* Iredale, 1924); and others.

Suborder: Ostreina

In contrast to the Pteriina, the left valve is attached to the substrate by a calcareous section. Byssus absent. Adults have no foot.

SUPERFAMILY: OSTREACEA (Oysters)
See Plate 57

Shell with an irregular outline and unequal valves, their structure somewhat lamellar. Hinge toothless (dysodont). Ligament in a triangular groove. Inner edge of the right valve often with small knobs, e.g. in *Lopha*, the other valve having corresponding pits. Mantle edge free, one adductor muscle.

Family: Gryphaeidae

Mainly fossil forms. Two Recent genera: *Hyotissa* Stenzel, 1971 (previously under *Lopha*); *Neopycnodonte* Stenzel, 1971 (previously under *Pycnodonte* Fischer v. Waldheim, 1835).

Family: Ostreidae (Oysters)

Left (attached) valve very convex. Shell with very variable ornament, its edge folded and lamellar. Cosmopolitan in shallow water. Genera: *Ostrea* Linné, 1758; *Alectryonella* Sacco, 1897; *Crassostraea* Sacco, 1897; *Lopha* Röding, 1798; *Saccostrea* Dollfus & Dautzenberg, 1920.

Subclass: Palaeoheterodonta

Excluding Unionioida (freshwater forms).

ORDER: TRIGONIOIDA

Shell triangular, with equal valves, mother-of-pearl inside. Two adductor muscles. Mantle open. Byssus absent.

SUPERFAMILY: TRIGONIACEA
See Plate 58

Shell rounded-triangular, closed, with umbones directed backwards. Ligament external, short. Shell interior with brilliant mother-of-pearl iridescence. Mantle edge free, with tentacles and eye-spots. Gill filaments only fused with one another at the edges.

Family: Trigoniidae

Numerous fossil forms, but only one recent genus: *Neotrigonia* Cossmann, 1912, off Australia.

Subclass: Heterodonta
ORDER: VENEROIDA

Shell with two equal valves, each with two fairly equal adductor muscle impressions. Mantle edges more or less fused, with or without siphons. Gills leaf-like.

SUPERFAMILY: LUCINACEA
See Plate 59

Shell small to very large, roundish to ovate, smooth, with concentric and radial ornament. Umbones small, directed forwards. Mantle with two openings at the rear, but no pallial sinus.

Family: Lucinidae (Lucinas or Platter shells)

With characters of the superfamily. Anterior adductor muscle impression more or less elongated. About 200 species. LUCININAE: shell circular, solid, with concentric and radial ornament. Anterior muscle scar impression. Genera: *Lucina* Bruguière, 1797, synonym: *Phacoides* Agassiz, 1845 (subgenus: *Lucinisca* Dall, 1901); *Callucina* Dall, 1901; *Codakia* Scopoli, 1777, synonym: *Lentillaria* Schumacher, 1817 (subgenus: *Epilucina* Dall, 1901); *Ctena* Mörch, 1861; *Epicodakia* Iredale, 1930; *Here* Gabb, 1866; *Linga* De Gregorio, 1884 (subgenera: *Bellucina* Dall, 1901; *Pleurolucina* Dall, 1901); *Loripes* Poli, 1791; *Megaxinus* Brugnone, 1880; *Parvilucina* Dall, 1901 (subgenus: *Cavilinga* Chavan, 1937); *Pillucina* Pilsbry, 1921 (subgenus: *Sydlorina* Iredale, 1930); *Wallucina* Iredale, 1930; and others. MYRTEINAE: shell thin, more or less angular, with concentric ornament. Anterior muscle impression medium-sized. Genera: *Myrtea* Turton, 1822; *Gonimyrtea* Marwick, 1929; *Lucinoma* Dall, 1901; *Monitilora* Iredale, 1930 (subgenus: *Prophetilora* Iredale, 1930); and others. MILTHINAE: shell relatively solid, compressed, with some concentric ornament. Anterior muscle impression long. Genera: *Miltha* H. & A. Adams, 1857; *Anodontia* Link, 1807 (subgenera: *Cavatidens* Iredale, 1930; *Loripinus* Monterosato, 1883); *Eamesiella* Chavan, 1951; and others. DIVARICELLINAE: shell circular, convex, with diverging or wavy ornament. Genera: *Divaricella* v. Martens, 1880; *Divalinga* Chavan, 1951; *Divalucina* Iredale, 1936; *Lucinella* Monterosato, 1883; and others.

Family: Fimbriidae

Shell squarish-ovate, thick, with concentric and radial ornament. Umbones almost central. Pallial sinus absent. Indo-Pacific. Genus: *Fimbria* Megerle v. Muhlfeld, 1911.

Family: Mactromyidae

One recent genus: *Bathycorbis* Iredale, 1930.

Family: Thyasiridae

Shell angular to ovate with the front edge indented. Hinge almost toothless. Genera: *Thyasira* Leach, 1818; *Adontorhina* Berry, 1947; *Axinopsida* Keen & Chavan, 1951; *Axinulus* Verrill & Bush, 1898; *Leptaxinus* Verrill & Bush, 1898; and others.

Family: Ungulinidae

Shell ovate to roundish, usually smooth, umbones low. Genera: *Ungulina* Roissy, 1805; *Diplodonta* Bronn, 1831; *Felania* Récluz, 1851; *Felaniella* Dall, 1899 (subgenus: *Zemysia* Finlay, 1926); *Numella* Iredale, 1924; and others.

SUPERFAMILY: CHAMACEA
See Plate 58

Shell with unequal valves, hinge rather thick. Pallial line without sinus. Shell attached to the substrate at the umbo of the left valve.

Family: Chamidae (Jewel boxes)

Shell irregularly formed, externally with elongated lamellae and spins. About 20 species. Genera: *Chama* Linné, 1758 (subgenus: *Psilopus* Poli, 1795); *Arcinella* Schumacher, 1817; *Pseudochama* Odhner, 1917 subgenus: *Eopseuma* Odhner, 1919).

SUPERFAMILY: GALEOMMATACEA
(ERYCINACEA, LEPTONACEA)

Shell very small to small, thin and translucent, sometimes covered by the mantle edge. Hinge simple, often rudimentary. Mantle with only one exhalant opening, the inhalant current of water for respiration entering at the front. Foot with byssus gland. These bivalves mostly live symbiotically with other marine animals, e.g. echinoderms, in the burrows of crabs and worms, etc., feeding on food particles left by the partner. There are several families which differ mainly in the construction of the hinge.

Family: Galeommatidae

Genera: *Galeomma* Sowerby, 1825; *Scintilla* Deshayes, 1856; and others.

Family: Erycinidae

Genera: *Erycina* Lamarck, 1805; *Lasaea* Brown, 1827; *Pythina* Hinds, 1844; and others.

Family: Kelliidae

Genera: *Kellia* Turton, 1822; *Bornia* Philippi, 1836; and others.

Family: Leptonidae

Genus: *Lepton* Turton, 1822; and others.

Family: Montacutidae

Genera: *Montacuta* Turton, 1822; *Mancikellia* Dall, 1899; *Mysella* Angas, 1877; and others.

SUPERFAMILY: CHLAMYDOCONCHACEA

Shell long and narrow, completely enclosed by the mantle, umbones close to the rear end. Adductor muscles absent.

Family: Chlamydoconchidae

A single genus: *Chlamydoconcha* Dall, 1844.

SUPERFAMILY: CYAMIACEA

Shell very small. Differs from Galeommatacea in having mantle openings at the rear. Mainly in southern seas.

Family: Cyamiidae

Genera: *Cyamium* Philippi, 1845; *Legrandina* Tate & May, 1901; and others.

Family: Turtoniidae

Genus: *Turtonia* Alder, 1845.

Family: Sportellidae

Genera: *Sportella* Deshayes, 1858; *Isoconcha* Dautzenberg & Fischer, 1911; and others.

Family: Neoleptonidae

Genus: *Neolepton* Monterosato, 1875; and others.

SUPERFAMILY: CARDITACEA
See Plate 58

Shell with equal valves, thick-walled, usually with radial ornament. Umbones in front of the centre, often far in front, and the posterior adductor muscle is correspondingly large. Mantle open up to the exhalant opening. Byssus gland present.

Family: Carditidae

Shell medium-sized, trapezoid or rounded-triangular, with marked radial ribs. Inner shell edge usually curved. Genera: *Cardita* Bruguière, 1792; *Beguina* Röding, 1798; *Cardiocardita* Anton, 1839 (subgenus: *Bathycardita* Iredale, 1925); *Carditamera* Conrad, 1838; *Carditella* Smith, 1881; *Cardites* Link, 1807; *Cyclocardia* Conrad, 1867 (subgenus: *Vimentum* Iredale, 1925); *Glans* Megerle v. Muhlfeld, 1811; *Megacardita* Sacco, 1899; *Milneria* Dall, 1881; *Miodontiscus* Dall, 1903; *Pleuromeris* Conrad, 1867; *Pteromeris* Conrad, 1862; *Thecalia* H. & A. Adams, 1858; *Venericardia* Lamarck, 1801; and others.

Family: Condylocardiidae

Shell small, triangular or ovate, usually taller than long, with radial and concentric ornament. Genera: *Condylocardia* Bernard, 1896; *Benthocardiella* Powell, 1930; *Condylocuna* Iredale, 1930; *Cuna* Hedley, 1902; *Radiocondyla* Iredale, 1936; and others.

SUPERFAMILY: CRASSATELLACEA
See Plate 58

Shell small to medium-sized, thick, with equal, triangular to trapezoid valves, and with concentric ornament. Umbones pointed, usually directed forwards. Muscle impressions prominent. Pallial line without sinus.

Family: Astartidae

Shell rounded-triangular, smooth or with concentric ornament, and with a dark brown periostracum. Umbones more or less turned forwards. Hinge large, ligament external. Genera: *Astarte* Sowerby, 1816; *Digitaria* Wood, 1853; *Gonilia* Stoliczka, 1871; *Goodallia* Turton, 1822; *Tridonta* Schumacher, 1817 (subgenera: *Nicania* Leach, 1819; *Rictocyma* Dall, 1872).

Family: Crassatellidae

Shell roundish-triangular to ovate, rounded at the front, more or less truncated at the rear, thick-walled, smooth or with concentric ornament. In warm seas. Genera: *Crassatina* Kobelt, 1881; *Crassinella* Guppy, 1874; *Eucrassatella* Iredale, 1924 (subgenus: *Hybolophus* Stewart, 1930); *Salaputium* Iredale, 1924; *Talabrica* Iredale, 1924; and others.

Family: Cardiniidae

A single Recent genus; *Tellidorella* Berry, 1963 (west coast of Central America).

SUPERFAMILY: CARDIACEA
See Plate 60

Shell varying in size, with equal valves and prominent radial ornament. Pallial line without a sinus. Animal with a short siphon.

Family: Cardiidae (Cockles)

Shell heart-shaped when seen from the side with both valves closed. Ribs developed to a varying extent, and sometimes also scales, knobs or spines. Ligament external, short and thick. Shell edges notched. The animal lives just below the surface of the sediment with the short siphons extended into the water above. The long, angled foot can be used to propel the animal across the surface of the sand, in leaps of some centimetres at a time. In cold and warm seas. CARDIINAE: shell semicircular to rounded-rectangular, rarely elliptical. Ribs smooth, with scales, knobs or spines. Rear edge of shell more or less notched, sometimes with tooth-like extensions. Hinge fairly straight. Genera: *Cardium* Linné, 1758 (subgenus: *Bucardium* Gray, 1853, synonym: *Ringicardium* Fischer, 1887); *Acanthocardia* Gray, 1851, synonym: *Sphaerocardium* Coen, 1933 (subgenus: *Rudicardium* Coel, 1914); *Parvicardium* Monterosato, 1884; *Plagiocardium* Cossmann, 1886 (subgenera: *Maoricardium* Marwick, 1944; *Papillicardium* Sacco, 1899); *Vepricardium* Iredale, 1929; and others. TRACHYCARDIINAE: shell ovate, the rear often with scales or spines and a toothed edge. Hinge relatively short, broad, straight or angled. Genera: *Trachycardium* Mörch, 1853 (subgenera: *Dallocardia* Stewart, 1930; *Mexicardia* (Stewart, 1930; *Phlogocardia* Stewart, 1930); *Acrosterigma*, Dall, 1900 (subgenera: *Regozara* Iredale, 1936; *Vasticardium* Iredale, 1927); *Papyridea* Swainson, 1840; and others. FRAGINAE: lower edge of shell angled. Ribs with knobs or scales. Genera: *Fragum* Röding, 1798 (subgenus: *Lunulicardia* Gray, 1853); *Corculum* Röding, 1798; *Ctenocardia* H. & A. Adams, 1857 (subgenera: *Afrocardium* Tomlin, 1931; *Microfragum* Habe, 1951); *Trigoniocardia* Dall, 1900 (subgena: *Americardia* Stewart, 1930; *Apiocardia* Olsson, 1961); and others. PROTOCARDIINAE: shell relatively angular, umbones almost in the middle. Ribs slightly spiny, mainly in the front part of the shell. Hinge long, slightly curved. Genera: *Nemocardium* Meek, 1876 (subgenera: *Discors* Deshayes, 1858; *Frigidocardium* Habe, 1951); *Keenaea* Habe, 1951; *Lophocardium* Fischer, 1887; *Lyrocardium* Meek, 1876; *Microcardium* Thiele, 1934; *Pratulum* Iredale, 1924; *Trifaricardium* Habe, 1951; and others. LAEVICARDIINAE: shell oblique-elliptical to roundish-rectangular, ribs more or less prominent with scales or knobs. No spines. Hinge long and curved. Genera: *Laevicardium* Swainson, 1840 (subgenera: *Dinocardium* Dall, 1900; *Fulvia* Gray, 1853); *Cerastoderma* Poli, 1795; *Clinocardium* Keen, 1936; *Serripes* Gould, 1841; and others.

SUPERFAMILY: TRIDACNACEA
See Plate 589

Shell medium-sized to very large (largest bivalves in the world), with prominent radial ornament. The front part of the hinge is reduced, so that only one cardinal tooth and the posterior lateral tooth are present. The animal lies within the mantle opening facing upwards. Lives on coral reefs.

Family: Tridacnidae (Giant clams)

Shell longish-triangular, very large, thick, the ribs and large folds with scales. *Tridacna* with a byssus, fastened to corals, *Hippopus* without byssus, with a closed shell when old, living in the sand. Indo-Pacific. Genera: *Tridacna* Bruguière, 1797 (subgenera: *Chametrachea* Mörch, 1853; *Persikima* Iredale, 1937); *Hippopus* Lamarck, 1799.

SUPERFAMILY: MACTRACEA
See Plate 62

Shell medium-sized, with equal, thin, procellanous valves. Ligament external. Siphons partly or completely fused. Pallial sinus deep and rounded. No byssus.

Family: Mactridae (Surf clams or Trough shells)

Shell ovate, triangular or longish. Umbones usually directed forwards. Periostracum smooth. Worldwide distribution. MACTRINAE: hinge well developed, siphons can be completely retracted into shell. Genera: *Mactra* Linné, 1767 (subgenera: *Coelomactra* Dall, 1895; *Cyclomactra* Dall, 1895; *Electomactra* Iredale, 1930; *Mactroderma* Dall, 1894; *Mactrotoma* Dall, 1894; *Nannomactra* Iredale, 1930; *Tumbeziconcha* Pilsbry & Olsson, 1935; and others); *Harvella* Gray, 1853; *Mactrellona* Marks, 1951; *Mulinia* Gray, 1837; *Rangia* Des Moulins, 1832 (subgenus: *Rangianella* Conrad, 1868); *Spisula* Gray, 1837 (subgenera: *Hemimactra* Swainson, 1840; *Mactromeris* Conrad, 1868; *Notospisula* Iredale, 1930; *Oxyperas* Mörch, 1853; *Pseudoxyperas* Sacco, 1901; *Standella* Gray, 1853; *Symmorphomactra* Dall, 1894); and others. LUTRARIINAE: shell gaping. Hinge with reduced lateral teeth. Siphons with rough epidermis, not completely retractile. Genera: *Lutraria* Lamarck, 1799 (subgenus: *Psammophila* Brown, 1827); *Eastonia* Gray, 1853; *Meropesta* Iredale, 1929; *Tresus* Gray 1853, synonym: *Schizothaerus* Conrad, 1853; and others. PTEROPSELLINAE: shell fairly well closed, thin. Siphons can be completely retracted into shell. Hinge relatively weak. Genera: *Anatina* Schumacher, 1817; *Raeta* Gray 1853 (subgenus: *Raetellops* Habe, 1952); and others. ZENATIINAE: shell compressed. Genera: *Zenatia* Gray, 1853; *Darina* Gray, 1853; *Resania* Gray, 1853; and others.

Family: Anatinellidae

Shell roundish-ovate, thin, rounded in the front, angular behind and somewhat gaping. Lateral hinge teeth lacking. A single genus: *Anatinella* Sowerby, 1833, Indo-Pacific.

Family: Mesodesmatidae

Shell small to medium-sized, wedge-shaped or roundish, longer in front than behind, somewhat compressed. Genera: *Mesodesma* Deshayes, 1832; *Anapella* Dall, 1895; *Atactodea* Dall, 1898; *Caecella* Gray, 1853; *Davila* Gray, 1853; *Donacilla* Philippi, 1836; *Ervilia* Turton, 1822; *Rochefortina* Dall, 1924; *Spondervilia* Iredale, 1930; and others.

SUPERFAMILY: SOLENACEA
See Plate 62

Shell elongated, with equal valves, gaping at both ends. Ligament external, byssus absent. Usually with a short pallial sinus.

Family: Solenidae (Razor shells, Jack-knife clams)

Shell long, fairly straight, truncated at the ends. Umbones near the front edge. Hinge with one tooth on either side. Burrowing in sand. Genera: *Solen* Linné, 1758; *Solena* Mörch, 1853 (subgenus: *Eosolen* Stewart, 1930).

Family: Cultellidae

Shell shorter, wider, compressed, rounded at the ends. Umbones not so far forward. Hinge with several teeth. Genera: *Cultellus* Schumacher, 1817 (subgenus: *Cultrensis* Coen, 1933), *Ensis* Schumacher, 1817; *Neosolen* Ghosh, 1920; *Pharella* Gray, 1854; *Phaxas* Gray, 1852; *Siliqua* Megerle v Muhlfeld, 1811 (subgenus: *Neosiliqua* Habe, 1965); and others.

SUPERFAMILY: TELLINACEA
See Plates 62 and 63

Shell small to medium-sized, usually ovate, laterally compressed, the rear often elongated to a kind of beak, and angled. Often rather asymmetrical. Ligament external, pallial sinus large, siphons separate.

Family: Tellinidae (Tellins)

Shell ovate to longish, the valves more or less equal. Over 200 species, mainly in warm seas. TELLININAE: variously ornamented. Hinge with lateral teeth. Genera: *Tellina* Linné, 1758 (subgenera: *Angulus* Megerle v. Muhlfeld, 1811; *Arcopagia* Brown, 1827; *Cadella* Dall, Bartsch & Rehder, 1938; *Cyclotellina* Cossmann, 1887; *Elliptotellina* Cossmann, 1887; *Eurytellina* Fischer, 1887; *Fabulina* Gray, 1851; *Hemimetis* Thiele, 1934; *Laciolina* Iredale, 1937; *Merisca* Dall, 1900; *Moerella* Fischer, 1887; *Nitidotellina* Scarlato, 1965; *Oudardia* Monterosato, 1884; *Peronidia* Dall, 1900; *Pharaonella* Lamy, 1918; *Phylloda* Schumacher, 1817; *Phyllodina* Dall, 1900; *Pinguitellina* Iredale, 1927; *Pseudarcopagia* Bertin, 1878; *Quadrans* Bertin, 1878; *Quidnipagus* Iredale, 1929; *Scissula* Dall, 1900; *Scutarcopagia* Pilsbry, 1918; *Semelangulus* Iredale, 1924; *Serratina* Pallary, 1922, synonym: *Striotellina* Thiele, 1934; *Tellinella* Mörch, 1853; *Tellinites* Lamarck, 1818; and others); *Strigilla* Turton, 1822 (subgenera: *Pisostrigilla* Olsson, 1961; *Simplistrigilla* Olsson, 1961); *Tellidora* H. & A. Adams, 1856; and others. MACOMINAE: ornament not prominent. Hinge without lateral teeth. Genera: *Macoma* Leach, 1819 (subgenera: *Cymatoica* Dall, 1890; *Psammacoma* Dall, 1900; *Rexithaerus* Tryon, 1869; *Temnoconcha* Dall, 1921; and others); *Apolymetis* Salisbury, 1929; *Florimetis* Olsson & Harbison, 1953; *Gastrana* Schumacher, 1817; *Psammotreta* Dall, 1900; and others.

Family: Donacidae (Wedge clams)

Shell usually small, wedge-shaped or triangular, obliquely truncated at the rear, long and pointed in front. Ligament external. Pallial sinus long. About 50 species, mostly tropical, living just below the surface of the sediment. Genera: *Donax* Linné, 1758 (subgenera: *Capsella* Gray, 1851; *Chion* Scopoli, 1777; *Cuneus* Da Costa, 1778; *Deltachion* Iredale, 1930; *Grammatodonax* Dall, 1900; *Hecuba* Schumacher, 1817; *Latona* Schumacher, 1817; *Machaerodonax* Roemer, 1870; *Paradonax* Cossmann & Payrot, 1910; *Plebidonax* Iredale, 1930; *Serrula* Mörch, 1853; *Tentidonax* Iredale, 1930); *Galatea* Bruguière, 1797, synonym: *Egeria* Roissy, 1805; *Hemidonax* Mörch, 1870; *Iphigenia* Schumacher, 1817; and others.

Family: **Psammobiidae** (Garidae) (Sunset shells)

Shell medium-sized, elongated, more or less gaping at the ends, thin, smooth or with fine ornament. Ligament external with thick ridges. Pallial sinus large. About 100 species, mostly tropical, on sandy or muddy shores. PSAMMOBIINAE: shell ovate-trapezoid, with equal valves, not gaping very much. Genera: *Gari* Schumacher, 1817, synonym: *Psammotaea* Lamarck, 1818 (subgenera: *Dysmea* Dall, Bartsch & Rehder, 1939; *Gobraeus* Brown, 1844; *Grammatomya* Dall, 1898; *Kermadysmea* Powell, 1958; *Psammobella* Gray, 1851; *Psammobia* Lamarck, 1818); *Amphichaena* Philippi, 1847; *Asaphis* Modeer, 1793, synonym: *Psammocola* Blainville, 1824 (subgenus: *Heteroglypta* v. Martens, 1880); *Ascitellina* Marwick, 1928; *Heterodonax* Mörch, 1853; *Orbicularia* Deshayes, 1850; and others. SANGUINOLARIINAE: longish-ovate, often beak-like at the rear, with the valves more or less unequal. Genera: *Sanguinolaria*; Lamarck, 1799 (subgenera: *Hainania* Scarlato, 1865; *Nuttallia* Dall, 1900; *Psammosphaerica* Jousseaume, 1894; *Psammotella* Herrmannsen, 1852; *Psammotellina* Fischer, 1887; *Soletellina* Blainville, 1824); and others.

Family: **Scrobiculariidae**

Shell medium-sized, roundish-ovate, thin, compressed, somewhat gaping, not curving laterally at the rear end. Hinge without lateral teeth. Pallial sinus large; the siphons can be extended to six times the length of the shell. Distributed particularly in European seas, usually on a muddy sea bed. Genus: *Scrobicularia* Schumacher, 1815.

Family: **Semelidae**

Similar to *Scrobicularia*, but often with the rear part of the shell showing a slight lateral curve. Hinge with lateral teeth. Mainly in warm seas. Genera: *Semele* Schumacher, 1817, synonym: *Amphidesma* Lamarck, 1818; *Abra* Lamarck, 1818, synonyms: *Abrina* Habe, 1952 and *Lutricularia* Monterosato, 1884 (subgenera: *Iacra* H. & A. Adams, 1856; *Syndosmya* Récluz, 1843); *Cumingia* Sowerby, 1883; *Leptomya* A. Adams, 1864; *Semelina* Dall, 1900; *Theora* H. & A. Adams, 1856; and others.

Family: **Solecurtidae** (Razor clams)

Shell rectangular, with rounded ends, gaping. Umbones near the middle. Genera: *Solecurtus* Blainville, 1824, synonym: *Solenocurtus* Blainville, 1826; *Azorinus* Récluz, 1869; *Pharus* Brown, 1844; *Tagelus* Gray, 1847; and others.

SUPERFAMILY: GAIMARDIACEA

Shell small, ovoid or trapezoid, thin, smooth or ribbed. Umbones far forwards. Byssus present. Usually on marine plants, in the central and southern Pacific.

Family: Gaimardiidae

Genera: *Gaimardia* Gould, 1852; *Costokidderia* Finlay, 1927; *Kidderia* Dall, 1876; *Neogaimardia* Odhner, 1924.

SUPERFAMILY: ARCTICACEA
See Plate 58

Shell medium-sized, ovate to elongated, usually with equal valves, the umbones fairly far forward. Ligament external. With a pallial sinus (no siphons).

Family: Arcticidae

Numerous fossil forms but only one Recent genus: *Arctica* Schumacher, 1817, synonym: *Cyprina* Lamarck, 1818.

Family: Bernardinidae

Shell very small. From the west coast of central America. Genera: *Bernardina* Dall, 1910; *Halodakra* Olsson, 1961.

Family: Trapeziidae

Shell medium-sized, longish, with the umbones near the front end. Living in holes in cliffs and reefs in warm seas. Genera: *Trapezium* Megerle v. Muhlfeld, 1811; *Coralliophaga* Blainville, 1924; *Isorropodon*, Sturany, 1896.

SUPERFAMILY: GLOSSACEA
See Plate 58

Shell small to medium-sized, with equal valves, the umbones conspicuously turned forwards. Smooth or with concentric sculpture. Ligament external. No pallial sinus.

Family: Glossidae (Isocardiidae)

Shell roundish to tongue-shaped. Umbones turned forward and rolled spirally inwards. Numerous fossil forms. Recent genus: *Glossus* Poli, 1795, synonym: *Isocardia* Lamarck, 1799 (subgenus: *Meiocardia* H. & A. Adams, 1857). *Glossus* (in the strict sense) in the North Atlantic, *Meiocardia* in the Indo-Pacific.

Family: Kelliellidae

Shell very small, roundish-ovate, umbones turned forward. North Atlantic, Australia. Genera: *Kelliella* Sars, 1870; *Pauliella* Munier-Chalmas, 1895; *Warrana* Laseron, 1953.

Family: Vesicomyidae

Shell small, longish-ovate to roundish. Lunule surrounded by a groove. No pallial sinus. Cosmopolitan. Genus: *Vesicomya* Dall, 1886; and others.

SUPERFAMILY: VENERACEA

See Plate 61

Shell medium-sized, squarish-ovate to longish, with equal valves. Ornament mainly concentric, but also ribbed, reticulate or smooth, with spines and scale-like lamellae, particular towards the rear. Umbones towards the front. Ligament external. Pallial sinus present. No byssus.

See Plate 61

Shell medium-sized, squarish-ovate to longish, with equal valves. Ornament mainly concentric, but also ribbed, reticulate or smooth, with spines and scale-like lamellae, particular towards the rear. Umbones towards the front. Ligament external. Pallial sinus present. No byssus.

Family: Veneridae (Venus clams)

Over 400 living species, with worldwide distribution, living in soft sea beds. VENERINAE: ornament radial and concentric. One lateral tooth in the front of the left valve. Genera: *Venus* Linné, 1758 (subgenera: *Antigona* Schumacher, 1817; *Ventricoloidea* Sacco, 1900); *Circomphalus* Mörch, 1853; *Globivenus* Coen, 1934; *Periglypta* Jukes-Browne, 1914; *Ventricolaria* Keen, 1954; and others. CIRCINAE: a few radial ribs are forked. Genera: *Circe* Schumacher, 1817; *Gafrarium* Röding, 1798; *Gouldia* C. B. Adams, 1847 (subgenus: *Gouldiopa* Iredale, 1924); and others. SUNETTINAE: smooth or with concentric ornament. Ligament sunken. Genera: *Sunetta* Link, 1807 (subgenera: *Cyclosunetta* Fischer-Piette, 1939; *Sunettina* Pfeiffer, 1869); and others. MERETRICINAE: shell longish-ovate, the ornament subdued or absent. Genera: *Meretrix* Lamarck, 1799; *Tivela* Link, 1807; *Transenella* Dall, 1883; and others. PITARINAE: umbones rather far forwards. Genera: *Pitar* Romer, 1857 (subgenera: *Lamelliconcha* Dall, 1902; *Pitarina* Jukes-Browne, 1913; *Tinctora* Jukes-Brown, 1914); *Amiantis* Carpenter, 1864 (subgenus: *Eucallista* Dall, 1902); *Callista* Poli, 1791 (subgenera: *Costacallista* Palmer, 1927; *Macrocallista* Meek, 1876); *Callocardia* A. Adams, 1864; *Lioconcha* Mörch, 1853; *Notocallista* Iredale, 1924; *Saxidomus* Conrad, 1837; and others. SAMARANGIINAE: shell more or less angular, without ornament. Genus: *Samarangia* Dall, 1902. DOSINIINAE: shell circular, with a heart-shaped lunule and concentric ornament. Pallial sinus deep and tongue-shaped. Genus: *Dosinia* Scopoli, 1777 (subgenera: *Pectunculus* Da Costa, 1778; *Phacosoma* Jukes-Browne, 1912); and others. CYCLININAE: similar to the preceding group. Genera: *Cyclina* Deshayes, 1850; *Cyclinella* Dall, 1902; and others. GEMMINAE: shell small, shiny, ventral margin crenulate. Genus: *Gemma* Deshayes, 1853; and others. CLEMENTIINAE: shell thin, without escutcheon, ornament vanishing. Genera: *Clementia* Gray, 1842; and others. TAPETINAE: shell longish-ovate, fairly smooth. Genera: *Tapes* Megerle v. Muhlfeld, 1811 (subgenus: *Ruditapes* Chiamenti, 1900); *Gomphina* Mörch, 1853 (subgenera: *Gomphinella* Marwick, 1927; *Macridiscus* Dall, 1902); *Irus* Schmidt, 1818 (subgenera: *Notirus* Finlay, 1928; *Notopaphia* Oliver, 1923); *Katelysia* Romer, 1857; *Liocyma* Dall, 1870; *Marcia* H. & A. Adams, 1857; *Paphia* Röding, 1798; *Venerupis* Lamarck, 1818, synonyms: *Polititapes* Chiamenti,

1900, and *Pullastra* Sowerby, 1826 (subgenus: *Paphirus* Finlay, 1927); and others. CHIONINAE: shell ovate-trigonal, thick, with concentric and radial ornament. Genera: *Chione* Megerle v. Muhlfeld, 1811 (subgenus: *Lirophora* Conrad, 1863); *Anomalocardia* Schumacher, 1817; *Bassina* Jukes-Browne, 1914 (subgenus: *Callanaitis* Iredale, 1917); *Chamelea* Mörch, 1853; *Mercenaria* Schumacher, 1817; *Placamen* Iredale, 1925; *Protothaca* Dall, 1902; *Tawera* Marwick, 1927; *Timoclea* Brown, 1827; and others.

Family: Petricolidae (False angel wings)

Shell elongate, narrower and gaping at the rear. These bivalves bore into soft limestone, coral, clay, etc. Genera: *Petricola* Lamarck, 1801 (subgenera: *Lajonkairia* Deshayes, 1854; *Petricolaria* Stoliczka, 1870; *Rupellaria* Fleuriau, 1802; and others); *Mysia* Lamarck, 1818.

Family: Cooperellidae

One genus: *Cooperella* Carpenter, 1864, off California.

ORDER: MYOIDA

Shell thin, without mother-of-pearl, hinge usually completely toothless or with 1-2 teeth. Siphons very well developed. Foot with or without byssus. The animals burrow in sand.

SUPERFAMILY: MYACEA
See Plate 63

Shell of varying sizes, elongate or ovate, with unequal gaping valves. Ligament mostly internal.

Family: Myidae (Soft-shell clams)

Shell medium-sized to large, longish-ovate, the rear pointed or truncated, and gaping. Hinge toothless. Pallial sinus large. Siphons long and fused, enclosed in a horny sheath. Only young individuals have a byssus. Widespread in sand and mud. Genera: *Mya* Linné, 1758 (subgenus: *Arenomya* Winckworth, 1930); *Cryptomya* Conrad, 1848; *Paramya* Conrad, 1861; *Platyodon* Conrad, 1837; *Sphenia* Turton, 1822; *Tugonia* Récluz, 1846; and others.

Family: Corbulidae (Corbula clams)

Shell small to medium-sized, ovate, with unequal valves, the rear angular or beaked. Genera: *Corbula* Bruguière, 1797; *Lentidium* Cristofori & Jan, 1832; and others.

Family: Sphaeniopsidae

Hinge with two teeth. Off California. Genus: *Grippina* Dall, 1912.

SUPERFAMILY: GASTROCHAENACEA

Shell small, thin, elongate with equal valves, gaping widely at the front. Hinge without teeth, ligament external. Pallial sinus large. Living in sand in warm seas.

Family: Gastrochaenidae

Genus: *Gastrochaena* Spengler, 1783, synonym: *Rocellaria* Blainville, 1829; and others.

SUPERFAMILY: HIATELLACEA
See Plate 63

Shell medium-sized, trapezoidal, but the outline is often irregular. Ligament external.

Family: Hiatellidae

Living free or attached by a byssus to rocks, bivalve shells, etc. often in caves. Circumpolar, arctic seas, east and west Atlantic, from Norway to the Mediterranean, in deep water off the West Indies and in the deeper parts of the North Pacific. Genera: *Hiatella* Bosc, 1801, synonym: *Saxicava* Fleuriau de Bellevue, 1802; *Cyrtodaria* Reuss, 1801; *Panomya* Gray, 1857; *Panopea* Ménard, 1807; *Saxicavella* Fischer, 1878; and others. There are two European species: *Hiatella arctica* (Linné, 1767), synonyms: *H. rugosa* (Linné, 1767) and *H. pholadis* (Linné, 1767) and *Hiatella striata* (Fleuriau de Bellevue, 1802), synonyms: *H. gallicana* (Lamarck, 1818) and *H. rugosa* of various authors. It is scarcely possible to distinguish old specimens of the two species. Young shells of *H. arctica* have 2 scaly toothed radial ribs at the rear. *H. arctica* lives free on marine plants or in rock crevices and breeds in summer, whereas *H. striata* almost always lives attached in holes which it has bored itself; it breeds in winter.

SUPERFAMILY: PHOLADACEA
See Plate 63

Shell thin, but very hard, elongate, gaping at both ends, surface ribbed, and having various accessory plates. Ligament absent. Shell interior with a spoon-shaped process, the apophysis, for the attachment of the foot muscle. These are widespread forms that bore into timber, soft limestone, coral, etc.

Family: Pholadidae (Angels wings or Piddocks)

Genera: *Pholas* Linné, 1758; *Barnea* Leach, 1826; *Cyrtopleura* Tryon, 1862; *Martesia* Sowerby, 1824; *Zirfaea* Leach, 1842; and others. *Cyrtopleura* occurs in the Caribbean, *Barnea* and *Zirfaea* on both sides of the Atlantic, *Zirfaea* also in the Mediterranean and off California, *Pholas* in northern Europe, Mediterranean and Caribbean.

Family: Teredinidae (Shipworms)

Animal elongate and worm-like, living in a calcareous tube that tapers to the rear. The very small valves cover only the front part of the body. The short siphons can be closed by two longish calcareous pallets. These bivalves bore in timber and often cause severe damage to harbour installations. Genera: *Teredo* Linné, 1758; *Bankia* Gray, 1842; and others.

Subclass: Anomalodesmata

Shell without or with only weak teeth. Ligament external or with an internal cartilage which has a calcareous plate, the lithodesma.

ORDER: PHOLADOMYOIDA

Shell thin, often with unequal valves, and with muscle impressions of approximately the same size, and mostly with mother-of-pearl. Siphons present, foot usually without a byssus. Shell free or attached (Myochamidae), or with a calcareous tube (Clavagellidae).

SUPERFAMILY: PHOLADOMYACEA

Shell medium-sized, with equal valves, ligament external.

Family: Pholadomyidae

Shell very thin, with radial ornament. Atlantic, Indo-Pacific, in deep water. Genus: *Pholadomya* Sowerby, 1823; and others.

SUPERFAMILY: PANDORACEA

Shell medium-sized, with unequal valves, the interior with or without mother-of-pearl.

Family: Pandoridae

Genus: *Pandora* Bruguière, 1797.

Family: Cleidothaeridae

Genus: *Cleidothaerus* Stutchbury, 1830.

Family: Laternulidae

Genus: *Laternula* Röding, 1798.

Family: Lyonsiidae

Genus: *Lyonsia* Turton, 1822.

Family: Myochamidae

Genera: *Myochama* Stutchbury, 1830; *Myadora* Gray, 1840.

Family: Periplomatidae

Genus: *Periploma* Schumacher, 1817.

Family: Thraciidae

Genus: *Thracia* Sowerby, 1823.

SUPERFAMILY: POROMYACEA (Septibranchia)

Shell small and thin. Gill cavity with a horizontal septum. Deep-sea forms.

Family: Poromyidae

Genus: *Poromya* Forbes, 1844.

Family: Cuspidariidae

Genus: *Cuspidaria* Nardo, 1840.

Family: Verticordiidae

Genus: *Verticordia* Sowerby, 1844.

SUPERFAMILY: CLAVAGELLACEA

Shell much reduced, with mother-of-pearl, and with one or both valves inside a calcareous tube ('secondary shell') secreted by the mantle. This tube has a sieve-like calcareous plate. Living vertically in the sediment, in the Red Sea and Indo-Pacific.

Family: Clavagellidae

Genera: *Clavagella* Lamarck, 1818; *Humphreyia* Gray, 1858; *Penicillus* Brugière, 1789.

Right: *Penicillus penis* (Linné, 1758), western Pacific (Taiwan), length 17cm. Below left: the sieve plate of the same, and right: the tiny shell valves fused with the calcareous tube (enlarged).

 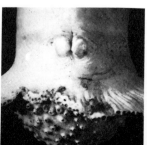

CLASS: SCAPHOPODA (Tusk shells)

See Plate 64

Marine molluscs with a tapering, tubular, slightly curved shell, open at both ends. The wider opening is at the front end, the narrower one to the rear, forming the apex. The latter usually has a smooth edge, often with a notch. The shell is positioned obliquely in the bottom with only the apex protruding above the surface of the substrate.

Scaphopods live almost exclusively in fairly deep water, only a few species occurring on the shore. Respiration takes place at the surface of the mantle for there are no gills. They feed on foraminiferans and similar micro-organisms.

Family: Dentaliidae

Shell tooth-shaped, smooth or ribbed. Widely distributed. Genus: *Dentalium* Linné, 1758 (subgenera: *Antalis* H. & A. Adams, 1854; *Fissidentalium* Fischer, 1885; *Fustiaria* Stoliczka, 1868; *Laevidentalium* Cossmann, 1888; *Pseudantalis* Monterosato, 1884; and others).

Family: Siphonodentaliidae

Shell small, smooth, somewhat convex in the middle. Genera: *Siphonodentalium* Sars, 1859; *Cadulus* Philippi, 1884; *Entalina* Monterosato, 1872; and others.

CLASS: CEPHALOPODA

See Plate 64

Marine molluscs with head and foot united. Shell external, internal or lacking. With gills and highly developed sense organs. Carnivorous.

Subclass: Nautiloidea

Shell spiral with numerous chambers. Mother-of-pearl.

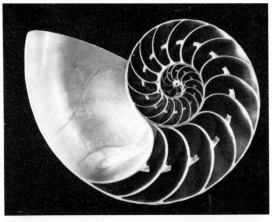

Longitudinal section through the shell of *Nautilus pompilius* Linné, 1758. The animal lives in the large chamber (to the left). The older chambers (to the right) normally contain gas and fluid and are in communication with one another by narrow tubes (siphuncle). Buoyancy can be adjusted by changes in the relative amounts of gas and fluid in the chambers.

Family: Nautilidae

Single genus: *Nautilus* Linné, 1758. Indo-Pacific.

Subclass: Coleoidea

Shell internal, often reduced or absent. Numerous orders and families. Those illustrated in Plate 64 are *Spirula* Lamarck, 1801 (family Spirulidae) and *Argonauta* Linné, 1758 (family Argonautidae).

COLOUR PLATES

In the descriptions which accompany each colour plate, the sizes given denote the greatest shell dimension (length or breadth).

Localities printed in parentheses after the general distribution area denote the source of the actual shell illustrated.

The common names of shells are printed in **bold** type.

1

1, 1a *Haliotis fulgens* Philippi, 1845. **Green Abalone.** Shell roundish-ovate, moderately deep with 5-7 slightly elevated open perforations. Prominent spiral ribs, close to one another. Colour dark-brown to greenish-brown. Inside with bright blue-green to pink mother-of-pearl. Conspicuous muscle impression. 10-20cm. California, in depths 3-6m. Synonym: *Haliotis splendens* Reeve, 1846.

2 *Haliotis rufescens* Swainson, 1822. **Red Abalone.** Shell thick ovate, not very deep, with 3-4 elevated, open perforations. Surface rough with numerous spiral ridges. Outside reddish, inside with pale mother-of-pearl. Muscle impression as though 'smeared'. Up to 30cm. California, more northerly than *H. fulgens*, in depths of about 7m. Synonym: *H. ponderosa* C. B. Adams, 1848.

3, 3a *Haliotis corrugata* Wood, 1828. **Pink Abalone.** Shell rather round, very convex, with 3-4 elevated, tubular, open perforations. Strong ribbing in both directions. Dark green to reddish-brown, inside with mother-of-pearl. 15-20cm. California, mainly among seaweeds. Synonyms: *H. diegoensis* Orcutt; *H. nodosa* Philippi, 1845.

4 *Haliotis (Euhaliotis) tuberculata* Linné, 1758. **The Ormer.** Shell longish-ovate, with 6-8 open perforations. Surface marbled dark brown with spiral grooves and radial folds. Inside pale mother-of-pearl. Up to 9cm, usually smaller. The only *Haliotis* on European coasts, from English Channel (not Britain) to Senegal, Canaries, Mediterranean. In Mediterranean, mainly the form *lamellosa* Lamarck, 1822, with stronger folds.

5 *Haliotis (Sulculus) diversicolor* Reeve, 1846. **Many-coloured Abalone.** Prominent ribs, 6-9 open perforations. Up to 9cm. Japan, southwards from the Kii Peninsula. *H. aquatilis* Reeve, 1846 is flatter, with less prominent ribs. *H. japonica* Reeve, 1846 is now a synonym.

6 *Haliotis (Haliotis) asinina* Linné, 1758. **Donkey's Ear.** Shell longish with relatively smooth surface, marbled olive-brown. Up to 10cm. Indo-Pacific (Cebu, Philippines).

7 *Haliotis (Sulculus) australis* Gmelin, 1791. **Silver Paua** (paua is Maori for an abalone). Surface yellowish with fine ornament. Inside pale silvery mother-of-pearl. 7-9cm. New Zealand (Lyall Bay, Washington, New Zealand).

8 *Haliotis (Marinauris) roei* Gray, 1827. Shell roundish-ovate, with thick, coarse spiral cords, marbled brownish-green. 7-9 open perforations. Up to 12cm. South and southwestern Australia (Fremantle).

2

1 *Scutus (Scutus) antipodes* Montfort, 1810. **Shield Shell, Duckbill, Elephant Snail.** Shell concentrically striped, with slight indentation in the front margin. Inside porcelain-white. The animal is large, dark with a proboscoid head. Up to 8cm. South and south-western Australia (Fremantle). Synonym: *S. anatinus* (Donovan, 1820).

2 *Scutus (Scutus) breviculus* (Blainville, 1817) 5-6cm. New Zealand (Timaru, New Zealand).

3 *Tugali (Tugali) cicatricosa* A. Adams, 1851. **Scarred Notched Limpet.** Coarse reticulate ornament, no indentation at front margin. 3cm. South and south-western Australia (Fremantle).

4 *Notomella dilecta* (A. Adams, 1851). **Delicate Slit Limpet.** Indian Ocean, south-western Australia (Hikkaduwa, Sri Lanka).

5 *Emarginula (Emarginula) elongata* (Da Costa, 1829). Shell translucent with reticulate ornament, interior white. On rocks and tangle-weeds. 9mm. Portugal, Canaries, Mediterranean (Sardinia). Synonym: *E. adriatica* (Da Costa). The related *E. fissura* Linné, 1758 from N.E. Atlantic (including Britain) has stronger ribs.

6 *Diodora (Diodora) italica* (Defrance, 1820). Reticulate ornament with low tubercles. 5cm. Mediterranean, Atlantic (Evboikos Kolpos, Greece).

7, 7a *Fissurella (Cremides) barbadensis* (Gmelin, 1791). **Barbados Keyhole Limpet.** Prominent, irregular radial ribs. Margin of inner callus green. Up to 3cm. Caribbean.

8, 8a *Fissurella (Cremides) nodosa* (Born, 1780). **Knobby Keyhole Limpet.** Tuberculate radial ribs, interior with strongly notched margin. Colour white to brown. Up to 3cm. Caribbean.

9, 9a *Fissurella (Cremides) gemmata* Menke, 1847. **White Keyhole Limpet.** Shell whitish-grey with tuberculate radial ribs. Inside white, the callus with greyish margin. Up to 3cm. West coast of Mexico.

10 *Diodora (Diodora) listeri* (d'Orbigny, 1853). **Lister's Keyhole Limpet.** Shell with white reticulation and a darkish margin. Up to 3cm. Caribbean.

11, 11a *Diodora (Diodora) gibberula* (Lamarck, 1822). Shell with curved base and fine ornament. Whitish-yellow with dark markings. Up to 2cm, usually smaller. Mediterranean. Atlantic, Canaries (Cyprus).

12, 12a *Diodora (Diodora) calzculata* (Sowerby, 1835). Strong radial ribs and reddish-white bands. Up to 2cm. South Africa (Jeffrey's Bay).

13 *Diodora (Diodora) aspera* (Eschscholtz, 1833). **Rough Keyhole Limpet.** White with dark bands. Up to 5cm. West coast of N. America.

14 *Fissurella (Cremides) rosea* (Gmelin, 1791). **Rosy Keyhole Limpet.** The inside of the perforation callus is green with a red margin. Otherwise similar to *F. barbadensis*. 2cm. West Indies, Caribbean Sea.

15 *Clypidina (Clypidina) notata* (Linné, 1758). **Black-ribbed False Limpet.** No perforation. 2cm. Indo-Pacific (Sri Lanka).

16 *Megathura crenulata* (Sowerby, 1825). **Great Keyhole Abalone.** Fine ornament and toothed margin. Up to 10cm. California.

3

1 *Patella (Patella) vulgata* Linné, 1758. **Common Limpet.** Shell yellowish-grey with brown flecks and strong radial ribs. Interior shiny with weak iridescence, the surface pattern showing through. Up to 6cm. British Isles, N.E. Atlantic, Mediterranean.

2 *Patella (Patella) aspera* Lamarck, 1822. **China Limpet.** Shell dirty yellowish-white, with coarse ornament and growth lines. Inside iridescent. Muscle impression orange. Up to 5cm. British coasts to Mediterranean.

3, 3a *Patella (Patella) caerulea* Linné, 1758. Shell fairly flat with strong radial ribs and weaker intermediate ridges, brownish-grey. Interior very iridescent. Up to 4cm. Mediterranean and adjacent Atlantic (Marbella, Spain).

4 *Patella (Patella) depressa* Pennant, 1777. Radial ribs extending beyond the shell margin. Interior orange and dark brown, with dark brown margin. 3cm. Britain, Atlantic, Mediterranean (Erqui, Brittany).

5 *Patella (Patellona) safiana* Lamarck, 1822. Shell fairly flat, with dense, equal ribs, dirty white with yellowish-brown rays, and translucent. Inside iridescent. 6-8cm. Northern and western coasts of Africa.

6 *Patella (Scutellastra) longicosta* Lamarck, 1819. Surface dark brownish-black, with strong ribs, overlapping the margin. Inside (shown here) bluish-white, with narrow dark margin. Up to 8cm. South Africa (Cape Province).

7 *Cellana toreuma* (Reeve, 1855). Shell flat, greenish to leather-coloured, with fine ornament. Colour and pattern very variable. Inside with silvery iridescence, the surface pattern showing through. Up to 4cm. Indo-Pacific.

8, 8a *Patella (Scutellastra) barbara* Linné, 1758. Shell flat, uniform pale brown, coarsely ribbed, but varying according to locality. Inside white, the muscle impression pinkish and the margin pale brown. Outline jagged. Up to 10cm. South Africa (Cape Province).

9 *Cellana tramoserica* (Holten, 1802). Shell strongly ribbed, colour variable, usually alternating pale and dark rays (yellow, orange, brown). Inside with a silky gloss. Up to 6cm. Australia.

10, 10a *Helcion (Ansates) pellucidus* (Linné, 1758). **Blue-rayed Limpet.** Shell translucent, smooth, horn-coloured, with fine, pale blue radial lines. Apex near the front end. Up to 2cm. Northern Europe to Portugal (Parede).

11 *Cellana exarata* (Reeve, 1854). **Black Limpet.** Shell convex, with numerous black radial ribs with rounded surfaces. Inside silvery-grey, the central callus black. Usually 4-6cm, sometimes up to 8cm. Hawaiian Islands (south coast of Big Island).

12 *Patella (Patellona) oculus* Born, 1788. Surface dark brown to grey-black, with alternating strong and weak ribs. Inside pale brown with broad blackish-brown margin, the muscle impression edged blue-grey. 11cm. South Africa.

13, 13a *Patella (Scutellastra) laticostata* Blainville, 1825. **Giant Limpet.** Shell tall, arched, pale greenish-grey with brown eyes, the top usually eroded. Up to 10cm. Australia (Onslow).

1 2 3 3a

4 5 6

7 8 8a

9

12

13

13a

4

1, 1a *Acmaea (Acmaea) mitra* Eschscholtz, 1833. **Whitecap Limpet.** Outside and inside pure white. Shell almost circular, with concentric growth lines, usually overgrown by algae. 3cm. West coast of N. America, Alaska to California (Kenai Peninsula, Alaska).

2, 2a *Acmaea (Collisella) limatula* Carpenter, 1864. **File Limpet.** Shell dark yellow or greenish-brown with fine scaly ribs. Interior bluish-white with brown margin. Up to 3cm. West coast of N. America (San Pedtro).

3 *Acmaea (Patelloida) alticostata* (Angas, 1865). **Ridged Limpet.** Shell with coarse ribs and dark growth lines, usually much eroded. Inside porcelain-white. Up to 4cm. Australia.

4, 4a *Acmaea (Notoacmea) persona* Eschscholtz, 1833. **Mask Limpet.** Shell relatively smooth, with greyish-white and brown flecks, the inside bluish-white with dark margin and muscle impression. 3cm. West coast of N. America (Neah Bay).

5, 5a *Acmaea (Notoacmea) insessa* Hinds, 1843. **Seaweed Limpet.** Shell tall, cap-shaped, smooth and shiny, uniform pale to dark brown. Inside dark brown with paler margin. Up to 2cm. West coast of N. America.

6, 6a *Acmaea (Notoacmea) testudinalis scutum* Eschscholtz, 1833. **Pacific Plate Limpet.** Shell flat, pale brown with dark rays often broken into spots. Interior bluish-white, the margin alternating pale and dark brown. Muscle impression dark. 4cm. West coast of N. America.

7 *Acmaea (Collisellina) saccharina* (Linné, 1758). **Sweet Limpet.** Conspicuous white ribs with dark ridges between, usually eroded. Interior white, the marginal notches with narrow black edges. 4cm. Indo-Pacific.

8, 8a *Acmaea (Collisella) antillarum* (Sowerby, 1831). **Antillean Limpet.** Outside with dark rays, inside porcelain-white, the margin with alternating brown and white. Muscle impression brown. 2cm. Florida, West Indies.

9, 9a *Acmaea (Collisella) dalliana* Pilsbry, 1891. **Dall's Limpet.** Shell flat, finely ribbed, brown with white flecks. Interior bluish-white, the external pattern showing through; the margin dark. Up to 5cm. West coast of central America (Guaymas).

10, 10a *Acmaea (Collisella) stanfordiana* Berry, 1957. Shell very flat with fine radial ornament, olive-brown with white flecks. Apex near the front end. Interior blue-green, the margin with alternating brown and white, muscle impression dark. 2·5cm. West coast of central America (Punta Penasco, Mexico).

11, 11a *Lottia gigantea* Gray, 1834. **Giant Owl Limpet.** Shell relatively large and low, pale brown with white flecks. Apex near front, usually eroded. Interior with large pale muscle impression, and broad, dark margin. 8cm. West coast of N. America (Monterey, California).

12 *Acmaea (Notoacmea) concinna* Lischke, 1870. Finely ribbed, brown with pale flecks. Interior (shown here) blue. 2cm. Japan (Kii).

13 *Acmaea (Notoacmea) concinna fuscoviridis* (Teramachi, 1949). Subspecies of No. 12, smaller (10-15mm), interior blue-green. Same distribution.

14 *Acmaea (Chiazacmea) pygmaea* (Dunker, 1882). Shell with radial brown rays. Interior (shown here) bluish-white, muscle impression brown. 8mm. Japan (Kii).

1 1a 2 2a
3 4 4a 5 5a
6 6a 7 8 8a
9 9a 11 12
10 10a 11a 13
14

5

1, 1a *Tectus (Rochia) conus* (Gmelin, 1791). Shell conical, with tuberculate spiral ridges, white with red markings. Base flat with red spiral bands. Columella ending with tooth. 5cm. Indo-Pacific, Red Sea (Eilat).

2 *Cantharidus (Cantharidus) purpureus* (Gmelin, 1791). **Red Top Shell.** On Seaweed. 2cm. New Zealand.

3 *Tectus (Tectus) dentatus* (Forskål, 1775). Conical with blunt tubercles. Base with concentric lines and a blue-green central area. Columella ending in a knob. 8cm. Indian Ocean.

4 *Bathybembix (Ginebis) argenteonitens hirasei* (Taki & Otuka, 1942). Shell thin, with external and internal mother-of-pearl. Small tubercles or whorl shoulders. 5cm. In depths 60-100m. Japan (Sagami Bay).

5 *Cantharidus (Cantharidus) ramburi* (Crosse, 1864). Pattern carmine and white. 2cm. South Australia.

6 *Tectus (Rochia) niloticus* (Linné, 1767). **Pearly Top Shell, Commercial Trochus.** Up to 15cm. Indo-Pacific.

7 *Calliostoma (Tristichotrochus) formosensis* (Smith, 1907). Whorls with slight shoulders. 6cm. In deep water off Taiwan.

8 *Calliostoma (Maurea) tigris* (Gmelin, 1791). **Tiger Top Shell.** Shell coeloconoid, with broad, rounded base, strikingly patterned brown and yellow. Up to 5cm. New Zealand.

A subspecies *chathamensis* Dell, 1950, Chatham Islands.

9 *Lischkeia (Lischkeia) alwinae* (Lischke, 1871). Shell whitish, with spiral ridges and tubercles, and a deep umbilicus. In depths of 60-100m. Japan, Taiwan.

10, 10a *Tectus (Tectus) pyramis* (Born, 1778). **Pyramid Top.** Shell with indistinct spiral ridges and small tubercles sutures. Base flat, white at centre, green at margin, without umbilicus. Up to 8cm. Indo-Pacific (Fremantle, Australia).

11 *Tegula (Chlorostoma) rugosa* (A. Adams, 1853). Whorls with spiral ridges and oblique folds. Umbilicus deep, white inside. 3cm. West coast of central America (Baja California del Norte).

12, 12a *Tegula (Chlorostoma) xanthostigma* (A. Adams, 1853). Deep black with weak spiral ridges. Base paler with green centre, and an umbilicus. 4cm. West Pacific (Kaohsiung, Taiwan).

13, 13a, 13b, 13c *Umbonium (Suchium) moniliferum* (Lamarck, 1822). Circular to lens-shaped, with variable colour and pattern. Base flat with an irregular callus over the umbilicus. 15mm. Indo-Pacific (Mikawa Bay, Japan).

14, 14a *Umbonium (Suchium) giganteum* (Lesson, 1831). **Button Shell.** Smooth with fine spiral grooves. Umbilicus sealed by a large callus plug. Up to 4cm. Indo-Pacific (Makawa Bay, Japan).

6

1 *Gibbula (Gibbula) magus* (Linné, 1758). Up to 30mm. Europe, English Channel to Mediterranean (Brittany).

2 *Gibbula (Forskalena) fanulum* (Gmelin, 1791). Up to 19mm. Mediterranean.

3 *Gibbula (Steromphala) umbilicalis* (Da Costa, 1778). 20mm. N.E. Atlantic coasts.

4 *Gibbula (Steromphala) cineraria* (Linné, 1758). **Grey Top.** 15mm. N.E. Atlantic coasts.

5, 5a *Clanculus (Clanculus) puniceus* (Philippi, 1846). **Strawberry Shell.** Up to 20mm. East Africa (Zanzibar).

6 *Clanculus (Clanculus) margaritarius* (Philippi, 1846). 15mm. Japan.

7 *Clanculus (Clanculus) pharaonius* (Linné, 1758). **Strawberry Top.** 15mm. Indian Ocean (Dar-es-Salaam).

8, 8a *Granata imbricata* (Lamarck, 1822). Scaly, grey, spiral ridges. Up to 30mm. Intertidal. Australia (Flinders Bay).

9 *Cantharidus (Phasianotrochus) bellulus* (Dunker, 1845). **Elegant Kelp Shell.** Up to 20mm. South Australia and Tasmania.

10 *Calliostoma (Calliostoma) ligatum* (Gould, 1849). Up to 25mm. Alaska.

11 *Cantharidus (Phasianotrochus) eximius* (Perry, 1811). Inside of aperture iridescent blue. 20mm. Southeast Australia (Long Reef, New South Wales).

12 *Diloma (Fractarmilla) rudis* (Gray, 1826). 20mm. Australia.

13 *Gaza sericata* Kira, 1959. Up to 20mm. Japan (Mikawa Bay, depth 90m).

14 *Calliostoma (Calliostoma) bonita* Strong, Hanna & Hertlein, 1933. Up to 24mm. West coast of central America (San Felipe, Baja California).

15 *Euchelus (Euchelus) atratus* (Gmelin, 1791). 17mm. West Pacific (Malaita).

16 *Monodonta (Monodonta) labio* (Linné, 1758). 15mm. Indo-Pacific (Kii, Japan).

17 *Calliostoma (Calliostoma) laugieri* (Payraudeau, 1826). 12mm. Mediterranean.

18 *Calliostoma (Ampullotrochus) granulatum* (Born, 1778). 33mm. Mediterranean.

19 *Calliostoma (Calliostoma) zizyphinus* (Linné, 1758). 25mm. English Channel to Mediterranean.

20 *Chrysostoma paradoxum* (Born, 1780). 20mm. Indo-Pacific (Malaita).

21 *Cantharidus (Phasianotrochus) rutilus* (A. Adams, 1851). **Pink-tipped Kelp Shell.** 12mm. South Australia (Sceale Bay).

22 *Cittarium pica* (Linné, 1758). **West Indian Top Shell.** Up to 8cm. South-east Florida and West Indies (Puerto Rico).

23 *Angaria tyria* (Reeve, 1842). 7cm. Australia (Fremantle).

24 *Angaria atrata* (Reeve, 1843). With short spines on shoulders, probably juvenile. 7cm. Japan (Kusui, Nada Cho). *A. atrata* has been regarded as a synonym of *A. delphinus*.

25 *Angaria delphinus* (Linné, 1758). **Dolphin Shell.** Up to 7cm. Indo-Pacific (Cebu, Philippines).

26 *Angaria melanacantha* (Reeve, 1842). 6cm. West Pacific (Palawan, Philippines).

7

1 *Turbo (Lunatica) marmoratus* Linné, 1758. **Green Turban.** Shell large, thick, marbled green, dark brown and white, with strong spiral cords. Young individuals smoother and rounder. Heavy calcareous operculum. Up to 20cm. Indian Ocean (Samar, Philippines). Synonym: *T. olearius* Linné, 1758.

2 *Turbo (Dinassovica) militaris* (Reeve, 1848). **Military Turban.** Smooth whorls, yellowish-green with dark brown spiral bands. 6-8cm. Rocky coasts of southern Queensland and New South Wales.

3, 3a, 4 *Turbo (Batillus) cornutus* (Lightfoot, 1786). **Horned Turban.** Last Whorl usually with 2 rows of hollow spines, but there are also spineless shells (4). Japanese investigations have shown that the spiny forms are mainly developed in unprotected places subjected to wave action, whereas spines are reduced or absent in sheltered localities. Coloration reddish or greenish according to the surrounding growth of plants on which the animal feeds. Calcareious operculum with granular surface (3a). Japan, 4-10m. (Kusui, Nada Cho).

5 *Turbo (Marmarostoma) argyrostomus* Linné, 1758. **Silver-mouthed Turban.** Yellow-brown with strong spiral cords. Umbilicus thick and granulose. Aperture pale silvery mother-of-pearl. 6-9cm. Indo-Pacific (Musqat, Arabian Gulf).

6 *Turbo (Marmarostoma) chrysostomus* Linné, 1758. **Gold-mouthed Turban.** With finer spiral cords than *T. argyrostomus.* Aperture golden-orange, mother-of-pearl. Up to 7cm. Indo-Pacific.

7 *Turbo (Callopoma) fluctuosus* Wood, 1828. Exterior very variable. Strong spiral cords with finer ribs between. Brown and white colour pattern runs spirally. Operculum with central granulose knob. No umbilicus. 7cm. West coast of central America (Mazatlan, Mexico).

8, 8a *Turbo (Lunella) coronatus* (Gmelin, 1791). Flat, conical yellow-brown or grey-green with fairly rounded whorls, the shoulders with jagged processes giving a crown-like appearance. Apex usually eroded to show mother-of-pearl and a hole at top of columella. Up to 40mm. Indian Ocean (Zanzibar).

9, 9a, 9b *Turbo (Ninella) whitleyi* Iredale, 1949. **Heavy Turbo.** Solid, flat, circular with wide, deep umbilicus. Ornament coarse, with tubercles on the shoulders and a deep channel along the suture. Coloration dirty grey to brownish, umbilical region white. Up to 9cm. West Australia (Fremantle). East Australian form is *T. (N.) torquata* (Gmelin, 1791).

10 *Turbo (Marmarostoma) pulcher* Reeve, 1842. **Beautiful Turban.** Brown and green with variable spiral ridges. 8cm. West Australia (Fremantle).

1

2

3a

3

5

6

4

8a

8

9

7

10

9a

9b

8

1 Turbo (Turbo) petholatus Linné, 1758. **Tapestry Turban, Cat's-eye Shell.** Smooth, glossy, red-brown to brownish-green with dark spiral bands. No umbilicus. Aperture edge and columellar callus yellow-green. Operculum massive, white outside with a blue-green centre, known as cat's eye. Up to 8cm. Indo-Pacific (Samar, Philippines).

2 Turbo (Turbo) reevei Philippi, 1847. Possibly only a red-brown variant of No. 1. West Pacific (Cebu, Philippines).

3, 3a Astraea (Bolma) rugosa (Linné, 1767). Angular whorls with tubercles or spines. Columellar callus, aperture edge and operculum (3a) orange-red. Up to 6cm. Mediterranean and adjacent Atlantic, Azores.

4, 4a Astraea (Astralium) phoebia Röding, 1798. Flat with triangular spines on edges of whorls. 2-4cm. South-east Florida, West Indies. Synonym: *A. longispina* (Lamarck, 1822).

5, 5a Astraea (Astralium) heimburgi (Dunker, 1882). Short flat apex and angular whorls, with folds and knobs. Base flat, with numerous granular spiral cords. Purplish-violet. 15mm. Japan (Kusui, Nada Cho).

6 Astraea (Astralium) calcar (Linné, 1758). Irregular leaf-like spines on edges of whorls. Base with coarse scaly cords, without umbilicus. 2-3cm. Indo-Pacific (Zamboanga, Philippines). Synonym: *A. laciniatus* (Gould, 1849).

7 Guildfordia triumphans (Philippi, 1841). Lower edge of body whorls with 7-9 long, hollow, finger-like spines which are removed as the shell grows, leaving small knobs. West Pacific, mainly Japan, 50-100m. (Kii, Japan). The larger, paler *G. yoka* Jousseaume, also from Japan, has longer spines.

8 Galeoastraea (Harisazaea) modesta (Reeve, 1848). Conical with tubercles or spines on whorl edges. Base orange-yellow without umbilicus. Up to 5cm. West Pacific, mainly Japan (Kii), depth 50–100m.

9 Astraea (Astralium) rotularia (Lamarck, 1822). **Knob Star Shell.** Conical, the whorl edges with coarse, spirally arranged folds. Base with scaly, spiral ribs, operculum smooth, red-brown or dark green. Up to 4cm. Australia (Broome).

10 Astraea (Astralium) haematragum (Menke, 1829). Conical, with prominent longitudinal folds forming knobs at the whorl edges. No umbilicus 2cm. West Pacific, mainly Japan (Kusui, Nada Cho).

11, 11a Astraea (Astraea) heliotropium (Martyn, 1784). Up to 10cm. On sandy bottoms, in moderate depths. New Zealand.

9

1, 2   *Phasianella australia* (Gmelin, 1791). **Australian Pheasant Shell.** Colour and pattern extremely variable. Up to 10cm. Tasmania and South Australia (Albany).

3   *Tricolia speciosa* (Mühlfeld, 1824). Yellowish with patterned brown spiral bands. 13mm. Mediterranean.

4   *Tricolia pulla* (Linné, 1758). 9mm. English coasts to Canaries, Mediterranean (Porto Ferro, Sardinia), Black Sea.

5   *Phasianella modesta* (Gould, 1861). 15mm. West Pacific (Solomons).

6, 6a   *Neritina (Provittoida) ziczac* (Lamarck, 1816). 18mm. West Pacific.

7   *Smaragdia viridis* (Linné, 1757). Yellowish-green. 5mm. West Indies and Mediterranean. The related *S. rangiana* (Récluz, 1842) is from the Indian Ocean and east African coast.

8   *Neritina (Vitta) piratica* Russell, 1940. Up to 20mm. West Indies.

9   *Theodoxus (Vittoclithon) luteofasciatus* Miller, 1879. Brown columellar callus. 12mm. West coast of Mexico (Mazatlan). Synonym: *Neritina picta* Sowerby, 1832.

10   *Puperita (Puperita) pupa* (Linné, 1767). About 8mm. West Indies.

11   *Neritodryas dubia* (Gmelin, 1791). 20mm. Indo-Pacific (Cebu, Philippines).

12   *Nerita (Nerita) peloronta* Linné, 1758. **Bleeding Tooth.** Reddish-orange marking around parietal teeth. 25mm. West Indies.

13, 13a   *Nerita (Amphinerita) polita* Linné, 1758. Flat spire, shiny surface, with broad parietal shield. 40mm. Indo-Pacific.

14   *Nerita (Amphinerita) polita australis* Wood, 1828. 20mm. Queensland.

15   *Nerita (Ritena) scabricosta* Lamarck, 1822. Rounded spiral cords. 30mm. West coast of Mexico. Synonym: *N. ornata* Sowerby, 1823.

16   *Nerita (Ritena) undata* Linné, 1758. Rounded spiral cords, colour variable, apex often orange. 44mm. Indo-Pacific.

17   *Nerita (Ritena) plicata* Linné, 1758. Strong spiral cords. Parietal are wrinkled. 25mm. Indo-Pacific.

18   *Nerita (Theliostyla) textilis* Gmelin, 1791. Up to 40mm. Indo-Pacific. *N. (T.) tessellata* Gmelin, 1791. 12-17mm. Florida, West Indies.

19   *Neritina (Dostia) crepidularia* Lamarck, 1822. Up to 15mm. Indo-Pacific.

20, 20a   *Nerita (Ritena) costata* Gmelin, 1791. 35mm. Indo-Pacific.

21, 21a   *Nerita (Theliostyla) squamulata* Le Guillou, 1841. 30mm. Indo-Pacific.

22   *Neritina (Vitta) virginea* (Linné, 1758). Colour and pattern very variable. About 10mm. Florida, Texas, West Indies (Haiti).

23   *Theodoxus (Pictoneritina) communis* (Quoy & Gaimard, 1832). Colour and pattern extremely variable. 15mm. West Pacific (Philippines). Synonym: *Neritina communis*.

24   *Neritina (Vittina) turrita* (Gmelin, 1791). Ovate, with short spire, 20mm. Indo-Pacific (Philippines).

1   *Littorina (Littorina) littorea* (Linné, 1758). **Common Winkle.** Up to 40mm. From the east coast of North America to western Europe (Heligoland).

2   *Littorina (Littorina) saxatilis* (Olivi, 1792). **Rough Winkle.** Up to 15mm. Female produces live young. North America to western Europe (Portugal).

3   *Littorina (Littorina) saxatilis rudis* (Maton, 1797). Up to 12mm. (Setubal, Portugal).

4, 4a   *Littorina (Littorina) obtusata* (Linné, 1758). **Flat Winkle.** Up to 15mm. North America to western Europe (Roscoff, Brittany). Also known as *L. littoralis*.

5   *Littorina (Littorina) scutulata* Gould, 1849. **Checkered Periwinkle.** 13mm. West coast of north America.

6   *Littorina (Austrolittorina) aspera* Philippi, 1846. Up to 16mm., usually smaller. West coast of central America (Mazatlan, Mexico).

7, 7a   *Littorina (Littorina) ziczac* (Gmelin, 1791). **Zebra Periwinkle.** 2cm. Caribbean.

8   *Littorina (Littorina) sitkana* Philippi, 1846. 17mm. West coast of North America.

9   *Littorina (Littorina) brevicula* (Philippi, 1844). Up to 22mm. Japan.

10, 10a   *Littorina (Littoraria) zebra)* (Donovan, 1825). 32mm. Costa Rica to Colombia (Canal Zone, Panama).

11   *Littorina (Littoraria) mauritiana* (Lamarck, 1822). 20mm. East Africa.

12   *Littorina (Austrolittorina) unifasciata unifasciata* Gray, 1826. 5-20mm. South and south-western Australia (Fremantle).

13   *Littorina (Littoraria) nebulosa* (Lamarck, 1822). 20mm. Gulf of Mexico.

14   *Littorina (Littorinopsis) irrorata* (Say, 1822). **Marsh Periwinkle.** Up to 20mm. New York to Florida (Atlantic City, N.J.).

15   *Littorina (Littorinopsis) scabra angulifera* (Lamarck, 1822). Up to 30mm. On mangroves, southern Florida (Tampa Bay) to Brazil.

16   *Littorina (Littorinopsis) scabra scabra* (Linné, 1758). **Rough Periwinkle.** 11-40mm. On mangroves. South Africa to southern Polynesia (Mile Bay, New Guinea).

17, 17a   *Littorina (Littoraria) undulata* Gray, 1839. 11-23mm. Rocky coasts, Madagascar to western Polynesia (Moragalla, Sri Lanka).

18, 18a   *Nodilittorina (Granulilittorina) exigua* (Dunker, 1860). 7-13mm. Coasts of China and Japan (Kii, Japan).

19   *Tectarius (Tectarius) pagodus* (Linné, 1758). 40mm. On rocks above high water. Indo-Pacific.

20   *Tectarius (Cenchritis) muricatus* (Linné, 1858). Up to 20mm. West Indies.

21   *Echininus (Echininus) cumingi spinulosus* (Philippi, 1847). 17mm. Japan.

22   *Nodilittorina (Nodilittorina) pyramidalis pyramidalis* (Quoy & Gaimard, 1833). 9-23mm. Indo-Pacific (Port Jackson, Australia).

23   *Tectarius (Tectarius) coronatus* Valenciennes, 1832. 10-40mm. Western Pacific (Malaita, Solomons).

24   *Tectarius (Tectarius) grandinatus* (Gmelin, 1791). 30mm. Pacific (Zamboanga, Philippines).

25   *Bembicium nanum* (Lamarck, 1822). 15mm. On rocks above high water. Southern Pacific (Catherine Island, South Australia).

11

1 *Architectonica perspectiva* (Linné, 1758). **Sundial Shell.** An additional spiral groove beneath the true suture. Umbilicus wide, deep, with brown edge. 5cm. Indo-Pacific (Taiwan).

2 *Architectonica maxima* (Philippi, 1848). Radial ornament more pronounced. Each whorl with true suture and 3 additional spiral grooves. Umbilicus with pale edge. 8cm. Indo-Pacific (Taiwan). Other species: *A. trochlearis* (Hinds, 1844). West Pacific; *A. nobilis* Röding, 1798. Florida, West Indies.

3, 3a *Heliacus stramineus* (Gmelin, 1791). Rounded whorls with spiral cords and fine radial lines. Umbilicus wide. 3·5cm. Indo-Pacific (Taiwan). Comparable species: *Grandeliacus mortensenae* Iredale, 1957, Australia.

4, 4a *Heliacus variegatus* (Gmelin, 1791). Each whorl with 4 spiral cords with alternate dark and light pattern. Umbilicus narrow, deep. Up to 20mm, usually smaller. Tropical Pacific (Malaita, Solomons).

5 *Turritella (Turritella) terebra* (Linné, 1758). **Auger Screw Shell.** Numerous convex whorls with strong spiral ribs. 12cm. Indo-Pacific (Palawan, Philippines).

6 *Turritella (Zaria) duplicata* (Linné, 1758). **Angled Screw Shell.** 12cm. Indian Ocean.

7 *Turritella (Turritella) communis* (Risso, 1826). **Common Screw Shell.** 5cm. European coasts, Mediterranean.

8 *Turritella (Zeacolpus) vittata* (Hutton, 1973). Flat whorls with numerous spiral lines. 4cm. New Zealand (Little Barrier Island, Hauraki Gulf).

9 *Turritella (Maoricolpus) rosea rosea* (Quoy & Gaimard, 1834). Body whorl sharply angled at base. 6cm. New Zealand (Timaru).

10 *Turritella (Turritella) gonostoma* Valenciennes, 1832. Flat whorls with fine spiral cords, marbled greyish-white and dark red-brown. 8cm. Gulf of California to Ecuador (San Carlos Bay, Mexico).

11 *Vermicularia spirata* Philippi, 1836. **Worm Shell.** Apical whorls tightly coiled (for c. 1cm), later ones grow distorted and completely separate from one another. 7-9cm. Caribbean. Other species: *V. knorri* Deshayes, 1843, smaller, paler, Florida; *V. fargoi* Olsson, 1950, rather larger than *V. spirata*, Florida, Texas.

12 *Bivonia triquetra* (Bivona, 1832). Shell a tube with triangular cross sections, diameter 6mm. Sessile on rocks, shells. North Sea, Atlantic. Mediterranean (Corsica).

13 *Lemintina arenaria* (Linné, 1758). Shell tube with rounded cross section, diameter 11-15mm. Mediterranean (Cannigione, Sardinia).

14 *Modulus modulus* (Linné, 1758). **Atlantic Modulus.** Axial ribs crossed by spiral cords. Umbilicus deep, narrow. 12mm. Texas, Florida, West Indies.

1 2 3 3a 4 4a 5 6 7 8 9 10 11 12 13 14 14a

12

1 *Telescopium telescopium* (Linné, 1758). **Telescope Creeper.** Conical with pronounced spiral ribs and grooves. Dark brown, often with pale spiral lines on whorls. Short siphonal canal. Columella twisted. Apex usually eroded. 10cm. Indo-Pacific (Cairns, Queensland).

2 *Terebralia sulcata* (Born, 1778). Shell usually chocolate-brown, sometimes grey-blue with brown bands. Outer lip wide and flared. Siphonal canal short. 6cm. Indo-Pacific.

3 *Terebralia palustris* (Linné, 1767). **Mud Creeper.** Conical with strong axial ribs. 8-12cm. Indo-Pacific (Malindi, Kenya).

4, 4a *Planaxis (Planaxis) sulcatus* (Born, 1780). **Ribbed Clusterwink.** Similar to *Littorina*. Lives gregariously. Up to 2cm. Tropical Pacific (Zamboanga, Philippines).

5 *Planaxis (Proplanaxis) planicostatus* Sowerby, 1825. Up to 20mm. Pacific coast of central America, Mazatlan to Peru (Panama Bay).

6 *Cerithium (Thericium) vulgatum* Bruguière, 1789. **Common Cerith.** Spiral ribs with tubercles. Siphonal canal short. 5cm. Mediterranean and adjacent Atlantic.

7 *Cerithium (Cerithium) nodulosum* Bruguière, 1792. **Giant Knobbed Cerith.** Broad spiral cords with tubercles. Outer lip much folded. Aperture splayed and notched. Up to 13cm. Indo-Pacific.

8 *Rhinoclavis vertagus* (Linné, 1767). Siphonal canal turned back at right angles to axis. 7cm. Indo-Pacific (Queensland).

9 *Rhinoclavis fasciatus* (Bruguière, 1792). Flat whorls with coloured banding. 8cm. Indo-Pacific (Tevenard Island, N.W. Australia).

10 *Batillaria (Velacumantus) australis* (Quoy & Gaimard, 1834). Strong radial ribs. 4cm. Australia.

11 *Tympanotonos fuscatus* (Linné, 1758). Spiral cords with tubercles and spines. Aperture rather small with short canal. 4·5cm. West Africa (Marshall Bay, Liberia).

12 *Rhinoclavis pulcher* (Sowerby, 1855). 6cm. **Beautiful Creeper.** Northern Australia and Queensland (Keppel Bay).

13 *Cerithium (Cerithium) columna* Sowerby, 1834. Up to 4cm. Tropical Pacific.

14 *Cerithium (Thericium) caeruleum* Sowerby, 1855. 3cm. East Africa, Red Sea.

15 *Cerithidea montagnei* (d'Orbigny, 2839). 3·5cm. California to Ecuador.

16 *Cerithium (Thericium) stercusmuscarum* Valenciennes, 1833. 2·5cm. California to Peru (Santa Cruz, Galapagos).

17 *Eulima (Balcis) grandis* (A. Adams, 1854). Smooth and glossy, without ornament except for an axial groove marking former aperture edges. 3·5cm. West Pacific (Taiwan).

13

1 *Epitonium (Epitonium) scalare* (Linné, 1758). **Precious Wentletrap.** Whorls rounded, loosely coiled, with regular, thin varices. Umbilicus present. 5-6cm. Indo-Pacific (Zamboanga, Philippines). Synonym: *Scalaria pretiosa* Lamarck, 1816.

2 *Epitonium (Clathrus) clathrus* (Linné, 1758). **Common Wentletrap.** Whorls with flattened varices. No umbilicus. 3cm. European coasts, mainly Mediterranean (Novigrad, Istria). Synonym: *Scalaria communis* Lamarck, 1801.

3 *Epitonium (Epitonium) pallasi* (Kiener, 1838). Similar to *scalare*, smaller, brownish. 3cm. Indo-Pacific (Keppel Bay, Queensland).

4 *Epitonium (Gyroscala) lamellosum* (Lamarck, 1822). About 3cm. Southern England to Mediterranean. Synonym: *Scala commutata* (Monterosato, 1887).

5 *Amaea (Amaea) magnifica* (Sowerby, 1844). 6-8cm. West Pacific, mainly Japan (Taiwan).

6 *Amaea (Acrilla) acuminata* (Sowerby, 1844). Distinct fine axial ribs. Brown with a white, spiral band. 4cm. Indo-Pacific (Taiwan).

7 *Trichotropis (Ariadna) borealis* Broderip & Sowerby, 1829. 2cm. North Europe (Iceland, depth 190m), Arctic.

8 *Janthina janthina* (Linné, 1758). **Violet Snail.** Up to 4cm. Lives afloat in warm seas. Synonyms: *J. fragilis* Lamarck, 1801, *J. communis*, Lamarck, 1822, *J. violacea* Röding, 1798.

9 *Janthina pallida* (Thompson, 1841). 2cm. All seas (Albufeira, Portugal).

10 *Janthina capreolata* Montrouzier, 1859. 25mm. South Australia.

11, 11a *Crepidula (Maoricrypta) monoxyla* (Lesson, 1830). Very flat, white, underside smooth. 3cm. New Zealand (Hauraki Gulf, Auckland).

12, 12a *Crepidula (Crepidula) fornicata* (Linné, 1758). **American Slipper Limpet.** 5cm. Introduced into Europe from North America. The animals form a chain, one above the other, the lowest attached to the substrate. The oldest (lowest) animals are females, the uppermost males, and the intermediate animals are hermaphrodites. A pest of oysters.

13 *Capulus (Capulus) ungaricus* (Linné, 1767). **Fool's Cap.** 5cm. S. Iceland to Mediterranean (Chioggia, Italy).

14, 14a *Calyptraea (Calyptraea) chinensis* (Linné, 1758). **Chinaman's Hat.** 15mm. N. Atlantic coasts and Mediterranean (Fuengirola, Spain).

15, 15a *Crucibulum scutellatum* (Gray, 1828). 3-5cm. California to Ecuador (Mazatlán, Mexico).

16, 16a *Crucibulum spinosum* (Sowerby, 1824). 3cm. West coast of central America.

17, 17a *Hipponix conicus* (Schumacher, 1817). 2cm. West Pacific (Fremantle).

18, 18a *Calyptraea (Trochita) trochiformis* (Born, 1778). 2-5cm. Ecuador to Peru.

14

1, 1a *Xenophora pallidula* (Reeve, 1842). **Pallid Carrier Shell.** Conical with a white to pale yellow-brown base with pronounced radial and spiral ornament. The animal collects bivalve and gastropod shells and stones and sticks these to the surface of its own shell, with a clear tendency to arrange them radially. Long, pointed objects such as gastropod shells are sometimes attached by one end, protruding like spokes, and bivalve shells so that the inside faces upwards. Shell diameter c. 5cm. West Pacific, mainly Japan (Kii) in depths of c. 50m. Related species: *X. corrugata* (Reeve, 1842), with brown radial curves at the base, 5cm, Indo-Pacific; *X. crispa* (König, 1831), synonym: *X. mediterranea*, 4cm, Mediterranean and adjacent Atlantic; *X. caperata* (Philippi, 1851), 2·5cm, and *X. senegalensis* Fischer, 1873, 4cm, both West Africa. Also two species off Australia and New Zealand. No umbilicus in genus *Xenophora*.

2, 2a *Stellaria solaris* (Linné, 1764). **Sunburst Carrier Shell.** Conical, pale brown thin-shelled, with hollow ray-like processes at periphery. The animal carries very few foreign objects or none. Umbilicus deep. 8·5cm. Indo-Pacific (Taiwan), South Africa. *Haliphoebus* P. Fischer, 1880 is a synonym of *Stellaria*.

3 *Aporrhais senegalensis* Gray, 1838. Each whorl with a row of tubercles spirally arranged. Outer lip with 3 more or less developed finger-like processes. 18-25mm. West Africa (Joal, Senegal).

4 *Aporrhais pespelecani* (Linné, 1758). **Pelican's Foot.** All whorls with pronounced tubercles. Body whorl with two additional rows of tubercles. Long siphonal canal (often erroneously regarded as a 'finger'). 4cm. N. Europe and Mediterranean, in depths 10-130m.

5 *Aporrhais serresianus* (Michaud, 1828). More finely, built with more numerous tubercles and 4 longer 'fingers' (apart from the long siphonal canal). 4cm. Mediterranean, in depths 75-2000m.

6 *Struthiolaria papulosa papulosa* (Martyn, 1784). 83mm. New Zealand (Timaru). Related species: *S. vermis* (Martyn, 1784), 45mm, New Zealand.

15

1 *Tibia fusus fusus* (Linné, 1767). **Spindle Tibia.** Shell spindle-shaped with pointed apex and extremely long thin siphonal canal, through which the animal extends its siphon while living deep down in the sand. The siphon brings it food and water for respiration. The first pale whorls have distinct ribs, later ones are smooth. Outer lip with 5 short projections. Total length about 23cm. Indo-Pacific, in depths of c. 40m (Bantayan Island, Philippines). Another Indo-Pacific subspecies, *T. f. melanocheilus* A. Adams, 1854 has a reddish-black aperture.

2 *Tibia insulaechorab* Röding 1798. **Arabian Tibia.** Shell solid, spindle-shaped with a shorter siphonal canal and very short projections on the somewhat thickened outer lip. Total length c. 15cm. Indo-Pacific, in relatively shallow water. Synonyms: *T. brevirostris* Schumacher, 1817; *T. curvirostris* Lamarck, 1822. The rarer subspecies *T. i. luteostoma* Angas, 1878, has a yellow aperture.

3, 3a *Tibia powisi* (Petit, 1842). Smaller than the preceding, with distinct spiral ornament, the body whorl with a shoulder. The uppermost projection on the outer lip is broader than the others and stumpy. Siphonal canal about as long as the aperture. 65mm. South Japan to Northern Australia in deep water (Tayabas Bay, Philippines). Synonym; *T. abyssicola* Schepman, 1909.

4, 4a *Lambis (Lambis) lambis* (Linné, 1758). **Common Spider Conch.** Outer lip wide with a thickened edge and 6 divergent, finger-like processes, and below a similarly shaped siphonal canal. Aperture uniform pale brown to orange-red. Female shells have a longish double tubercle on the shoulder and the 'fingers' turn upwards. Male shells are smaller, have 2 equal-sized single tubercles on the shoulder and the finger are not raised. 10-20cm. Indo-Pacific, on reef flats and coral sand.

5 *Lambis (Lambis) truncata truncata* (Humphrey, 1786). **Giant Spider Conch.** The stumpy apex is characteristic (the first 5 whorls lie in the same plane). Up to 40cm. Indian Ocean (Mozambique), depth 20-30m. *L. (L.) t. sebae* has a more pointed apex, and occurs in the south Pacific.

6 *Terebellum terebellum* (Linné, 1758). **Little Auger Shell.** Up to 60mm. Indo-Pacific (Sulu Sea, Philippines).

1

3

3a

4

2

4a

5

6

16

1 *Strombus (Strombus) alatus* Gmelin, 1791. **Florida Fighting Conch,** so called from the powerful strokes of the animal's foot during flight and defence. Apical whorls have axial ribs, later ones have spiral ridges and a row of shoulder tubercles, increasing in size towards the base. Outer lip wing-like with characteristic 'stromboid notch'. Coloration creamy-white to dark brown, inner lip and columellar callus shiny orange-brown. 8cm. Caribbean. Possibly a subspecies of No. 2.

2 *Strombus (Strombus) pugilis* Linné, 1758. **West Indian Fighting Conch.** Shell form as *alatus*, usually pale orange. 8cm. Caribbean to Brazil (Puerto Rico). *S. (S.) p. nicaraguensis* Fluck, 1905 on east coast of Nicaragua, 4-6cm.

3 *Lambis (Harpago) chiragra chiragra* (Linné, 1758). **Chiragra Spider Conch.** Female shell 15–25cm, aperture pale flesh pink, the last two shoulder tubercles larger than the others. Male shell 10-17cm, aperture more brightly coloured, shoulder tubercles all about the same size. Southern Pacific, depths c. 20m.

4 *Lambis (Harpago) chiragra arthritica* Röding, 1798. No difference between male and female shells, both like male of No. 3, but with orange aperture. The parallel streaks on the parietal area run parallel to the spiral folds on the back of the shell. 12-17cm. East Africa to Maldives in shallow water.

5 *Strombus (Doxander) vittatus campbelli* Griffith & Pidgeon, 1834. 5cm. Northern Australia. See also Plate 17/4, 11. Another geographically restricted subspecies is *S. (D.) vittatus japonicus* Reeve, 1851, south of Honshu and Kyushu, Japan.

6 *Lambis (Millepes) scorpius scorpius* (Linné, 1758). **Scorpion Conch.** With 6 'fingers' and a curved, finger-like siphonal canal. Aperture brownish-orange to violet. 10-16cm. Western Pacific (Sulu Sea, Philippines). The Indian Ocean has *L. (M.) scorpius indomaris* R. T. Abbott, 1961.

7 *Lambis (Lambis) crocata crocata* (Link, 1807). **Orange Spider Conch.** 10-15cm. Indo-Pacific (Zanzibar). *L. (L.) crocata pilsbryi* R. T. Abbott, 1961, in the Marquesas Islands.

8 *Strombus (Canarium) urceus* Linné, 1758. **Little Bear Conch.** Colour and ornament variable, aperture pale (white mouth form). 6cm. Western Pacific, 20m depth.

9 *Strombus (Canarium) urceus* Linné, 1758. **Little Bear Conch.** Aperture dark (black mouth form).

10 *Strombus (Tricornis) gigas* Linné, 1758. **Pink Conch, Queen Conch.** Up to 30cm. Caribbean.

17

1 *Strombus (Tricornis) sinuatus* Humphrey, 1786. Outer lip with 4 leaf-like processes. Aperture brownish to purplish-red. 10cm. West Pacific (Bohol I., Philippines), on coral sand, depth 20m.

2, 2a *Strombus (Euprotomus) aurisdianae* Linné, 1758. Upper edge of outer lip with a lobe-like process. Aperture orange. 6cm. Indo-Pacific. Related to *S. (E.) aurisdianae aratrum* (Röding, 1798), Australia and *S. (E.) bulla* (Röding, 1798), Samoa westwards.

3 *Strombus (Tricornis) raninus* Gmelin, 1791. **Hawk-wing Conch.** Shoulder of body whorl with 2 large tubercles. Aperture reddish. Up to 8cm. South-east Florida, West Indies (Granada). Synonym: *S. bituberculatus* Lamarck, 1822.

4 *Strombus (Doxander) vittatus vittatus* Linné, 1758. Spire tall with pronounced axial ribs. Very variable. 11cm. South China, Malaya, Melanesia, on sand or mud, to 40m.

5 *Strombus (Conomurex) luhuanus* Linné, 1758. **Strawberry or Blood-mouth Conch.** Columellar lip dark brown, inner lip reddish. 3-6cm. West Pacific (Samar I., Philippines), living in colonies.

6, 6a *Strombus (Laevistrombus) canarium* Linné, 1758. **Yellow or Dog Conch.** Aperture white. Shell yellow-brown, smooth, varying in size, form and coloration. Synonyms: *Lambis turturella* Röding, 1798; *Strombus isabella* Lamarck, 1822. 3-9cm. West Pacific, in large colonies on sandy mud.

7 *Strombus (Gibberulus) gibberulus gibberulus* Linné, 1758. **Humped Conch.** An abnormal shell, the result of irregular whorls and sutures. Varices on the upper whorls. Yellow-brown to grey-brown with numerous white spiral lines. Aperture purplish-violet. 3-7cm. Indian Ocean (Zanzibar). Very common in shallow water. *S. (G.) gibberulus albus* Mörch, 1850, is smaller, white, with carmine aperture, Red Sea, Gulf of Aden. *S. (G.) gibberulus gibbosus* (Röding, 1798) has the aperture white, yellow, orange or pale violet. Indo-Pacific, Ryukyu Is. to Indonesia.

8 *Strombus (Conomurex) decorus decorus* (Röding, 1798). **Mauritian Conch.** Shell with shoulder tubercles. Inner lip white. 3-6cm. Indian Ocean. *S. (C.) decorus persicus* Swainson, 1821, Arabia, Persian Gulf.

9 *Lambis (Millepes) millepeda* (Linné, 1758). **Millepede Spider Conch.** 9-14cm. Indo-Pacific (Cebu, Philippines), in shallow water.

10 *Strombus (Canarium) labiatus labiatus* (Röding, 1798). Whorl shoulders angled, ribs prominent. 2-4cm. West Pacific (Honshu, Japan). Synonym: *Strombus plicatus* Lamarck, 1816. The other subspecies *S. (C.) labiatus* Lamarck, 1816. The other subspecies *S. (C.) labiatus olydius* Duclos, 1844, East Africa to Sri Lanka.

11 *Strombus (Doxander) listeri* Gray, 1852. 12cm. Only in the Bay of Bengal, in depths of 70m. (Mergui Island, Andamans).

18

1 *Globularia fluctuata* (Sowerby, 1825). **Waved Moon Shell.** 50mm. Philippines (Siasi, Sulu Archipelago).

2, 2a *Polinices (Polinices) aurantius* (Röding, 1798). **Orange Moon Shell.** Yellow to orange. Umbilicus covered 40mm. South-west Pacific.

3 *Polinices (Polinices) powisiana* (Récluz, 1844). Umbilicus partially blocked. Brown bands. 50mm. Indian Ocean, West Pacific (Sibuyan, Philippines).

4 *Natica (Naticarius) cruentata* (Gmelin, 1791). Umbilicus open. 45mm. On muddy bottoms in deep water, Mediterranean and adjacent Atlantic. Synonyms: *Natica hebraea* (Martin, 1789); *Natica maculata* (v. Salis, 1793).

5 *Natica (Naticarius) stercusmuscarum* (Gmelin, 1791). Up to 50mm. Mediterranean and adjacent Atlantic. Commoner than *N. cruentata*. Synonym: *Natica millepunctata* Lamarck, 1822.

6 *Polinices (Mammilla) mammatus* (Röding, 1798). Ovate, rather thin, with dark brown bands and chocolate-brown apertural callus. Lower third of outer lip slightly angular. Up to 50mm. Indo-West-Pacific.

7 *Natica stellata* Hedley, 1913. **Stellate Moon Shell.** Umbilicus open. Up to 50mm. Indo-Pacific (Samar Island, Philippines).

8 *Natica (Naticarius) alapapilionis* (Röding, 1798). **Butterfly Moon Shell.** With 4 narrow bands with alternate brown and white markings.

Up to 30mm. Indo-Pacific.

9 *Natica lineata* (Röding, 1798). Up to 30mm. Indo-Pacific (Taiwan).

10 *Sinum concavum* (Lamarck, 1799). Ear-shaped, brownish, with spiral ornament, base pale. Up to 30mm. West Africa (Angola).

11 *Lunatia catena* (Da Costa, 1778). **Necklace Shell.** Suture with a band of brown markings. Umbilicus open. Up to 40mm. Mediterranean, Atlantic, rare in North Sea.

12 *Natica (Naticarius) onca* (Röding, 1798). **China Moon.** Five bands with trapezoid, brown markings. Up to 30mm. Indo-Pacific.

13 *Natica undulata* (Röding, 1798). **Zebra Moon Shell.** Wavy pattern. 30mm. West Pacific. Synonym: *Notocochlis zebra* (Lamarck, 1822).

14 *Polinices (Neverita) josephina* (Risso, 1826). Very flat. Umbilicus filled with a brown button-like callus. Up to 40mm. Mediterranean. (Sicily), intertidal.

15 *Polinices (Neverita) peselephanti* (Link, 1807). Cream, yellow or orange. Apex and columella base white. Up to 40mm. South-west Pacific (Queensland).

16 *Polinices (Conuber) conicus* (Lamarck, 1822). Up to 45mm. Australia.

17 *Natica fasciata* (Röding, 1798). **Solid Moon Shell.** Up to 25mm. South-west Pacific (Long Reef). Synonym: *Natica solida* Blainville, 1825.

18 *Polinices (Neverita) duplicata* (Say, 1822). **Shark's Eye.** Umbilicus with large callus. 50mm. Florida (Boga Siega Bay).

19

1 *Ovula ovum* (Linné, 1758). **Egg Cowry.** Outside smooth and white, inside orange-brown. Up to 90mm. Indo-Pacific (Solomon Islands).

2 *Ovula costellata* (Lamarck, 1810). Inside pink. Up to 50mm. Indo-Pacific (Bur Sudan, Red Sea).

3 *Diminovula sinensis* (Sowerby, 1874). Back smooth, aperture narrow. Up to 25mm. China Sea (Taiwan).

4 *Calpurnus verrucosus* (Linné, 1758). Ends reddish, with warty tubercles. Up to 30mm. Indo-Pacific. (Solomons).

5 *Prionovolva marginata* (Sowerby, 1830). Up to 20mm. Indo-Pacific (Taiwan).

6, 6a *Simnia spelta* (Linné, 1758). 15-22mm. Mediterranean and adjacent Atlantic (Almeria, southern Spain).

7 *Volva volva* (Linné, 1758). Ends much elongated. Usually without teeth on lips. Up to 12cm. Indo-Pacific (Taiwan).

8, 8a *Cyphoma gibbosum* (Linné, 1758). **Flamingo Tongue.** 30mm. S.E. coast of North America to West Indies.

9, 9a *Prionovolva cavanaghi* Iredale, 1931. Back coloured, base white. Up to 15mm. Mauritius to eastern Australia (Mackay, Queensland).

10 *Pseudosimnia carnea* (Poiret, 1789). Yellow, reddish or violet. Up to 20mm. Mediterranean, North Africa, West Indies.

11, 11a *Triviella aperta* (Swainson, 1828). Brownish to reddish, with shiny back. Base white. Up to 20mm. South Africa (Jeffrey's Bay).

12 *Niveria (Niveria) quadripunctata* (Grey, 1827). Pink with 4 brown, dorsal spots. Up to 7mm. Caribbean (Puerto Rico).

13, 13a *Trivia (Trivia) monacha* (Da Costa, 1778). **Common European Cowry.** Greyish-pink with dark markings. Base white. Up to 13mm. European coasts (Morgat, Brittany).

14, 14a *Niveria (Niveria) pediculus* (Linné, 1758). Back pale brown, with 3 pairs of dark spots. Up to 15mm. Caribbean.

15 *Trivia (Trivia) europaea* (Montagu, 1808). No dorsal spots. Up to 15mm. European coasts (Wales). Synonym: *T. arctica* (Montagu, 1803).

16 *Trivia (Trivia) europaea mediterranea* (Risso, 1826). Mediterranean subspecies with dark dorsal spots. Synonym: *T. tripunctata* (Requien).

17 *Trivia (Sulcotrivia) pulex* (Gray, 1827). Back shiny, sides and base pale. Up to 12mm. Mediterranean and adjacent Atlantic (Sicily).

18 *Pustularia (Pustularia) cicercula* (Linné, 1758). Up to 25mm. Cocos-Keeling Island to Polynesia (Samar, Philippines). Synonym: *P. bistrinotata* Schilder, 1937.

19 *Pustularia (Pustularia) lienardi* (Jousseaume, 1874). Up to 25mm. Indo-Pacific. (Pulau Langkawi, Malaysia).

20, 20a *Pusula (Pusula) radians* (Lamarck, 1811). 20mm. West coast of Panama.

21 *Jenneria pustulata* (Lightfoot, 1786). 25mm. West coast of central America.

22 *Staphylaea (Nuclearia) nucleus* (Linné, 1758). Up to 30mm. Indo-Pacific.

23 *Staphylaea (Staphylaea) limacina* (Lamarck, 1810). 30mm. Indo-Pacific.

20

1 *Cypraea (Cypraea) tigris* Linné,
1758. **Tiger Cowry.** Roundish-
ovate, almost pear-shaped. Colour
very variable, usually whitish or pale
brown with dark spots and blotches.
Base white. 4-14cm. In shallow or
deep water, often among corals,
feeding on the polyps. Widespread in
the Indo-Pacific (Great Barrier Reef,
Australia).

2 *Cypraea (Cypraea) tigris* Linné,
1758. A colour variant from East
Africa (Zanzibar).

3 *Lyncina pantherina* (Lightfoot,
1786). Panther Cowry. Smaller and
more slender than *Cypraea tigris*.
Aperture curved, apex much sunken,
the end of the shell somewhat beak-
like. Ground colour greyish-white to
golden-brown with smallish more
uniform markings. 5-8cm. Only Red
Sea and the adjacent Gulf of Aden
(Dahlak Archipelago, Ethiopia).

4 *Mauritia (Mauritia) mauritiana*
(Linné, 1758). **Hump-back Cowry.**
Broad, heavy, with tall back, well
defined margin and flat base. Margin
and base a uniform chocolate-brown,
back often paler with roundish, pale
markings, and usually with signs of
injuries (from the hard conditions in
the intertidal zone). 6-12cm. Indo-
Pacific, 4m and deeper (Samar Island, Philippines).

5 *Lyncina camelopardalis* (Perry,
1811). Brownish-grey with white
markings, margin and base pale

beige. Columellar teeth separated by
black spaces. 30-70mm. Red Sea
(Dahlak) and adjoining Gulf of Aden.
Synonym: *Cypraea melanostoma*
Sowerby, 1825.

6 *Umbilia hesitata* (Iredale, 1916).
Wonder Cowry. Large, pear-
shaped, with the ends beak-like and
the back very convex in the middle.
Apex deeply sunken. Back and base
creamy-white with pale brown markings. Up to 10cm. South-east Australia (Eden, N.S.W.), 60-200m.

7 *Umbilia hesitata beddomei Schilder*, 1930. Probably a dwarf form
from further north in New South
Wales, or possibly the female of *U.
hesitata*.

8 *Mauritia (Leporicypraea) mappa*
(Linné, 1758). **Map Cowry.** Back
brownish, the dorsal line pale with
short, rounded branches. 50-90mm.
Indo-Pacific (Samar Island, Philippines).

9, 9a *Erosaria (Ravitrona) caput-
serpentis* (Linné, 1758). **Snake's
Head Cowry.** Back brown with
white markings, margin a uniform
chocolate-brown. Base flat. 25-
40mm. Indo-Pacific (Samar Island,
Philippines).

10 *Chelycypraea testudinaria*
(Linné, 1758). Longish-cylindrical,
creamy-white to brown, and with
dark brown spots and small white
dots 8-13cm. Indo-Pacific (Samar
Island, Philippines).

21

1 *Macrocypraea cervus* (Linné, 1771). 9-15cm. Only southern Florida (Key Largo), Bahamas and Yucatan. Related species: *Macrocypraea cervinetta* (Kiener, 1843), west coast of central America; *Macrocypraea zebra* (Linné, 1758), Caribbean and N.E. coast of South America.

2 *Mauritia (Arabica) histrio* (Gmelin, 1791). Back brown with closely packed white markings. Base pale. 30-70mm. Only in Indian Ocean (Zanzibar). Related species: *M. (A.) depressa* (Gray, 1824), east Africa to central Pacific; *eglantina* (Duclos, 1833), west Pacific; *grayana* Schilder, 1930, Red Sea and Persian Gulf; *maculifera* Schilder, 1930, central Pacific.

3 *Mauritia (Arabica) arabica* (Linné, 1758). **Arabian Cowry.** Back with brown markings resembling hieroglyphics, with white spots showing through. Base pale, tooth intervals brown. 30-80mm. Indo-Pacific.

4 *Talparia (Talparia) talpa* (Linné, 1758). **Mole Cowry.** Cylindrical and pale with 4 brown cross bands. Base uniform dark brown. Lips with fine teeth. 25-90mm. Indo-Pacific (Zanzibar).

5 *Mauritia (Arabica) scurra* (Gmelin, 1791). **Jester Cowry.** Cylindrical and greyish with a network of pale brown markings. Base reddish-brown, sides with dark brown dots. Tooth intervals brown. 30-50mm. Indo-Pacific (Singapore).

6 *Talparia (Arestorides) argus* (Linné, 1758). Cylindrical with 3 brown cross bands and numerous brown circles of different sizes. 65-90mm. Indo-Pacific (Samar Island, Philippines).

7, 7a *Zoila decipiens* (Smith, 1880). Back unusually tall, and pale with dark chocolate-brown markings. Sides and base uniform dark brown. Base flat. 50-70mm. North-west Australia (Broome). Related species. *Z. friendii* (Gray, 1831); *marginata* (Gaskoin, 1848); *venusta* (Sowerby, 1846); *rosselli* (Cotton, 1948); all Australian.

8, 8a *Erosaria (Erosaria) erosa* (Linné, 1758). **Eroded Cowry.** Back ochre-yellow with small white dots and darker blotches. Base pale beige, each side with a darkish rectangular marking. 20-50mm. Indo-Pacific (Samar Island, Philippines).

9, 9a *Lycina lynx* (Linné, 1758). **Lynx Cowry.** Back brown, bluish and orange with large and small brown markings. Base pale. Tooth intervals orange. 20-60mm. Indo-Pacific (Zanzibar).

10 *Luria (Luria) lurida* (Linné, 1758). Grey-brown, with two paler cross bands. Ends orange, each with 2 black markings.

11, 11a *Erosaria (Erosaria) lamarcki* (Gray, 1825). **Lamarck's Cowry.** White dots on an ochre-coloured background. Sides pale, with brown spots. Base pale. 30-50mm. Western Indian Ocean (Mozambique).

12, 12a *Zonaria (Zonaria) pyrum* (Gmelin, 1791). **Pear Cowry.** Back with dark cross bands and red-brown markings. Sides and base orange-brown. 25-40mm. Mediterranean (Rhodes) and N.W. Africa.

13 *Lyncina vitellus* (Linné, 1758). **Pacific Deer Cowry.** Back brown with white spots. Base pale. 30-60mm. Indo-Pacific (Zanzibar).

22

1, 1a *Lyncina carneola* (Linné, 1958). **Carnelian Cowry.** Greyish-red with pale bands. Tooth intervals violet. 20-70mm. Indo-Pacific.

2 *Palmadusta (Palmadusta) lutea* (Gmelin, 1791). Base orange-brown with black markings. 10-20mm. Philippines (Zamboanga) to western Australia.

3, 4 *Monetaria (Monetaria) moneta* (Linné, 1758). **Money Cowry.** Two colour variants. Up to 38mm. Indo-Pacific.

5 *Monetaria (Ornamentaria) annulus* (Linné, 1758). **Gold Ringer.** Up to 30mm. Indo-Pacific.

6 *Blasicrura (Bistolida) kieneri* (Hidalgo, 1906). Up to 22mm. Indo-Pacific.

7 *Palmadusta clandestina* (Linné, 1767). Up to 20mm. Indo-Pacific.

8 *Erosaria (Erosaria) ocellata* (Linné, 1758). Base pale with brown spots. 20-30mm. Indian Ocean (Hikkaduwa, Sri Lanka).

9 *Erosaria (Ravitrona) spurca* (Linné, 1758). **European Yellow Cowry.** Up to 30mm. Mediterranean (Haifa), West Africa, Caribbean.

10 *Erosaria (Erosaria) boivinii* (Kiener, 1843). Up to 35mm. Southwest Pacific.

11 *Erronea (Erronea) caurica* (Linné, 1758). 25-30mm. Indo-Pacific.

12 *Zonaria (Pseudozonaria) arabicula* (Lamarck, 1811). **Little Arabian Cowry.** 2cm. West coast of central America.

13 *Erosaria (Erosaria) eburnea* (Barnes, 1824). Albino form. 30-50mm. West Pacific (Solomons).

14, 14a *Cribraria (Ovatisa) chinensis* (Gmelin, 1791). Up to 45mm. West Pacific.

15 *Blasicrura (Blasicrura) coxeni* (Cox, 1873). 15-25mm. New Guinea to Solomons (Rabaul, New Britain).

16 *Palmadusta (Palmadusta) asellus* (Linné, 1758). **Asellus Cowry.** With 3 dark bands. Sides and base white. 14-22mm. Indo-Pacific (Cebu).

17 *Cribraria (Cribraria) cribraria* (Linné, 1758). **Sieve Cowry.** Up to 36mm. Indo-Pacific.

18 *Blasicrura (Blasicrura) quadrimaculata* (Gray, 1824). Four-spotted Cowry. Each end with a pair of black markings. Up to 30mm. South-west Pacific (Zamboanga, Philippines).

19 *Erosaria (Ravitrona) helvola* (Linné, 1758). **Honey Cowry.** Back blue-green with dark markings. Sides and base orange-brown. 10-30mm. Indo-Pacific.

20 *Luria (Basilitrona) isabella* (Linné, 1758). 10-50mm. Indo-Pacific (Beruwala, Sri Lanka).

21 *Palmadusta (Palmadusta) ziczac* (Linné, 1758). **Zigzag Cowry.** With 3 white cross bands of V-shaped markings. Indo-Pacific (Philippines).

22 *Palmadusta diluculum* (Reeve, 1845). Back pattern brownish-velvet. Base white with brown spots. 15-30mm. East Africa (Mozambique).

23 *Zonaria (Neobernaya) spadicea* (Swainson, 1823). **Chestnut Cowry.** 35-60mm. South California, Monterey to San Benito Island (Palo Verde).

24 *Erronea (Adusta) onyx* (Linné, 1758). **Onyx Cowry.** 25-46mm. Indo-Pacific (Philippines).

25 *Erronea (Adusta) walkeri* (Sowerby, 1832). Up to 35mm. Seychelles to northern Australia.

26 *Blasicrura (Blasicrura) cylindrica sowerbyana* (Schilder, 1932). Australia.

23

1 *Galeodea echinophora* (Linné, 1758). Whorls with spiral rows of tubercles. Pale orange-brown, aperture white. Outer lip with teeth inside. Columellar callus broad. Up to 10cm. Mediterranean and adjacent Atlantic, to 10m. Sold in fish markets.

2 *Galeodea tyrrhena* (Gmelin, 1791). Similar to the preceding, but spire taller, shoulders less prominent, ornament finer, no tubercles. Up to 13cm. Mediterranean and adjacent Atlantic. 100-2000m. Synonym: *Cassidaria rugosa* (Linné, 1758).

3 *Phalium (Semicassis) saburon* (Brugière, 1792). Pale brownish with spiral ornament. Parietal callus broad. Up to 80mm. Western Mediterranean and adjacent Atlantic (Canaries), to 100m.

4 *Phalium (Tylocassis) granulatum granulatum* (Born, 1778). **Scotch Bonnet.** Reticulate ornament, frequently with more prominent spiral ridges. Parietal callus warty. 4-10cm. East coast of America, North Caroline to Brazil.

5 *Phalium (Phalium) decussatum* (Linné, 1758). Bluish-white with a pattern of brown markings, and reticulate ornament. Varices on the shoulder somewhat pointed. Up to 70mm. South-east Asia and Indonesia.

6 *Phalium (Phalium) strigatum* (Gmelin, 1791). **Striped Bonnet.** With reddish-brown stripes. Up to 10cm. China, Taiwan (Pescadores), Honshu.

7 *Phalium (Semicassis) semi-granosum* (Lamarck, 1822). Pale orange-brown, the upper parts of the whorls granulose. Up to 60mm. Southern Australia (Tasmania).

8 *Cypraecassis (Levenia) coarctata* (Sowerby, 1825). Longish, with chocolate-brown markings. Upper part of the outer lip turned inwards. Up to 70mm. Gulf of California (Guaymas, western Mexico) to northern Peru.

9 *Morum (Oniscidia) cancellatum* (Sowerby, 1824). Ornament coarse with pointed tubercles. 50mm. Coasts of China (Taiwan).

10 *Phalium (Phalium) glaucum* (Linné, 1758). Bluish-grey tinged with yellowish-orange. Whorl shoulders with fine tubercles. Outer lip slightly toothed, and with 3-4 spines at the lower edge. Parietal callus with folds. Up to 12cm. Indo-Pacific (Siasi, Philippines). Similar species: *P. (P.) bandatum* (Perry, 1811), longer with spiral band pattern of square yellow-brown markings. Southern Japan, Indonesia, northern Australia.

11 *Casmaria erinaceus erinaceus* (Linné, 1758). Form *vibex*, shiny, pale without shoulder tubercles (a difference from the nominate form). Up to 70mm. Indo-Pacific (Cebu, Philippines).

12 *Phalium (Tylocassis) granulatum undulatum* (Gmelin, 1791). With rounded, spiral ribs and a warty parietal callus. Up to 11cm. Mediterranean and adjacent Atlantic (Malta). Synonym: *Cassis sulcosa* (Brugiuère, 1792).

24

1 *Cassis (Cassis) cornuta* (Linné, 1758). **Horned Helmet.** Shell heavy, with row of large or small shoulder tubercles and a solid, flat, longish parietal shield. Aperture narrow. Outer lip flat at the edge with 5-7 large, whitish inner teeth. Columella orange-yellow, the lower half with whitish spiral folds. The whorls also have spiral ridges with tubercles. In the male the shoulder tubercles are long, slightly curved and relatively far apart. Female shells have smaller and more numerous shoulder tubercles. The intervening surface areas have web-like reticulation. Juvenile shells lack the fully developed parietal shield and have a rounder shoulder with 9-13 rather small, equally sized spines and a more distinct colour pattern (creamy-white with semicircular chocolate-brown markings). Up to 35cm, male shells smaller. Indo-Pacific. Related species: *C. (C.) madagascariensis* Lamarck, 1822, shell more rounded, with more numerous, small shoulder tubercles, the aperture black and parietal shield pink. Up to 30cm. South-east coast of North America, Bermuda, West Indies; *C. (C.) tessellata* (Gmelin, 1791), shell thin, longish, shoulder with very small tubercles in 2-3 spiral rows. Up to 27cm. West Africa, Senegal to Angola.

2, 2a *Cypraecassis (Cypraecassis) rufa* (Linné, 1758). **Bull Mouth, Red Helmet.** Shell thick (used for cameos) with large blunt tubercles and rows of finer spirally arranged tubercles. Aperture narrow. Outer lip broad. Parietal callus large and thick. Reddish-brown with paler areas. Up to 18cm. Indo-Pacific, but not in Micronesia or Hawaii.

3 *Cassis (Cassis) tuberosa* (Linné, 1758). **King Helmet.** Upper surface reticulate. Parietal shield triangular with blackish columella. Edge of outer lip with black markings. Up to 20cm. Florida, West Indies, Brazil. Related species: *C. (C.) flammea* (Linné, 1758), parietal shield oval, outer lip without black markings. 8-13cm. Florida, Bermuda, Lesser Antilles.

4 *Tonna galea* (Linné, 1758). **Giant Tun.** Shell roundish-ovate, brownish-yellow, thin-walled but firm, with rather low spire, 7 whorls and a large body whorl. Suture grooved. Apex dark brown and smooth. Later whorls with alternate thick and thin spiral ridges. Aperture wide, inside white. Outer lip slightly thickened and wavy at the edge. Columella much twisted. Up to 25cm, usually less. Widespread in tropical Pacific and Caribbean, extending to coasts of Portugal and north-west Africa. Related species: *T. olearium* (Linné, 1758), dark brown, with shallower ornament, finer intermediate ridges. Japan, Philippines, Indonesia.

5 *Tonna luteostoma* (Kuster, 1857). Spire very low. Spiral ridges broad, and separated by deep channels. Creamy-white with spiral pattern of brown markings. Up to 18cm. Japan to New Zealand.

25

1   *Tonna cepa* (Röding, 1798). **Can-aliculated Tun.** Shell thin, ovate, with low spire, roundish whorls and a shiny surface. Spiral ridges broad and flat, with narrow but shallow intermediate channels. Axial ornament lacking. Suture deep (canaliculated). Aperture wide, brownish inside. Coloration creamy-white, yellowish or pale brown, with an irregular pattern of brown markings. Up to 12cm. Indo-Pacific. Synonym: *Tonna olearium* Bruguière, 1789).

2   *Tonna perdix* (Linné, 1758). **Partridge Tun.** Shell strikingly thin, with taller spire, a deep suture and large body whorl. Spiral ridges broad and flat with a pattern of dark brown markings. The intermediate grooves narrow, shallow and mostly pale. Up to 20cm. Indo-Pacific. Related species: *T. maculosa* (Dillwyn, 1817), western Atlantic, Caribbean.

3   *Tonna sulcosa* (Born, 1778). Shell with a relatively taller spire and deeper suture. Spiral ridges rounded, flattish, the intermediate grooves about the same breadth. Outer lip prominent, its inner edge with paired teeth. Shell surface white with 3-4 brown spiral stripes. Up to 12cm. Indo-Pacific. Synonym: *T. fasciata* Brugière, 1789.

4   *Malea pomum* (Linné, 1758). Spiral ridge below the suture angled, the later ones rounded, flattish. Grooves shallow. Aperture narrow. Outer lip more developed below, with a wavy edge and large teeth inside. Columellar callus white. Shiny, creamy-white with irregular brown and white markings. Up to 80mm. Tropical Pacific.

5   *Tonna allium* (Dillwyn, 1817). Spiral ridges rounded with broad intermediate channels. Coloration yellowish to bluish-white, with brown markings on the ridges. Apical region purplish-brown. Up to 90mm. Indo-Pacific.

6   *Ficus subintermedius* (d'Orbigny, 1852). Spire low and sunken. Surface finely reticulate. Suture deep. Axial ribs uniformly prominent, but spiral ridges differing. Coloration pale to violet-brown, with 4-5 pale spiral bands and widely separated dark markings. Aperture whitish-violet inside, grading to brownish further in. Columella slender and elegantly curved. Up to 10cm. Indo-Pacific (Taiwan), 10-20m. Synonyms: *F. ficoides* Lamarck, 1822 and *F. communis* Röding, 1798, both now known to refer to an intermediate form and so are incorrect. Related species: *F. variegata* Röding, 1798, with a more inflated shell, which is dark violet inside, New Guinea, Indonesia, Philippines.

7   *Ficus gracilis* (Sowerby, 1892). Similar to *F. subintermedius* but the apex not so sunken. Coloration pale brown. Spiral ridges more pronounced than axial ribs. Up to 15cm. Japan (Taiwan), 200m.

26

1 *Charonia (Charonia) tritonis* (Linné, 1758). **Pacific Triton.** Spire very tall with broad, flat spiral ridges. Creamy-white with a pattern of brown, halfmoon-shaped markings. Aperture orange-brown inside. Outer lip edge toothed. Columella folded. Up to 40cm. Indo-Pacific (Tonga).

2 *Charonia (Charonia) tritonis variegata* (Lamarck, 1816). **Atlantic Triton.** Very similar to the nominate form but with irregular, usually slightly shouldered whorls. Body whorl more convex. Up to 40cm. Caribbean (Puerto Rico), East Atlantic, Mediterranean. Synonym: *C. tritonis seguenzae* (Aradas & Benoit, 1870).

3 *Charonia (Charonia) rubicunda* (Perry, 1811). **Knobbed Triton.** Whitish with red-brown markings. Up to 25cm. Mediterranean, East Atlantic, Indo-Pacific. Synonym: *C. nodifera* (Lamarck, 1822).

4 *Cymatium (Septa) pileare* (Linné, 1858). **Common Hairy Triton.** Periostracum hairy. Up to 10cm. Caribbean and Indo-Pacific (Bazaruto Bay, Mozambique).

5 *Cymatium (Cymatium) lotorium* (Linné, 1767). Varices with pale and dark markings. Siphonal canal long. Orange-brown with a white aperture. Up to 16cm. Indo-Pacific (Samar Island, Philippines).

6 *Cymatium (Septa) parthenopus* (v. Salis, 1793). Raised spiral ridges with wide intervening spaces. Up to 15cm. Mediterranean, Caribbean, Indo-Pacific. Synonyms: *C. amer-icanum* (d'Orbigny, 1842); *C. australasiae* (Perry, 1811); *C. brasilianum* (Gould, 1849); *C. echo Kuroda & Habe, 1950.*

7 *Argobuccinum (Ranella) olearium* (Linné, 1758). Whorls convex, tuberculate, with spiral ornament and a deep suture. Varices prominent. Aperture wide with toothed outer lip. Up to 200cm. Mediterranean (Sardinia), East Atlantic, Southern Africa, Australia, New Zealand, Synonym: *Ranella gigantea* Lamarck, 1816.

8 *Bursa rana* (Linné, 1758). **Elegant Frog Shell.** Varices positioned opposite one another. Spirally arranged tubercles and fine granular ridges. Upper canal opening behind the first spire on the lip edge. Columella folded. Up to 80mm. Indo-Pacific.

9 *Distorsio (Rhysema) clathrata* (Lamarck, 1816). Up to 7cm. Caribbean, East Atlantic (a few localities). Related species: *D. (R.) reticulata* Röding, 1798; *D. (D.) anus* (Linné, 1758); both in tropical Pacific.

10 *Gyrineum (Biplex) perca* (Perry, 1811). **Winged Frog Shell.** 5cm. Southern Japan to Australia (Taiwan).

11 *Bursa bubo* (Linné, 1758). With tuberculate spiral ornament and a folded columella. Up to 20cm. Indo-Pacific. Synonym: *B. rubeta gigantea* Smith, 1914. Dealers sometimes call it *B. lampas.*

12 *Bursa bufo* Röding, 1798. Similar to No. 11, but less tuberculate, with a smooth columella. Up to 14cm. Indo-Pacific (Kusui, Japan).

27

1 *Trunc(ul)ariopsis trunculus* (Linné, 1758). Shell convex and spindle-shaped, usually with 6 tuberculate or spiny varices. Body whorl with three brown bands. Up to 80mm. Mediterranean and adjacent Atlantic. Used in ancient times for production of the dye Tyrian purple.

2 *Murex (Bolinus) brandaris* Linné, 1758. Shell club-shaped with relatively low spine, the base extended into a long canal. Body whorl with tubercles or spines. Up to 80mm. Mediterranean, adjacent Atlantic, West Africa. Also produces purple dye.

3 *Murex (Bolinus) cornutus* Linné, 1758. **African Horned Murex.** Similar to No. 2, but much larger, with very flat spire, weak spinal ornament, each body whorl edge with 6 long, curved spines. Also spines on the canal base. 20cm. West Africa (Senegal). Variant form: *M. (B) cornutus tumulosus* Sowerby, 1841, with almost straight spines, south to Angola.

4 *Murex (Murex) brevispina* Lamarck, 1822. **Short-spine Murex.** Three much rounded varices with spiny tubercles. Base of the body whorl and of the canal with short spines. 65mm. East Africa, Mozambique to Natal (Mozambique).

5 *Murex (Haustellum) haustellum* Linné, 1758. **Snipe's Bill.** Whorls convex with 3 large varices. Brown pattern. Aperture orange. 10-15cm.

Red Sea to West Pacific (Zamboanga, Philippines). Synonym: *M. (H.) kurodai* Shikama, 1964.

6 *Murex (Murex) rectirostris* Sowerby, 1841. Spine relatively tall, whorls convex with 3 tall varices, each with a short spine. 70mm. China, Japan and adjacent Pacific (Taiwan).

7 *Murex (Murex) nigrispinosus* Reeve, 1845. **Black-spine Murex.** Whorls roundish with tuberculate spinal ornament and varices. Spines varying in length, fairly straight at the tip and dark. 10cm. Indo-Pacific (Samar Island, Philippines).

8 *Murex (Murex) pecten* (Lightfoot, 1786). **Venus Comb Murex.** Spire relatively tall, body whorl convex, ornamented with finely tuberculate spiral ridges. Three varices, each with a dense row of long, curved spines. Up to 13cm. Indo-Pacific. Synonyms: *M. (M.) tenuispina*, Lamarck, 1822; *M. (M.) triremis* (Perry, 1811).

9 *Murex (Murex) scolopax* Dillwyn, 1817. Whorls with weak widely spaced spiral ridges, and relatively few spines. 13cm. Indo-Pacific (Musquat, Arabian Sea).

10 *Chicoreus (Siratus) aguayoi* Clench & Peréz-Farfante, 1945. Unlike the similar *C. (S.) antillarum* (Hinds, 1843) this species has curved spines and a recurved siphonal canal. Up to 65cm. Caribbean (Puerto Rico).

28

1 *Hexaplex regius* (Swainson, 1821). **Regal Murex.** Aperture with bright pink lips and dark brown markings on the parietal shield. An exhalation canal in the upper part of the aperture. 10-12cm. Southern part of Gulf of California to Peru, in shallow water. The *Hexaplex* group is closely related to the genus *Phyllonotus* (Swainson, 1833) and some authorities combine the two groups. (*Hexaplex* has 5-7 varices per whorl, *Phyllonotus* 3-4).

2 *Hexaplex erythrostomus* (Swainson, 1831). **Pink-mouthed Murex.** Shell surface rough and chalky-white with very fine spiral ornament. Aperture shiny pink inside. Parietal shield much expanded. Up to 12cm. Gulf of California to Peru. Synonym: *Murex bicolor* Valenciennes, 1832.

3 *Hexaplex brassica* (Lamarck, 1822). **Cabbage Murex.** Shell white to pale or reddish-brown, with 3 brown bands. Edges of the varices and aperture bright orange-pink. Varices not so strongly folded as in the other *Hexaplex* species. 10-15cm. Gulf of California (Guaymas, Mexico) to Peru, down to 50m. Synonym: *Murex ducalis* Broderip, 1829.

4 *Hexaplex cichoreus* (Gmelin, 1791). **Endive Murex.** Shell white with dark brown bands, ornamented with alternate strong and weak spiral ridges. Aperture white. Up to 70mm. Indo-Pacific. Synonyms: *Murex endivia* Lamarck, 1822; *M. foliacea* Perry, 1811.

5 *Muricanthus ambiguus* (Reeve, 1845). Very similar in form to two related species, the more southerly *M. radix* and the more northerly *M. nigritus*, and possibly just a transitional form between them. Compared with *M. nigritus* the present shell is more rounded with shorter apex and canal, and has more spines. Compared with *M. radix* it is larger and less pear-shaped. Up to 17cm (usually less). West coast of central America, southern Mexico to Panama. Synonym: *Murex melanoleucus* Mörch, 1860.

6 *Muricanthus nigritus* (Philippi, 1845). **Black Murex.** Apex and canal somewhat longer than in *M. radix* and *M. ambiguus*. Varices with fewer spines. Juvenile shells almost white, becoming black with age. Up to 15cm. Gulf of California.

7 *Muricanthus radix* (Gmelin, 1791). **Root Murex.** Shell pear-shaped, basically white with numerous closely packed black spines. Up to 10cm. Panama to southern Ecuador. In the trade, the term 'radix' is applied to all 3 species.

29

1 *Homalocantha anatomica zamboi* Burch & Burch, 1960. Shell greyish-white, with loose coils, a long siphonal canal, and 4-5 varices each with 3 long processes with fan-shaped ends. Aperture orange-pink. Up to 6cm. Restricted to Honshu and the Philippines (Palawan). In the nominate form *H.a. anatomica* (Perry, 1811) the processes are long and forked, those of *H.a. pele* (Pilsbry, 1921) are short. Both in the Indo-Pacific.

2 *Chicoreus (Chicoreus) torrefactus* (Sowerby, 1841). **Scorched Murex.** Shell longish with fine, dark and pale spiral ornament, and 3 varices per whorl. Aperture white or creamy-orange. Up to 10cm. Indo-Pacific (Kii, Japan).

3 *Chicoreus (Chicoreus) palmarosae* (Lamarck, 1822). **Rose-branch Murex.** Pale brown, with fine dark brown spiral ridges, 3 varices, a pink apex and white aperture. The tips of the spines are usually white, but occasionally red. 10cm. Indo-Pacific (Cebu, Philippines).

4 *Chicoreus (Chicoreus) brunneus* (Link, 1807). Grey with dark brown spiral ornament and 3 varices. Aperture edge pink, the inside white. Up to 70mm. Indo-Pacific. Synonym: *C. adustus* (Lamarck, 1822).

5 *Chicoreus (Chicoreus) cervicornis* (Lamarck, 1822). **Two-forked Murex.** 6cm. Australia. Similar species: *C. axicornis* (Lamarck, 1822), Indo-Pacific; *C. damicornis* (Hedley, 1903) and *C. recticornis* (v. Martens, 1880), Australia.

6 *Pterynotus (Pterynotus) bipinnatus* (Reeve, 1845). White, with a very long spire, and fine spiral ridges, mainly on the leaf-like varices. Aperture pale violet. 40-65mm. Indo-Pacific (Philippines). Related species: *P. elongatus* (Lightfoot, 1786), 65mm, Indo-Pacific.

7 *Chicoreus (Siratus) pliciferoides* Kuroda, 1942. A few varices with spines of varying length. Siphonal canal recurved. Aperture white. 13cm. Japan (Taiwan).

8 *Pterynotus (Pterynotus) alatus* (Röding, 1798). White with spiral ornament and 3 varices with thin, folded lamellae. 60mm. Indo-Pacific (Ryukyu). Synonym: *P. pinnatus* (Swainson, 1822).

9 *Homalocantha scorpio* (Linné, 1758). Strong spiral ridges and 4-8 varices. Outer lip with long T-shaped processes. Aperture white. 30mm. Indo-Pacific (Zamboanga, Philippines).

10 *Chicoreus (Chicoreus) florifer arenarius* Clench & Peréz Farfante, 1945. Varix lamellae almost equal in size. 60mm. A local form from Sanibel Island, Florida. In the nominate form *C. (C.) f. florifer* (Reeve, 1846) the lamellae are not equal in size, West Indies.

11 *Chicoreus (Chicoreus) ramosus* (Linné, 1758). **Giant Murex.** White, often with brown stripes, and 3 varices carrying long, curved spines. Aperture edge shiny pink, white inside. 15-20cm. Indo-Pacific. Synonym: *C. inflatus* (Lamarck, 1822).

30

1 *Thais (Stramonita) haemastoma* (Linné, 1767). **Rock Shell.** Spiral rows of tubercles. Aperture orange-red. 80mm. Mediterranean, Atlantic, West Indies, intertidal on rocks.

2 *Purpura persica* (Linné, 1766). Alternating coarse and fine spiral ridges, and tubercles. Outer lip folded. Up to 50mm or more. Indo-Pacific. Similar species: *P. rudolphi* (Lamarck, 1822), same form, but more tuberculate.

3 *Purpura patula* (Linné, 1758). **Wide-mouthed Purpura.** With 6–7 spiral rows of tubercles. Columella salmon-pink. 50mm. Southeast Florida, West Indies (Puerto Rico).

4 *Nucella lapillus* (Linné, 1758). **Dog-whelk.** 40mm. Atlantic, North Sea (Heligoland).

5 *Ocenebra (Hadriania) craticulata* (Brocchi, 1814). 38mm. Mediterranean (Elba).

6 *Nucella lamellosa* (Gmelin, 1791). **Frilled dog-whelk.** Very variable in form, ornament and coloration. 60mm. West coast of N. America (Washington).

7 *Drupa (Drupa) morum* Röding, 1798. 20-40mm. Indo-Pacific.

8 *Drupa (Drupina) grossularia* Röding, 1798. 20-30mm. Indo-Pacific.

9 *Drupa (Ricinella) rubusidaeus* Röding, 1798. 30-50mm. Indo-Pacific.

10 *Drupa (Drupa) ricinus* (Linné, 1758). 20-30mm. Indo-Pacific.

11 *Thais (Mancinella) alouina* (Röding, 1798). Pale orange, 5 rows of tubercles, aperture orange, the inside striped. Up to 50mm. Indo-Pacific (Taiwan).

12 *Thais (Thais) echinata* (Blainville, 1832). 5 spiral rows with spiny tubercles. 20-50mm. Indo-Pacific (Broome, N.W. Australia).

13 *Eupleura muriciformis* (Broderip, 1833). Very variable in form and coloration. Up to 38mm. California to Ecuador, on shore and in deeper water.

14 *Eupleura nitida* (Broderip, 1833). Spiral ridges, axial ribs and 2 lateral, wing-like varices. 20mm. Mexico to Panama (Montiso Bay).

15 *Nassa serta* (Brugière, 1789). Creamy-white, with irregular red-brown bands and blotches. Spiral ornament and axial ribs (growth lines). Columella whitish. Up to 5cm. Indo-Pacific (Taiwan).

16 *Muricopsis zeteki* Hertlein & Strong, 1961. White, with brown spines. Aperture bluish-white. 20-30mm. West coast of central America (Guaymas, Mexico).

17 *Nucella canaliculata* (Duclos, 1832). Spiral ornament and a deep suture. Up to 30mm. Alaska (Cook Bay) to California.

18 *Morula margariticola* (Broderip, 1832). Body whorl with a prominent axial ribs, and spiral ornament. Aperture violet-brown. Up to 20mm. North coast of Australia (Port Hedland, N.W. Australia).

19 *Trophon (Zeatrophon) ambiguus* (Philippi, 1844). Female shell strongly reticulate, male relatively smooth. 50mm. New Zealand (Timaru).

20 *Cymia mutabilis* (Link, 1807). 50mm. Indo-Pacific (Taiwan).

31

1 *Ceratostoma burnetti* (A. Adams & Reeve, 1849). Three leaf-like varices with strong spiral folds. A prominent tooth on edge of outer lip. 10cm. China, Japan (Honshu) and Korea, on rocks, 20m.

2 *Pteropurpura plorator* (A. Adams & Reeve, 1849). With 3 wing-like varices. 40mm. Japan (Sagami Bay), 50–200m.

3 *Pteropurpura centrifuga* (Hinds, 1844). West coast of central America, Magdalena Bay to Panama (Perlas I.), 60–180m.

4 *Trophonopsis (Pagodula) carinata* (Bivona, 1832). 30mm. Mediterranean (Isola Caprara, Adriatic), Atlantic, in deep waters.

5 *Ocenebra (Ocenebra) erinacea* (Linné, 1758). **Sting-winkle.** Very variable. Up to 60mm. Mediterranean (Fuengirola, Spain), European Atlantic coasts, W. Scotland to Azores, to 50m. An oyster pest.

6 *Vitularia salebrosa* (King & Broderip, 1832). Up to 60mm. West coast of central America, California to Colombia (Pedro Gonzales, Panama).

7 *Ceratostoma nuttalli* (Conrad, 1837). 30mm. California (White's Point).

8 *Pteropurpura (Ocinebrellus) adunca* (Sowerby, 1834). 30mm. Japan (Taiwan), 40m.

9 *Coralliophila (Latimurex) costularis* (Lamarck, 1816). Spiral ridges and axial folds. Up to 60mm. Indo-Pacific (Eilat, Red Sea).

10 *Quoyula madreporarum* (Sowerby, 1832). Up to 30mm. Indo-Pacific and west coast of central America (Guaymas, Mexico).

11 *Coralliophila (Latimurex) meyendorffi* (Calcara, 1845). 35mm. Mediterranean (Greece), Canaries, N.W. Africa.

12 *Coralliophila (Coralliophila) violacea* (Kiener, 1836). Aperture violet. Up to 35mm. Indo-Pacific (Batayan I., Philippines). Synonym: *C. squamulosa* (Reeve, 1846).

13 *Coralliophila (Coralliophila) abbreviata* (Lamarck, 1816). **Short Coral Shell.** With rounded shoulder, coarse spiral ornament consisting of numerous small scales. Aperture reddish-white. Up to 30mm. South-east Florida (Delray Beach), West Indies.

14 *Coralliophila (Coralliophila) caribaea* Abbott, 1958. Up to 20mm. Caribbean (Portobello, Panama).

15 *Coralliophila* species. A shell found in 1971 in a tidal pool at Punta Bique, Panama, and not yet identified.

16 *Coralliophila (Pseudomurex) costata* (Blainville, 1832). Shell white, biconical, with axial ribs and fine spiral ornament. 25mm. California to Panama (San Luis Gonzaga, Mexico).

17 *Latiaxis (Tolema) pagodus* (A. Adams, 1853). With flat, curved spines on the whorl shoulders. 20mm. Indo-Pacific, Japan.

18 *Columbarium pagoda* (Lesson, 1831). Up to 10cm. South of Japan (Taiwan). Related species *C. spinicinctum* (v. Martens, 1881), Australia.

32

1, 1a *Latiaxis (Latiaxis) mawae*
(Griffith & Pidgeon, 1834). Upper
whorls flat, forming a broad shoulder, the last two being loosely attached. Lobes along the shoulder, and an umbilicus. 50mm. South of Japan (off Taiwan), 100-150m. *L. (L.) pilsbryi* (Hirase, 1908), is smaller in depths down to 200m.

2 *Rapa rapa* (Linné, 1758).
Papery Rapa. Shell bulbous, with flat spire, short siphonal canal, and spiral ornament. 50m. Indo-Pacific (Zamboanga, Philippines), living in soft corals.

3 *Coralliophila (Lataxiena) fimbriata* (Hinds, 1844). Reticulate ornament with spiny tubercles. Slit-like umbilicus. 30mm. (Taiwan).

4, 4a *Neorapana muricata* (Broderip, 1832). Spire low, with strong spiral folds, overlapping like scales on the tubercles. Usually c. 60mm, but may be more. Mexico (Guaymas) to Ecuador. Often known in the trade as *Acanthina muricata*.

5 *Latiaxis idoleum* (Jonas, 1846).
White, spindle-shaped with convex whorls showing close spiral ridges and weak axial ribs. Umbilicus almost covered by the columellar callus. 45mm. Indo-Pacific, Japan (Taiwan). 90-150m. Synonym: *L. eugeniae* (Bernardi, 1853).

6 *Latiaxis (Tolema) japonicus*
(Dunker, 1882). White with fairly tall spire, and angular whorls, the shoulder having a double ring of spines. Flat, scaly spiral ornament. Um-

bilicus open. 50mm. Japan, 100-200m.

7 *Latiaxis (Tolema) lischkeanus*
(Dunker, 1882). Milky-white, translucent, the spiral ornament with scaly points. Shoulder with a ring of spines curved upwards. Umbilicus open, and columella more slender than in *L. japonicus*. 40mm. Japan, c. 200m.
Related species in Japanese waters: *L. winkworthi* Fulton, 1930; *L. kinoshitai* Fulton, 1930; *L. tosanus* Hirase, 1908; *L. kawamurai* Kira, 1954; *L. deburghiae* (Reeve, 1857); *L. kiranus* Kuroda, 1959.

8 *Latiaxis crebrilamellosus* (Sowerby, 1913). With sharp, scaly spiral ornament, axial ribs and a deep suture. 40mm. Japan.

9 *Rapana venosa* (Valenciennes, 1846). Whorl shoulder with tubercles. Aperture very large, bright orange-red. 10cm. The species comes originally from Japan, but was introduced into the Black Sea with a load of oyster spat. Bulgarian coast (Varna, taken by divers). Synonym: *R. thomasiana* (Crosse, 1861).

10 *Rapana bezoar* (Linné, 1758).
With spiral ornament and small varices on the shoulder. 60mm. Japan, West Pacific (Taiwan), 10m.

11 *Rapana rapiformis* (Born, 1778).
Shell large with short spines on the whorl edge, particularly on the shoulder. Lower half of shell showing spiral ornament. Aperture flesh-pink to orange. 11cm. South of Japan to Philippines (Tayabas Bay).

33

1 *Columbella major* Sowerby, 1832. About 27mm. West coast of central America.

2 *Columbella haemastoma* Sowerby, 1832. Up to 25mm. West coast of America.

3 *Pyrene ocellata* (Link, 1807). Up to 20mm. West Pacific (Japan).

4 *Pyrene ocellata* (Link, 1807). Another pattern.

5 *Parametaria dupontii* (Kiener, 1849). Up to 28mm. Mexico (Guaymas).

6 *Strombina turrita* (Sowerby, 1832). About 30mm. West Panama.

7 *Pyrenepunctata*(Bruguière,1789). About 20mm. West Pacific (Japan).

8 *Columbella rustica* (Linné, 1758). About 20mm. Mediterranean and adjacent Atlantic.

9 *Columbella labiosa* Sowerby, 1822. About 20mm. West coast of central America.

10 *Anachis (Costoanachis) fluctuata* (Sowerby, 1832). 18mm. West Panama.

11 *Mitrella scripta* (Linné, 1758). Up to 15mm. Mediterranean (Sicily).

12 *Strombina (Strombina) fusinoidea* Dall, 1916. 50mm. West coast of central America.

13 *Columbella strombiformis* (Lamarck, 1822). Up to 30mm. West coast of central America.

14 *Anachis (Costoanachis) varia* (Sowerby, 1832). Up to 20mm. West Mexico.

15 *Buccinulum (Euthria) corneum* (Linné, 1758). Spindle-shaped with short curved canal. Suture deep. Up to 70mm. Mediterranean (Sardinia), under rocks down to 30m.

16 *Buccinum (Buccinum) undatum* Linné, 1758. **Common Northern Whelk.** Up to 10cm. North Atlantic, North Sea (not Mediterranean) on sand and muddy ground.

17 *Buccinum (Buccinum) groenlandicum* Jeffreys, 1877. Yellowish-white under a hairy periostracum. Growth lines and indistinct ribs. Irregular spiral ridges. 40mm. Arctic seas (Godthaab, Greenland).

18 *Sipho gracilis* (Da Costa, 1778). Longish, spindle-shaped, with periostracum. Up to 80mm. North Atlantic, North Sea, east coast of England. In 30-200m. More northerly species: *S. islandicus* (Gmelin).

19 *Siphonorbis (Colicryptus) fusiformis* (Broderip, 1830). Shell thin, with very convex whorls, curved ribs and a periostracum. Up to 25mm. North Atlantic (Vikurall, Iceland).

20 *Plicifusus (Microfusus) latericus* (Möller, 1842). Ribs only on upper whorls. Aperture edge sharp. Canal short, but rather broad. Periostracum. Up to 26mm. North Atlantic (Jokuldjup, Iceland).

21 *Buccinum (Madiella) humphreysianum fusiforma* (Kiener, 1834). Thin, transparent, horny, yellow-brown. 60mm. Mediterranean form, more convex than *B. humphreysianum* Bennet, North Atlantic, Portugal to Norway.

22 *Neptunea despecta* (Linné, 1758). Whorls angular. 16cm. North Atlantic (Iceland). Possibly only a northern variety of *N. antiqua*.

23 *Neptunea antiqua* (Linné, 1758). About 13cm. North Atlantic, North Sea, western Baltic.

34

1 *Babylonia areolata* (Link, 1807). Whorls separated by a fairly deep suture. Easily recognisable by pattern of markings arranged in spiral rows. Umbilicus present. 90mm. Indo-Pacific (Taiwan), 10-20m.

2 *Babylonia japonica* (Reeve, 1842). Roundish whorls, normally covered with a thick, dark periostracum. Umbilicus present. 80mm. Japan (Kii) 10-20mm.

3 *Babylonia canaliculata* (Schumacher, 1817). Whorls with an angular shoulder and deep suture, forming a spiral groove. Umbilicus present 50mm. Indian Ocean (Sri Lanka).

4 *Siphonalia signum* (Reeve, 1843). Whorls angular, with tubercles on the shoulder. Body whorl large. Siphonal canal curved. 60mm. Japan (Mikawa Bay).

5 *Siphonalia trochulus* (Reeve, 1843), forma *tokaiensis* Kira, a local form of the paler *trochulus*. Honshu, Japan.

6 *Siphonalia pfeifferi* (Sowerby). 60mm. Japan.

7 *Siphonalia cassidariaeformis* (Reeve, 1843). Extremely variable in form and coloration. Prominent tubercles on the shoulder. 40mm. Japan.

8 *Cantharus (Gemophos) ringens* (Reeve, 1846). With prominent spiral ornament and a deep exhalation canal at the upper end of the aperture. Outer lip edge thickened with teeth inside. 28mm. West coast of central America (Mexico).

9 Pisania (Pisania) pusio (Linné, 1758). **Miniature Triton Trumpet.** About 30mm. S.E. Florida

(Elliott Key) to West Indies.

10 *Pisania (Pisania) striata* (Gmelin, 1791). Colour and pattern variable: yellowish-white or olive to reddish-brown. 20mm. Mediterranean and adjacent Atlantic (Canaries), on rocks in shallow water.

11 *Pisania (Ecmanis) tritonoides* (Reeve, 1846). About 40mm. Indo-Pacific (Japan).

12 *Phos (Phos) senticosus* (Linné, 1758). Sharp tubercles at the intersections of axial and spiral ornament. 35mm. Indo-Pacific (N.W. Australia).

13 *Volutharpa ampullacea perryi* (Jay, 1857). Shell thin, olive-coloured with a hairy periostracum. 45mm. East coast of Honshu, Japan. The nominate form *V. a. ampullacea* (Middendorf, 1848), N. Pacific, is smaller.

14 *Cantharus (Pollia) mollis* (Gould, 1860). Whorls with flat ribs and narrow spiral ridges. 30mm. Japan, among rocks on the shore.

15 *Cantharus (Cantharus) erythrostomus* (Reeve, 1846). Broad axial ribs crossed by wavy spiral ridges. Aperture edge and columellar callus bright orange-red. Up to 30cm. Indo-Pacific (Broome, N.W. Australia).

16 *Hindsia sinensis* (Sowerby, 1876). Shell conical with reticulate ornament. Aperture circular, with a varix at the outer edge. 35mm. China, Taiwan.

17 *Penion maxima* (Tryon, 1881). Whorls angular, siphonal canal long. 25cm. Queensland to Tasmania (Nelson's Bay, Australia).

35

1 *Fasciolaria (Pleuroploca) trapezium* (Linné, 1758). Whorls angular, with tubercles on the shoulder, and paired spiral stripes. Outer lip sharp, columella folded. Periostracum. Up to 20cm. Indo-Pacific (Madagascar), under corals.

2 *Fasciolaria (Pleuroploca) australasia* (Perry, 1811). **Australian Tulip Shell.** Whorl with fewer tubercles, but numerous fine spiral ridges, and 2-3 columellar folds. Pale brown, with a thin periostracum. Up to 30mm. Australia (Flinders Bay, Victoria).

3 *Peristernia incarnata* (Kiener, 1840). Relatively small with weak spiral ridges and massive axial ribs. Outer lip sharp. Up to 30mm. Indian Ocean to Western Australia (Port Hedland).

4 *Latirus (Latirus) polygonus* (Gmelin, 1791). Whorls angled with spiral ridges and prominent axial ribs. Two rows of tubercles on body whorl. 4-5 columellar folds. Periostracum. Up to 70mm. Indo-Pacific.

5 *Fassiolaria (Pleuroploca) filamentosa* (Röding, 1798). Spiral ridges prominent, shoulder somewhat angled with stumpy tubercles. Reddish-brown markings. Up to 15cm. Indo-Pacific (Queensland).

6 *Fusinus (Fusinus) nicobaricus* (Röding, 1798). **Nicobar Spindle.** Upper whorls with tubercles. Spiral ridges and a brown pattern running axially. Outer lips with teeth. Up to 15cm. Eastern Australia.

7 *Fusinus (Fusinus) dupetitthouarsi* (Kiener, 1840). White under a greenish-yellow periostracum. Up to 25cm. West coast of central America. California to Ecuador, down to 50m.

8 *Fusinus (Fusinus) salisburyi* Fulton, 1930. Older whorls roundish with broad axial ribs, which become separate tubercles lower down. Body whorl angular. 20cm. Queensland, 100-200m.

9 *Fusinus (Fusinus) colus* (Linné, 1758). **Distaff Spindle.** Older whorls ribbed, later ones tuberculate. Siphonal canal very long and slender. Up to 20cm. Indo-Pacific (Bazaruto Bay, Mozambique).

10 *Fusinus (Fusinus) australis* (Quoy & Gaimard, 1833). Tuberculate ribs only on the upper whorls. Body whorl with angular spiral ridges. Periostracum thick and brown. Up to 10cm. Western Australia.

11 *Leucozonia cerata* (Wood, 1828). Biconical with prominent tubercles and periostracum. Up to 50mm. West Mexico to Panama, and Galapagos.

12 *Latirus (Latirulus) nagasakiensis* Smith, 1880. Prominent axial ribs. 30mm. South of Honshu.

13 *Fusinus (Simplicifusus) simplex* (Smith, 1879). Whorls roundish with prominent sharp axial ribs. Brownish-grey periostracum. Up to 70mm. South of Honshu.

14 *Granulifusus nipponicus* (Smith, 1879). Shell thin with spiral ornament and slender siphonal canal. Up to 70mm. South of Honshu.

15 *Leucozonia (Latirolagena) smaragdula* (Linné, 1758). Roundish, with fine spiral ridges. Up to 50mm. Indo-Pacific. (Zamboanga, Philippines).

16 *Opeatostoma pseudodon* (Burrow, 1815). Aperture with a very large tooth. Periostracum dark. Up to 70mm. Gulf of California to Peru.

36

1 *Fasciolaria (Cinctura) tulipa*
(Linné, 1758). **True Tulip Shell.**
Whorls rounded, pattern variable,
periostracum thin. Up to 20cm.
Caribbean (Puerto Rico), to 10m.

2 *Fasciolaria (Cinctura) hunteria*
(Perry, 1811). **Branded Tulip
Shell.** Periostracum thin. About
70mm. Gulf of Mexico.

3 *Volema (Hemifusus) colossea* (Lamarck, 1816). **Giant Stair Shell.**
Columella almost straight, with
callus, without folds. Periostracum
hairy. Over 30cm. Japan.

4 *Nassarius (Zaphon) fossatus*
(Gould, 1849). **Giant Western
Nassa.** Up to 45mm. American Pa-
cific coast, Vancouver to California
(Newport Bay).

5 *Nassarius (Zeuxis) olivaceus*
(Bruguière, 1789). Up to 40mm.
Indo-Pacific (Taiwan), on reefs,
under rocks, in muddy sand.

6 *Bullia rhodostoma* (Gray, 1847).
40mm. South Africa, False Bay to
Natal (Port Alfred), on sandy bottoms in shallow water.

7 *Bullia annulata* (Lamarck, 1822).
Up to 40mm. South Africa (Jeffrey's
Bay, eastern Cape Province), on
sandy bottoms in shallow water.

8, 8a *Nassarius arcularius arcularius*
(Linné, 1758). With prominent ribs
and parietal shield. Base with c. 4
spiral grooves 20-30mm. West Pacific (Cebu).

9, 9a *Nassarius arcularius plicatus*
(Röding, 1798). A related subspecies,
with spiral ornament on the whole
whorl surface. East Africa (Massawa,
Eritrea). Synonym: *Nassarius pullus*
(Linné, 1758).

10 *Sphaeronassa mutabilis* (Linné,
1758). Up to 30mm. Mediterranean
(Sicily) and adjacent Atlantic, on
sandy and muddy bottoms in shallow
water.

11 *Nassarius (Niotha) variegatus*
(A. Adams, 1852). Surface moderately granular, suture channelled.
20-30mm. Indo-Pacific (Mozambique). Synonyms: *Niotha clathrata*
(Lamarck, 1816); *Niotha gemmulata*
(Lamarck, 1822).

12 *Nassarius (Alectrion) glans glans*
(Linné, 1758). Lip edge serrated. Up
to 50mm. Indo-Pacific. *N. (A.) glans
particeps* (Hedley, 1915) has smooth
lip edge.

13 *Nassarius (Uzita) clathratus*
(Born, 1778). 36mm. Mediterranean
(Malta) and adjacent Atlantic. Syn-
onym: *Hinia (Uzita) limata*
(Chemnitz, 1780).

14, 14a *Nassarius (Nassarius) coronatus* (Bruguière, 1789). Axial
ornament only as shoulder tubercles.
20-30mm. Indo-Pacific (Madagascar).

15 *Amyclina corniculum* (Olivi,
1792). Colour and ornament very
variable. Up to 20mm. Mediterranean (Sardinia), in quiet water
among rocks with seaweeds.

16 *Nassarius (Hinia) incrassatus*
(Strom, 1768). Columella and outer
lip whitish. 12-15mm. European
coasts (Biscay), including Mediterranean.

17 *Nassarius (Hinia) reticulatus*
(Linné, 1758). **Netted Dog Whelk.**
Up to 30mm. European coasts (Brit-
tany), Mediterranean.

18, 18a *Cyclope neritea* (Linné,
1758). Up to 25mm. Mediterranean
(Grado, Adriatic) and adjacent Atlantic, on sandy and muddy ground
in shallow water.

19, 19a *Cyclope (Panormella) pel-
lucida* (Risso, 1826). Thin, translucent with yellowish pattern. Up to
8mm. Mediterranean (Spain), in
shallow water.

37

1 *Volema (Hemifusus) ternatana* (Gmelin, 1791). Shell large, thin, pale, flesh-coloured. Columella relatively straight, slender, without siphonal swelling. Periostracum velvety. Shoulder tubercles may be absent. Up to 20cm. South of Honshu, in quiet waters, to 20-50m depth.

2 *Volema (Pugilina) cochlidium* (Linné, 1758). **Winding Stair Shell.** Columella with siphonal swelling. Shell solid, the shoulder usually with tubercles. Periostracum present. 15cm. Indian Ocean (Port Darwin). Synonym: *Volegalea wardiana* Iredale, 1938.

3 *Volema (Hemifusus) carinifera* (Habe & Kosuge, 1965). **Angulate Stair Shell.** Up to 15cm. West Pacific (Manila Bay, Philippines).

4 *Volema (Volema) myristica* Röding, 1798. **Heavy Crown Shell.** Whorls flat, with pointed folds on suture. Columella with callus. With brown stripes inside, occasionally also outside. 80mm. Japan.

5 *Volema (Volema) pyrum* (Gmelin, 1791). Shell roundish, shiny, yellowish to nut-brown, sometimes with dark ·bands. Periostracum brown. 70mm. East Africa (Mozambique). Synonym: *V. paradisiaca* (Röding, 1798).

6 *Volema (Pugilina) morio* (Linné, 1758). Shell thin, chocolate-brown with a white band below the shoulder edge. Columella relatively slender, without siphonal swelling. Periostracum present. 12cm. West Africa (Senegal).

7, 7a *Volema (Melongena) melon-gena* (Linné, 1758). **West Indian Crown Conch.** Shell massive, pear-shaped, with deep suture and pale bands. Spines, if present, relatively short, on base and whorl edges. Up to 10cm. Juvenile shells (7a) without spines. Restricted to the Caribbean islands, the Gulf Coast and northern South America, in low salinity coastal waters. The subgenus *Melongena* is often regarded as a full genus.

8 *Volema (Melongena) corona corona* (Gmelin, 1791). **American or Florida Crown Conch.** Shoulder angular, usually with crown of erect spines. Shells vary in whorl height, shape and spine development. Up to 10cm. Florida to Mexico, West Indies.

9 *Volema (Melongena) corona altispira* (Pilsbry & Vanatta, 1934). Probably only a variant (not a true subspecies) from the same range as No. 8 (Lake Worth, Florida).

10 *Volema (Melongena) patula* (Broderip & Sowerby, 1829). Periostracum dark. Shoulder with tubercles or blunt spines. 12-17cm. California to Panama.

11 *Busycon contrarium* (Conrad, 1867). **Lightning Whelk.** Shell usually sinistral (left-handed), and used by the animal to open closed bivalves. Up to 17cm. South Carolina, Florida (Sanibel Island), Gulf Coast, in shallow water.

12 *Busycon canaliculatum* (Linné, 1758). **Channelled Whelk.** Shoulder with weak tubercles, suture deep, aperture yellowish. Up to 18cm. East coast of N. America, Cape Cod to Florida.

38

1 *Voluta musica musica* Linné, 1758. Shell heavy with thick, flat ribs forming tubercles at the shoulder. Aperture long, relatively narrow with deep exhalant channel. Columella with several sharp folds. Pattern of spiral lines and dots resembling musical notation. 40-90mm. Caribbean Sea, Puerto Rico to Venezuela (Virgin Islands) on sandy ground, to 10m. *V. musica demarcoi* Olsson, 1965, is rather more slender, with less striking pattern, Mexico, to 100m.

2 *Lyria (Lyria) delessertiana* (Petit de la Saussaye, 1842). Shell with conical spire, prominent ribs, a thickened outer lip and numerous closely packed columellar folds. Inside white. 40-50mm. North from Madagascar (Nossi Be), Comoros, Seychelles.

3 *Lyria (Lyria) mitraeformis* (Lamarck, 1811). **Southern Lyre Shell.** Differing from No. 2 in having a stouter spire, coarser and less dense ribs, and weaker columellar folds. 30-50mm. South coast of Australia (Port Lincoln), in 20m.

4 *Ternivoluta studeri* (von Martens, 1897). Shell relatively light, with short spire and a smooth, spherical apex. Ribs only on the early whorls. Body whorl smooth with fine spiral ridges at the base. Inside of aperture creamy-orange. Outer lip and lower columella white. 40-50mm. East coast of Australia (Cape Moreton, Queensland), 20-200m.

5 *Ericusa (Ericusa) sericata* Thornley, 1951. Shell light, with a large dome-shaped apex, with few whorls and a flat area below the suture. Columella with 4 prominent folds. 70-125mm. Queensland, 70-200m.

6 *Fulgoraria (Fulgoraria) hamillei* (Crosse, 1869). Shell with angular ribs and fine spiral ridges. Apex spherical, the first whorl at an angle to the vertical axis. 10-15cm. South Honshu to Taiwan, 10-40m.

7 *Fulgoraria (Musashia) formosense* Azuma, 1967. First whorls with coarse ribs, the remainder with fine spiral ribs and axial growth lines forming reticulate ornament. 70-90mm. Only in the Taiwan Strait, on muddy ground, 100m.

8 *Cymbium olla* (Linné, 1758). Shell relatively light, with a large knob-like apex and a deep suture above the body whorl. 90-115mm. Spanish south coast (Cadiz) and north-west Africa, 50-100m.

9 *Cymbium pepo* (Lightfoot, 1786). Shell rather broad with sunken apex. Outer lip widely flared. Columellar edge concave. 15-25mm. Rio de Oro to Gulf of Guinea (Senegal).

10 *Cymbium cymbium* (Linné, 1758). **Elephant's Snout Volute.** Shell sub-cylindrical, with sunken apex. Shoulder sharply keeled. 10-15cm. Canary Islands to Senegal.

39

1 *Cymbiola (Cymbiolena) magnifica* (Gebauer, 1802). Shell large, globose, with short spire and smooth, rounded apex. Shoulder slightly angled, the last part of the body whorl with flat tubercles. Aperture very wide, its inside flesh-pink or pale orange. Columella slightly curved with 4 folds. 20-30cm. Eastern Australia (Cape Moreton), to 100m.

2 *Cymbiola (Aulica) nobilis* (Lightfoot, 1786). Shell heavy, variable in size and pattern. Apex usually brown, dome-shaped, consisting of 3-4 smooth whorls. Shoulder slightly concave. Columella with 4 folds. Parietal region very shiny white. General coloration pale ochre. Axial zigzag lines. 10-18cm. Indo-Pacific, to 70m.

3 *Cymbiola (Aulicina) rutila norrisii* (Gray, 1838). **Blood-red Volute.** Extremely variable in colour, pattern and occurrence of shoulder tubercles. Apex with 3 slightly tuberculate whorls. Shoulder tubercles not usually pronounced. Columella with 4 folds, the callus area orange-brown. 60-80mm. New Guinea eastwards to Solomons (Guadalcanal), to 40m. *C (A.) rutila rutila* (Broderip, 1826), coasts of N. Queensland.

4 *Melo (Melo) melo* (Lightfoot, 1786). Shell globose, the body whorl accounting for the total length. Aperture wide, with 3 columellar folds and orange-brown callus. Parietal region very shiny. General coloration yellowish-orange, often with bands of brown markings. 17-23cm. South China Sea (Singapore), to 10m.

5 *Melo (Melocorona) broderipi* (Griffith & Pidgeon, 1834). Shell truncated above, with a circle of small spines. Apex large, dome-shaped, slightly projecting above the spines. 25-35cm. New Guinea to Philippines. Possibly a subspecies of the Indonesian *M. (M.) aethiopica* (Linné, 1758).

6 *Cymbiola (Aulica) imperialis* (Lightfoot, 1786). Shell heavy, with flat, conical spire and curved spines on the shoulder, becoming even longer towards the aperture. Apex dome-shaped; smooth, dark brown. Columella with 4 folds. 20-25cm. Sulu Archipelago (Zamboanga, Mindanao), 20m.

7 *Cymbiola (Aulicina) nivosa* (Lamarck, 1804). Extremely variable. Apex stumpy, with 2-3 tuberculate whorls. Aperture dark brown inside. Columella with 4 folds, its callus orange-brown. 60-80mm. Western Australia, to 40m.

8 *Cymbiola (Aulicina) vespertilio* (Linné, 1758). **Bat Volute.** Extremely variable. Apex stumpy with 3 tuberculate whorls. Aperture dirty brown inside. Columella with 4 folds. 45-115mm. Philippines (Cebu) and northern Australia, to 20m.

9 *Melo (Melocorona) amphora* (Lightfoot, 1786). Shell very large. Apex dome-shaped, smooth. Shoulder with long spines. Coloration variable. 30-45cm. Western Australia to New Guinea, 10m. Synonym: *Melo diadema* (Lamarck, 1811).

40

1 *Cymbiolista hunteri* Iredale, 1931. **Marked Volute.** Shell relatively large and light with conical apex, somewhat concave shoulder and small, pointed tubercles on the shoulder which do not continue as axial ribs. Outer lip with a broad, angular edge. Columella with 4 oblique folds. Up to 17cm. East coast of Australia (Cape Moreton), 30-150m.

2 *Scaphella (Scaphella) junonia* (Lamarck, 1804). **Juno's Volute.** Shell with stumpy apex, the first whorls finely reticulate, the body whorl smooth. Columella with 4 folds. 80-130cm. Several varieties in an extended geographical range. Caribbean, 20-80m.

3 *Volutoconus bednalli* (Brazier, 1878). Shell with rounded apex and attractive pattern. 90-130mm. Arafura and Timor Seas (Port Darwin), 10-40m.

4 *Amoria (Amoria) ellioti* (Sowerby, 1864). **Elliot's Volute.** Shell longish-ovate, smooth, pale with axial lines. Apex wart-like, flesh-coloured. Aperture brown inside. 70-110mm. North-western Australia (Pretty Pool), on sand at extreme low tide.

5 *Ampulla priamus* (Gmelin, 1791). Shell rather thin, smooth, glossy, yellowish-brown with darker regularly arranged markings. Columella without folds. 60-80mm. Off the coast of southern Spain and N.W. Africa. The only species in the genus, it was formerly placed in the genus *Halia* Risso, 1826.

6 *Amoria (Relegamoria) molleri* (Iredale, 1936). Shell long, fairly light, with short spire. Apex conical. Aperture long and narrow, the outer lip with callus on the inner edge. Columella with 4 prominent folds, and secondary folds. 80-125mm. East coast of Australia, 100-200m.

7 *Amoria (Amoria) maculata* (Swainson, 1822). Shell longish-ovate, smooth, pale with spiral pattern of markings and a wart-like apex. 50-75mm. Queensland (Fitzroy Reef), to 20m.

8 *Amoria (Amorena) undulata* (Lamarck, 1804). **Wavy Volute.** Form and coloration variable. Shell with orange-brown wavy lines. Aperture apricot-coloured inside. 80-120mm. South coast of Australia (Port Lincoln), on sandy flats, to 400m.

9 *Harpulina lapponica* (Linné, 1767). Shell rather globose, the wartlike apex sitting on 3 smooth whorls. First whorl with indistinct spiral tubercles, later ones smooth. Columella with 7-8 folds. 60-100mm. Southern India (Kilakarai) and Ceylon, to 15m.

10 *Nannamoria parabola* Garrard, 1960. Shell narrowing towards the base, with a low spire and wart-like apex. Shoulder with c. 10 pointed tubercles. Columella with 7-11 weak folds. 30-35mm. Hitherto only found off Cape Moreton, Queensland, in 100-200m.

41

1 *Alcithoe (Alcithoe) arabica* (Gmelin, 1791). Extremely variable in size, colour, form and the extent of the shoulder tubercles. Spire long, with wart-like apex. Columella with 4-5 oblique folds. 80-190mm. New Zealand, mainly off the west coast of North Island and the northern part of South Island (Cape Farewell), to 100m. Synonym: *Voluta pacifica* (Perry, 1810).

2 *Amoria (Zebramoria) zebra* (Leach, 1814). Shell relatively small and solid, longish-ovate, with conical spire. Apex small, smooth, consisting of 2-3 roundish, often dark whorls. Upper whorls ribbed, body whorl smooth, without shoulder. Columella with 4 oblique folds. Ground coloration pale beige, with pattern of red-brown lines. Very variable. 35-55mm. North-east Australia (Clairview, Queensland), to 50m.

2a *Amoria (Zebramoria) zebra* (Leach, 1814). Dark, so-called 'black', colour variety (Cape Capricorn, Queensland).

2b *Amoria (Zebramoria) zebra* (Leach, 1814). Pale, so-called 'gold' colour variety, with subdued pattern (Curtis Island, Queensland).

3 *Cymbiola (Aulica) flavicans* (Gmelin, 1791). **Yellow Volute.** Shell heavy, roundish, with short spire, and a wart-like apex consisting of 3 smooth whorls. Whorls usually smooth or slightly tuberculate. Columella white, with 4 oblique folds. Outer lip creamy-white, but dark violet-brown inside. 10cm. Northern Australia (Port Darwin) to southern New Guinea, to 100m.

4 *Cymbiolacca peristicta* McMichael, 1963. Shell longish-ovate, with short spire and a shoulder bearing small, pointed tubercles. Reddish-white with brown dots. Columella with 4 folds. 60-75mm. Queensland (Big Sandy Cay), 5m.

5 *Cymbiolacca pulchra* (Sowerby, 1825). Possibly the same species as No. 4. South of Swain Reefs to Bustard Bay (Queensland).

6 *Amoria (Amoria) damonii* Gray, 1864. Relatively large for the genus. Apex whitish. Early whorls shiny, smooth, grey-brown with a white suture. Later whorls creamy-white or tan-coloured, with irregular brown pattern. Body whorl with 3 dark spiral bands. Aperture pale brown inside. 40-140mm. Rottnest Island, S.W. Australia to Cookstown, Queensland (Broome, Western Australia), 100m.

7 *Cymbiola (Aulicina) deshayesi* (Reeve, 1855). Shell somewhat pointed below, and white with orange-brown pattern. Apex dome-shaped, with 3 pale yellow, slightly tuberculate whorls. Shoulder with stumpy tubercles. Columella straight, with 4 oblique folds. 70-100mm. North-west of New Caledonia, on intertidal coral sand.

8 *Amoria (Amoria) grayi* Ludbrook, 1953. Shell uniformly beige-grey, rather more slender than No. 6. Upper whorls with brown angular lines. 50-100mm. Western Australia (Thevenard Island, Onslow), to 40m.

42

1, 1a *Harpa major* Röding, 1798. The brown marking on the columellar callus is more or less divided into two. 50-90mm. East Africa to Marquesas Islands and Hawaii, in 50-100m. Related species: *H. davidis* (Röding, 1798). 50-90mm. Bay of Bengal.

2 *Harpa amouretta* Röding, 1798. Apex small, narrow, reddish-brown. 20-60mm. Indo-Pacific. Related species: *H. gracilis* Broderip & Sowerby, 1829, apex white, Ellice Island, Tuamotus, Clipperton Island.

3, 3a *Harpa harpa* (Linné, 1758). **Common Harp.** Three separate, brown parietal markings. More slender than Nos. 1 and 4. 50-80mm. Indo-Pacific. Synonym: *H. nobilis* Röding, 1798.

4 *Harpa ventricosa* Lamarck, 1816. Shell outline rather rectangular, with sharp rib spines on the upper part of the whorls. Two separate parietal markings and a small basal spot. Callus usually yellowish-orange. 50-100mm. East Africa, Red Sea, Seychelles, Mauritius, 20m.

5 *Harpa crenata* Swainson, 1822. 40-90mm. West coast of N. America (La Paz, Mexico), 50m.

6, 6a *Marginella glabella* (Linné, 1758). Shell pear-shaped, shiny, pale reddish-brown, with pale markings. Outer lip toothed. Four columellar folds. 40mm. North-west Africa (Cap Blanc), to 70m.

7, 7a *Bullata (Cryptospira) elegans* (Gmelin, 1791). Spire low. Body whorl large, smooth, shiny, narrower below. Pale and dark grey reticulate pattern. Callus and outer lip edge red-brown. Columella with 6 pale folds. 30mm. Indo-Pacific (Andaman Islands).

8, 8a *Bullata (Cryptospira) elegans* (Gmelin, 1791). A pale grey form with axial zigzag lines, and without reticulate pattern. Callus and outer lip edge yellowish-orange. 35mm. Indo-Pacific (Penang), to 10m.

9 *Glabella adansoni* (Kiener, 1835). Spire conical. Shoulder ribbed. Outer lip edge thickened and toothed. Olive-grey markings and dark lines on a pale ground. 25mm. West Africa (Senegal), 20m.

10, 10a *Persicula persicula persicula* (Linné, 1758). Shell ovate with flat spire. Aperture long, narrow, with parallel edges. Columella white, callused, with 8 folds. Exhalation groove extending to apex. 20mm. West Africa (Niodor, Senegal). Related subspecies: *P. p. avellana* (Lamarck, 1822), with smaller spots.

11, 11a *Persicula cornea* (Lamarck, 1822). Yellowish-brown with darker bands. 25mm. West Africa (Niodor, Senegal).

12 *Bullata (Glosia) bernardi* (Largilliert, 1845). Shell grey with long outer lip. 25mm. South-west of Taiwan (Kao-hsiung), 40m.

13, 13a *Persicula cingulata* (Dillwyn, 1817). Shell as No. 10, creamy-yellow, with orange-red lines. 20mm. West Africa (Dakar). Synonym: *Persicula lineata* (Lamarck, 1822).

14, 14a *Marginella (Austroginella) muscaria* (Lamarck, 1822). **Fly-like Marginella.** 12mm. South-east Australia (Boydtown, N.S.W.), to 10m.

43

1 *Oliva (Oliva) porphyria* (Linné, 1758). **Tent Olive.** 10cm. Gulf of California to Galapagos, mainly in Gulf of Panama (Pedro Gonzales).

2 *Olivella (Callianax) biplicata* (Sowerby, 1825). **Purple Dwarf Olive.** Two narrow basal folds. Up to 27mm. Western coast of N. America (San Diego).

3 *Ancilla (Baryspira) albocallosa* (Lischke, 1870). 70mm. South of Honshu, Japan.

4 *Ancilla (Ancillista) velesiana* Iredale, 1936. **Girdled Ancilla.** Up to 10cm. Eastern Australia (Mackay, Queensland). *A. (A.) cingulata* (Sowerby and Broderip, 1830) has a blue-grey apex (typical of the N. Australian coast).

5 *Oliva (Oliva) miniacea* (Röding, 1798). Form *marrati* Johnson, 1817. Philippines.

6 *Oliva (Oliva) tremulina* Lamarck, 1810. Aperture white inside. 50-80mm. Indo-Pacific (Taiwan).

7 *Oliva (Oliva) miniacea* (Röding, 1798). **Red-mouthed Olive.** The nominate form. Aperture dark orange inside. 50-90mm. Philippines (Cebu) and Fiji.

8 *Oliva (Oliva) sayana* Ravenel, 1834. **Lettered Olive.** 40–80mm. West Indies (Sanibel Island).

9 *Oliva (Neocylindrus) lignaria* Marrat, 1868. Form *cryptospira* Ford, 1891. 40-60mm. Aperture lavender-blue to deep violet inside. Indo-Pacific.

10 *Oliva (Carmione) reticulata* (Röding, 1798). **Blood Olive.** Up to 50mm. Indo-Pacific.

11 *Oliva (Oliva) incrassata* (Lightfoot, 1786). Spire flat conical, body whorl with shoulder. 50-80mm. West coast of central America.

12 *Oliva (Carmione) elegans* Lamarck, 1811. Up to 40mm. Indo-Pacific.

13 *Oliva (Oliva) annulata* Gmelin 1791. Form *carnicolor* Dautzenberg, 1927. Uniformly coloured, in contrast to nominate form. 40-60mm. Philippines (Siasi Island).

14 *Oliva (Oliva) reticularis* Lamarck, 1810. Form *olorinella* Duclos, 1835. **Pearl Olive.** White, up to 50mm. West Indies (Puerto Rico).

15 *Oliva (Oliva) caribaeensis* Dall & Simpson, 1901. 40mm. Caribbean.

16 *Oliva (Neocylindrus) tesselata* Lamarck, 1811. Up to 35mm. Indo-Pacific (Solomon Is.).

17 *Oliva (Oliva) caerulea* (Röding, 1798). Aperture deep violet. 40-50mm. Indo-Pacific (Solomons). Synonym: *O. (O.) episcopalis* Lamarck, 1811.

18 *Oliva (Carmione) bulbosa* (Röding, 1798). 35-50mm. East Africa (Mozambique) to Bali. Many colour variants: *immaculata* Vanatta, 1915, pure white; *fabagina* Lamarck, 1811, dark brown; *inflata* Lamarck, 1811, blue-grey, spotted; *tuberosa* Röding, 1798, with 2 golden stripes or bands; see also No. 19.

19 *Oliva (Carmione) bulbosa*, form *bicingulata* Lamarck, 1811, with 2 brown bands.

20 *Oliva (Galeola) carneola* (Gmelin, 1791), form *unizonalis* Dautzenberg, 1927, with one white band. 14-24mm. Indo-Pacific (Marau Sound, Solomons).

21 *O. (G.) carneola* (Gmelin, 1791). Nominate form (Philippines).

22 *O. (G.) carneola*, form *candidula* Dautzenberg, 1927. White band indistinct.

23 *O. (G.) carneola*, form *bizonalis* Dautzenberg, 1927, with 2 bands.

44

1 *Turbinella laevigata* Anton, 1839. **Brazilian Chank.** Shell pointed-ovate, with tall spire. Whorls with fine spiral ridges, almost smooth. Body whorl globose, with short neck. Three rather pronounced parietal folds. Yellowish-white, usually below a periostracum. 10cm. Brazilian coast (Salvador, Bahia). Another western Atlantic species: *T. angulata* (Lightfoot, 1786), the **West Indian Chank, Lamp Shell,** with prominent shoulder tubercles, down to 25m. Gulf of Mexico, southern Florida, Bahamas, northern Cuba.

2 *Turbinella pyrum* (Linné, 1758). **Indian Chank.** Shell solid, pear-shaped, porcellanous below a thick periostracum. Lower part of body whorl with weak spiral ornament. Cream to reddish-white, the apex and body with brown markings. Up to 12cm. Ceylon and Bay of Bengal. In the Hindu religion, the shell is regarded as a symbol of the God Vishnu and his incarnation Krishna. Sinistral (left-handed) shells, of which only about 20 are known, are particularly important.

3 *Tudicula (Tudicula) armigera* (A. Adams, 1855). **Spined Whelk.** Shell pear-shaped, with a long siphonal canal and shoulder spines. 50-75mm. Queensland, down to 40m.

4 *Tudicula (Tudicula) rasilistoma* Abbott, 1959. Shell spinkle-shaped, with rather tall spire. Columellar callus expanded to form shield. Up to 80mm. Queensland (Cape Moreton) to New South Wales, in 30-70m.

5 *Afer cumingii* (Reeve, 1847). Shell spindle-shaped, with long siphonal canal, shoulder tubercles, and spiral ridges. Columella with 1-2 folds. 70mm. China and Taiwan (Kaohsiung) in 20-30m.

6 *Vasum (Vasum) turbinellum* (Linné, 1758). Shell solid with prominent spines. Spire rather low. 50-85mm. Indo-Pacific (Zanzibar), in 3-50m.

7 *Vasum (Vasum) ceramicum* (Linné, 1758). Spire tall. Columella with 3 prominent, but narrow folds. Outer lip with paired teeth on its inner edge. 80-150mm. Indo-Pacific (Philippines), in 6-50m.

8 *Vasum (Vasum) tubiferum* (Anton, 1839). Unlike Nos. 6 & 7, this species has a funnel-shaped umbilicus and reddish-violet markings on the parietal callus, but no black markings on the inner edge of the outer lip. 70-120mm. Restricted to shallow water off Cuyo I., Philippines.

9 *Vasum (Vasum) muricatum* (Born, 1778). Shoulder tubercles short, stumpy. Inside porcelain-white. 50-80mm. South Florida (Sanibel Island) and West Indies, among corals or on rocky bottoms, in 8-12m.

10 *Vasum (Vasum) rhinoceros* (Gmelin, 1791). Shell variable in shape and spire form. Parietal callus brown. 50-90mm. East Africa (Zanzibar).

11 *Vasum (Vasum) rhinoceros* (Gmelin, 1791). The so-called yellow form. Parietal callus white. A single colony off Zanzibar.

45

1 *Mitra (Strigatella) decurtata* Reeve, 1844. 35mm. (Pescadores Island, Taiwan).

2 *Mitra (Nebularia) cucumerina* Lamarck, 1811. 20mm. Indo-Pacific (Tahiti).

3 *Vexillum (Pusia) ebenus* (Lamarck, 1811). Glossy black with a narrow spiral, yellow band. 20mm. Mediterranean (Spain).

4 *Mitra (Mitra) papalis* (Linné, 1758). **Papal Mitre.** With pointed shoulder folds near the suture, and fine spiral ridges. 11cm. Indo-Pacific (Samar Island, Philippines).

5 *Mitra (Mitra) mitra* (Linné, 1758). **Episcopal Mitre.** Whorls rounded, smooth, without shoulder folds, and with large markings. Up to 18cm. Indo-Pacific.

6 *Mitra (Mitra) stictica* (Link, 1807). **Pontifical Mitre.** Shoulder with more pronounced folds than in No. 4. An orange colour variant. Up to 70mm. (Queensland).

7 *Mitra (Mitra) stictica* (Link, 1807). A reddish-orange colour variant (Queensland).

8 *Mitra (Mitra) eremitarum* Röding, 1798. 65mm. West Pacific (Cebu, Philippines).

9 *Vexillum (Costellaria) costatum* (Gmelin, 1791). 50mm. (Fitzroy Reef, Queensland).

10 *Vexillum (Vexillum) gruneri* (Reeve, 1844). Ribs sharp, shoulder pronounced. Three red-brown spiral lines. Brown inside. 30mm. (Marau Sound, Solomons).

11 *Vexillum (Vexillum) plicarium* (Linné, 1758). 50mm. Indo-Pacific.

12 *Vexillum (Vexillum) rugosum* (Gmelin, 1791). 50mm. Indo-Pacific.

13 *Vexillum (Costellaria) granosum* (Gmelin, 1791). Grey, with a single white, spiral band. 30mm. Mauritius to Fiji (Sulu Archipelago).

14 *Mitra (Strigatella) litterata* La-marck, 1811. Irregular brown markings. 27mm. Indo-Pacific.

15 *Scabricola (Swainsònia) fissurata* (Lamarck, 1811). 50mm. Indian Ocean.

16 *Vexillum (Vexillum) caffrum* (Linné, 1758). 50mm. **Negro Mitre.** West Pacific (Queensland).

17 *Cancilla (Domiporta) praestantissima* (Röding, 1798). Spiral ridges nut-brown. 35mm. (Solomons).

18 *Cancilla (Domiporta) filaris* (Linné, 1758). 30mm. Indo-Pacific.

19 *Vexillum (Costellaria) exasperatum* (Gmelin, 1791). 30mm. (Queensland).

20 *Pterygia fenestrata* (Lamarck, 1811). 25mm. (Marau Sound, Solomons).

21 *Mitra (Strigatella) paupercula* (Linné, 1758). Black with wavy white, axial stripes. 20mm. Indo-Pacific (Taiwan).

22 *Mitra (Nebularia) ferruginea* Lamarck, 1811. Prominent spiral lines with rust-brown markings. Aperture golden-brown. 35mm. Indo-Pacific (Tahiti).

23 *Pterygia nucea* (Gmelin, 1791). Shell smooth, with 2 brown bands and fine spiral lines. Outer lip edge with brown granulations. 40mm. Indo-Pacific (Guadalcanal, Solomons).

24 *Mitra (Mitra) variabilis* Reeve, 1844. 35mm. (Hazel Wood I., Queensland).

25 *Mitra (Mitra) cornicula* (Linné, 1758). 20mm. Mediterranean (Sardinia).

26 *Neocancilla clathrus* (Gmelin, 1791). 30mm. Indo-Pacific (Solomons).

27 *Vexillum (Vexillum) coccineum* (Reeve, 1844). 80mm. Indo-Pacific.

28 *Cancilla (Cancilla) isabella* Swainson, 1840. 80mm. Indo-Pacific.

46

1 *Cancellaria (Euclia) cassidiformis* Sowerby, 1832. 35mm. West Mexico, 40m.

2 *Cancellaria (Merica) asperella* Lamarck, 1822. 40mm. Japan (Kii), 40m.

3 *Narona (Solatia) nodulifera* (Sowerby, 1825). 45mm. Japan.

4 *Cancellaria (Cancellaria) obesa* Sowerby, 1832. 35mm. California.

5 *Cancellaria (Cancellaria) urceolata* Hinds, 1843. 33mm. West Mexico, 73m.

6 *Trigonostoma rugosa* (Lamarck, 1822). 35mm. Virgin Islands, West Indies.

7 *Trigonostoma (Ventrilia) scalariformis* (Lamarck, 1822), 25mm. Taiwan.

8 *Aphera (Sydaphera) spengleriana* (Deshayes, 1830), 45mm. Japan (Mikawa).

9 *Cancellaria (Bivetia) identata* Sowerby, 1832, 32mm. Gulf of California.

10 *Cancellaria (Cancellaria) reticulata* (Linné, 1767). 40mm. Caribbean.

11 *Terebra (Strioterebrum) dislocata* Say, 1822. Fine spiral ridges and prominent axial ribs. Colour variants (white, grey, orange-brown). 40mm. Caribbean (Bahamas).

12 *Hastula rufopunctata* (E. A. Smith, 1877). Fairly smooth. 35mm. Indo-Pacific (S.W. Australia). *H. strigilata* (Linné, 1758) has a similar pattern, Indo-Pacific.

13 *Hastula lanceata* (Linné, 1767). Glossy white, with wavy, reddish-brown axial lines. 70mm. Indo-Pacific (Philippines).

14 *Duplicaria duplicata* (Linné, 1758). With a second spiral groove below the suture. 70mm. Indo-Pacific (Mozambique).

15 *Duplicaria evoluta* (Deshayes, 1859). 70mm. West Pacific (Taiwan).

16 *Terebra (Perirhoe) babylonia* Lamarck, 1822. Whorls with numerous spiral grooves. 80mm. Indo-Pacific (Solomons). Synonym: *T. acus* (Gmelin, 1791).

17 *Terebra (Oxymeris) felina* (Dillwyn, 1817). With one spiral groove below the suture. 50-70mm. Indo-Pacific.

18 *Impages hectica* (Linné, 1758). Ribs indistinct. Aperture enlarged below. 50mm. Indo-Pacific (Rabaul).

19 *Terebra (Terebra) subulata* (Linné, 1767). Body whorl with 3 rows of markings. 15cm. Indo-Pacific (Zamboanga).

20 *Terebra (Subula) areolata* (Link, 1807). Body whorl with 4 rows of markings. 11cm. Indo-Pacific (Philippines).

21 *Terebra (Subula) dimidiata* (Linné, 1758). Pale colour variant. 11cm. Indo-Pacific (Philippines).

22 *Terebra (Subula) dimidiata* (Linné, 1758). Dark colour variant.

23 *Terebra (Subula) strigata* Sowerby, 1825. 13cm. West coast of central America (Panama).

24 *Terebra (Oxymeris) maculata* (Linné, 1758). Apical whorls with axial ornament. 11cm. Indo-Pacific (Northern Reefs, Queensland).

25 *Terebra (Oxymeris) crenulata* (Linné, 1758). With pointed folds beneath the suture. 10cm. Indo-Pacific (Guadalcanal, Solomons).

47

1 *Conus (Conus) marmoreus* Linné, 1758. Type of the subgenus. Spire rather low. Shoulder with weak tubercles. Pale and dark reticulate pattern, mainly with roundish triangular white markings. 5-10cm. Indo-Pacific (Philippines).

2 *Conus (Conus) nicobaricus* Hwass in Bruguière, 1792. Fine reticulation, 2-3 dark bands. 5-10cm. East Indies and Philippines (Siosi).

3 *Conus (Conus) marchionatus* Hinds, 1843. Distinct reticulate pattern. 30mm. Only off Marquesas Islands (Nukuhiva).

4 *Conus (Rhombus) imperialis* Linné, 1758. **Imperial Cone.** Type of the subgenus. Spire very flat. Shoulder with a row of tubercles. Sides fairly straight. Up to 10cm. Indo-Pacific (Guadacanal, Solomons).

5 *Conus (Rhombus) viridulus* Lamarck, 1810. Up to 70mm. Apparently only off East Africa (Zanzibar).

6 *Conus (Rhombus) fuscatus* Born, 1778. Up to 70mm. Off East Africa (Mauritius).

7 *Conus (Lithoconus) leopardus* Röding, 1798. Type of the subgenus. Shell solid. Spire fairly flat, with smooth shoulder. Spotted pattern variable, less dense than in No. 8. No yellow bands. Old shells up to 20cm. Indo-Pacific (Cebu). Synonym: *C. millepunctatus* Lamarck, 1822.

8 *Conus (Lithoconus) litteratus* Linné, 1758. Letter-marked Cone. Shoulder sharply angled. Spotted

pattern variable. With dark yellow bands. Up to 12cm. Indo-Pacific (Michaelmas Reef, Queensland).

9 *Conus (Lithoconus) eburneus* Hwass in Bruguière, 1792. Pale with rounded shoulder and less dense pattern. Up to 50mm. Indo-Pacific (Philippines).

10 *Conus (Lithoconus) tessulatus* Born, 1778. Spire concave, shoulder rounded. Orange linear pattern, the aperture and base lavender-blue. 45mm. Indo-Pacific (New Guinea).

11 *Conus (Lithoconus) tessulatus* Born, 1778. A colour variant, with broader pattern. 35mm. Pacific (Guadalcanal, Solomons).

12 *Conus (Puncticulis) arenatus* Hwass in Bruguière, 1792. Sand-dusted Cone. Type of the subgenus. Spire low, conical, with a row of tubercles above the shoulder. Sides slightly convex. Marked with numerous small dots. 20-40mm. Indo-Pacific (Queensland).

13 *Conus (Puncticulis) zeylanicus* Gmelin, 1791. Only East Africa and neighbouring islands (Mauritius).

14 *Conus (Puncticulis) pulicarius* Hwass in Bruguière, 1792. Prominent tubercles at the shoulder. Colour and pattern variable. 40mm. Indo-Pacific (Taiwan).

15 *Conus (Puncticulis) stercusmuscarum* Linné, 1758. Aperture deep orange right inside. Up to 50mm. Indo-Pacific (Malaita, Solomons).

16 *Conus (Lithoconus) papillionaceus* Hwass in Bruguière, 1792. Spire flat, shoulder roundish. 5-10cm. West Africa (Senegal).

48

1 *Conus (Virroconus) ebraeus* Linné, 1758. **Hebrew Cone.** Type of the subgenus. Spire fairly flat, shoulder with stumpy tubercles. 35mm. Indo-Pacific (Philippines) and west coast of central America.

2 *Conus (Virroconus) chaldeus* Röding, 1798. Indo-Pacific (Zanzibar), including Clipperton and Galapagos Is.

3 *Conus (Virroconus) miliaris* Hwass in Bruguière, 1792. 25mm. (Zanzibar).

4 *Conus (Pionoconus) perplexus* Sowerby, 1857. Apex sharp. 27mm. California.

5 *Conus (Chelyconus) monachus* Linné, 1758. Spire slightly convex. Shoulder roundish. Body whorl smooth, with a few flat, spiral ridges at the base. 40mm. Indo-Pacific (Philippines).

6 *Conus (Chelyconus) achatinus* Gmelin, 1791. **Agate Cone.** Body whorl with spiral ridges. 60mm. (N.W. Australia).

7 *Conus (Leptoconus) generalis* Linné, 1767. Apex sharp, spire somewhat concave, the shoulder angular. 75mm. Indo-Pacific (Philippines).

8 *Conus (Leptoconus) ammiralis* Linné, 1758. 65mm. Indo-Pacific (Philippines).

9 *Conus (Leptoconus) monile* Hwass in Bruguière, 1792. 50mm. East Indies and Philippines (Straits of Malacca).

10 *Conus (Cheloconus) catus* Hwass in Bruguière, 1792. Extremely variable. 40mm. Indo-Pacific (Lady Musgrave I., Queensland).

11 *Conus (Leptoconus) regularis* Sowerby, 1833. Very variable. 40-60mm. California to Panama (Mulege, Mexico).

12 *Conus (Leptoconus) spurius atlanticus* Clench, 1942. In contrast to the nominate form *C. spurius* Gmelin, 1791, the markings are arranged in groups. 50-80mm. Western Atlantic, Florida (Sanibel Island).

13 *Conus (Leptoconus) thalassiarchus* Sowerby, 1834. Spire flat, apex pointed, shoulder angular. 70mm. Only off Philippines (Sorsogon Bay).

14 *Conus (Stephanoconus) princeps* Linné, 1758. **Prince Cone.** Apex small, spire very flat, shoulder with tubercles. Up to 50mm. West coast of central America (Guaymas).

15 *Conus (Pionoconus) magus* Linné, 1758. 55mm. Indo-Pacific.

16 *Conus (Pionoconus) pertusus* Hwass in Bruguière, 1792. 30mm. (Hawaii).

17 *Conus (Dauciconus) furvus* Reeve, 1834. 50mm. Philippines (Sorsogon Bay).

18 *Conus (Rhizoconus) mustelinus* Hwass in Bruguière, 1792. 75mm. (Siasi I.).

19 *Conus (Rhizoconus) capitaneus* Linné, 1758. 65mm. Indo-Pacific.

20 *Conus (Rhizoconus) miles* Linné, 1758. **Soldier Cone.** Type of the subgenus. Spire flat and broad. 65mm. Indo-Pacific (Philippines).

21 *Conus (Dauciconus) litoglyphus* Hwass in Bruguière, 1792. 50mm. Indo-Pacific.

22 *Conus (Dauciconus) planorbis* Born, 1780. 45mm. Indo-Pacific.

23 *Conus (Regiconus) aulicus* Linné, 1758. **Courtly Cone.** 85mm. Indo-Pacific (Samar Island).

24 *Conus (Gastridius) geographus* Linné, 1758. **Geographer Cone.** Shell light, with shoulder tubercles. 10cm. Indo-Pacific (Philippines).

49

1 Conus *(Virgiconus) virgo* Linné, 1758. Type of the subgenus. Base violet. 10cm. Indo-Pacific.

2 Conus *(Cylinder) telatus* Reeve, 1848. Spire tuberculate. Ornament resembling textile. 60mm. Off Philippines (Giumaros Island). Probably synonymous with No. 4.

3 Conus *(Cylinder) victoriae* Reeve, 1843. Colour very variable. 60mm. Western Australia (Port Hedland).

4 Conus *(Cylinder) textile* Linné, 1758. Type of the subgenus. Spire slightly concave, with sharp apex. 80mm. Indo-Pacific (Mozambique).

5 Conus *(Tuliparia) tulipa* Linné, 1758. Type of the subgenus. Shell thin, the spire with tubercles. 60mm. Indo-Pacific.

6 Conus *(Darioconus) omaria* Hwass in Bruguière, 1792. Type of the subgenus. 70mm. Indo-Pacific (Philippines).

7 Conus *(Darioconus) praelatus* Hwass in Bruguière, 1792. Blue-grey shadows in the white markings. 60mm. East Africa (Mozambique).

8 Conus *(Darioconus) pennaceus* Born, 1778. Similar to No. 6. 40mm. Hawaii (Oahu).

9 Conus *(Cylinder) complanatus* Sowerby, 1866. 60mm. Western Australia (Broome).

10 Conus *(Floraconus) novaehollandiae* A. Adams, 1859. Probably only a subspecies of the more slender and less densely patterned *C. (F.) anemone* Lamarck, 1810. 40mm. Western Australia (Port Hedland).

11 Conus *(Textilia) pica* A. Adams & Reeve, 1848. Shell thick, inflated. 35mm. West Pacific (Philippines).

12 Conus *(Lautoconus) mediterraneus* Hwass in Bruguière, 1792. Type of the subgenus. Spire fairly tall, pointed. Whorls slightly convex. Olive and brown pattern, usually with a white band. Very variable. Lip to 60mm (usually less). Mediterranean (Sardinia) and adjacent Atlantic.

13 Conus *(Hermes) nussatella* Linné, 1758. Type of the subgenus. Spire rather tall, pointed. Shell slender, with spiral ornament. 40-50mm. Indo-Pacific (Philippines).

14 Conus *(Strioconus) striatus* Linné, 1758. Type of the subgenus. Spire low, the shoulder keeled. Fine spiral lines. 75mm. Indo-Pacific (New Island, Queensland).

15 Conus *(Endemeconus) sieboldi* Reeve, 1848. 60mm. China Sea (Taiwan).

16 Conus *(Asprella) orbignyi* (Audouin, 1831. 65mm. China Sea (Taiwan).

17 Conus *(Cleobula) glaucus* Linné, 1758. Spire very short, with pointed apex. Whorls slightly convex, smooth, 40mm. West Pacific (New Guinea).

18 Conus *(Cleobula) quercinus* Lightfoot, 1786. 65mm. Indo-Pacific.

19 Conus *(Cleobula) figulinus* Linné, 1758. Type of the subgenus. Brown with darker spiral lines. 65mm. Indo-Pacific (Solomons).

20 Conus *(Cleobula) betulinus* Linné, 1758. Up to 12cm. Indo-Pacific.

50

1, 1a *Thatcheria mirabilis* Angas,
1877. **Japanese Wonder Shell,
Miraculous Thatcheria.** Shell
thin, with a striking pagoda-like
spire. Shoulder keeled and angular.
Surface smooth, matt, with very fine
ornament. Outside pale sandy-
yellow, inside white, with enamel-
like sheen. Up to 10cm. South coast
of Honshu and Shikoku, Japan, 120-
180m.

2 *Polystira oxytropis* (Sowerby,
1834). Shell whitish to creamy-
yellow with a thick spiral ridge. Up to
45mm. California to Ecuador, 110m.

3 *Cochlespira pulchella pulcher-
issima* (Kuroda, 1959). Shell small,
pagoda-like, differing from other
subspecies mainly in the form and
number of the shoulder tubercles
(24-30, small, stumpy). 40mm. Japan
(Kao-hsiung, Taiwan), 120-180m.

4 *Knefastia tuberculifera* (Broderip
& Sowerby, 1829). Robust, with
coarse shoulder tubercles and finer
spiral ridges. 65mm. Gulf of California (Mazatlán, Mexico).

5 *Lophiotoma (Lophioturris) indica*
(Röding, 1798) Shell with a sharp
spiral ridge an a long siphonal canal.
Up to 95mm. Ceylon to Fiji (Philippines).

6 *Gemmula congener cosmoi* (Sykes,
1930). Shell white, with a spiral keel
consisting of vertically connected
pairs of tubercles. 60mm. Japan.

7 *Oenopota (Propebela) turricula
nobilis* (Möller, 1842). 21mm.

Circum-arctic (Faxaflói, Iceland),
150m.

8 *Fusiturris undatiruga* (Bivona,
1832). 50mm. Yellow-brown, often
with a brown band above the shoulder. Mediterranean (Messina) and
adjacent Atlantic. Synonym: *F. simi-
lis* Dautzenberg, 1891.

9 *Leucosyrinx queenslandica* Powell,
1969. 60mm. (Cape Moreton,
Queensland).

10 *Hormospira maculosa* (Sowerby,
1834). 60mm. West coast of central
America.

11 *Polystira picta* (Reeve, 1843).
Larger than No. 2, with brown
markings on the spiral ridges. 60mm.
Gulf of California (Guaymas), 20-
70m.

12 *Gemmula (Unedogemmula) unedo* (Kiener, 1840). Spiral keel with
small double tubercles. Suture deep.
80-100mm. Persian Gulf, East Indies, Japan (Taiwan), 100-300m.

13 *Benthofascis biconica* (Hedley,
1903). Spindle-shaped with stumpy
apex. 40mm. Southern Queensland
(Cape Moreton) to Tasmania, 20-
200m.

14 *Daphnella nobilis* Kira, 1954.
Shell thin, with roundish whorls and
a deep suture. 30mm. Japan (Tosa),
100-150m.

15 *Bathytoma (Micantapex) ag-
nata* Hedley & Petterd, 1906. Spirally
arranged coarse and fine tubercles.
30mm. Eastern Australia (Cape Moreton) and New Zealand.

51

1 *Pyramidella (Voluspa) acus* (Gmelin, 1791). 55mm. Indo-Pacific. Synonyms: *P. maculosa* Lamarck, 1822; *P. punctata* Schubert & Wagner, 1829.

2 *Kleinella (Leucotina) gigantea* (Dunker, 1882). With spiral ridges and an umbilicus. 30mm. Japan (Mikawa Bay).

3 *Pyramidella terrebelloides* (A. Adams, 1855). 30mm. Japan.

4, 5 *Pupa solidula* (Linné, 1758). Up to 35mm. Tropical Pacific.

6 *Pupa sulcata* (Gmelin, 1791). Up to 30mm. Tropical Pacific.

7 *Acteon tornatilis* (Linné, 1767). Lip extended at base, columella twisted. Up to 25mm. European coasts, Mediterranean (Viareggio, Italy).

8 *Pupa nitidula* (Lamarck, 1816). 20mm. Tropical Pacific.

9 *Acteon siebaldii* (Reeve, 1842). Up to 25mm. Japan (Mikawa Bay).

10 *Melampus coffeus* (Linné, 1758). Up to 2cm. Florida, West Indies, in mangrove swamps.

11 *Hydatina albocincta* (van der Hoeven, 1839). Shell very thin, apex sunken. Up to 60mm. West Pacific (Kii, Japan).

12 *Bulla punctulata* A. Adams, 1850, in Sowerby. Spire sunken. Up to 30mm. West Pacific (Queensland), Japan, west coast of central America.

13 *Bulla ampulla* Linné, 1758. Up to 60mm. Indo-Pacific (Ceylon).

14 *Bulla botanica* Hedley, 1918. Up to 60mm. South and western Australia.

15 *Cylichna arachis* (Quoy & Gaimard, 1833). Cylindrical, with sunken spire and a periostracum. 25mm. South and western Australia (Albany).

16 *Haminoea virescens* (Sowerby, 1833). **Sowerby's Paper-bubble.** Shell thin, transparent, greenish. Apex sunken. 20mm. West coast of northern America.

17 *Haminoea hydatis* (Linné, 1758). 11mm. European coasts, Mediterranean.

18 *Atys (Atys) naucum* (Linné, 1758). Shell thin, translucent, apex sunken, and fine ornament. Up to 45mm. Tropical Pacific (Zamboanga).

19 *Atys (Aliculastrum) cylindricus* (Helbling, 1779). 30mm. Tropical Pacific.

20 *Scapander lignarius* (Linné, 1758). Ovate, narrowing above, with sunken apex and brown periostracum. Up to 60mm. European coasts.

21, 21a *Trimusculus garnoti* (Payraudeau, 1826). Dish-shaped, with the apex curved backwards. 10mm. Mediterranean (Marseilles).

22, 22a *Siphonaria pectinata* (Linné, 1758). 30mm. Mediterranean and adjacent Atlantic (Parede, Portugal), Florida, Texas, West Indies. Synonym: *S. algesirae* Quoy & Gaimard, 1833.

23, 23a *Siphonaria laciniosa* (Linné, 1758). 30mm. West Pacific.

24 *Trimusculus reticulatus* (Sowerby, 1835). 25mm. West coast of northern America.

25, 25a *Siphonaria deflexa* (Helbling, 1779). 30mm. South Africa.

26 *Siphonaria capensis* Quoy & Gaimard, 1833. 28mm. South Africa.

27 *Siphonaria gigas* Sowerby, 1825. 50mm. West coast of central America.

52

1 *Nucula (Nucula) nucleus* (Linné, 1769). **Common Nut Clam.** Rounded-triangular, longer in front than behind, lower edge toothed. Mother-of-pearl inside. Hinge angled, with numerous small, sharp, interlocking teeth. Periostracum yellow. 10mm. European coasts, Mediterranean (Chioggia, Italy), in mud and sand, 10-100m.

2 *Nuculana (Saccella) acuta* (Conrad, 1831). **Pointed Nut Clam.** Rear of shell beaked. Concentric ribs. 10mm. American east coast (Florida), West Indies. 230m.

3 *Nuculana (Nuculana) pernula* (Müller, 1771). **Muller's Nut Clam.** White with dark periostracum. 20mm. Arctic seas, North Atlantic, North Pacific (Cook Inlet, Alaska).

4 *Nuculana (Nuculana) minuta* (Fabricius, 1776). Ribs prominent. 15mm. Arctic seas, between Nova Scotia and San Diego (Puget Sound, Washington).

5 *Yoldia hyperborea limatuloides* Ockelmann, 1954. Flat, longish, gaping. 36mm. Iceland (Faxaflói), Arctic seas, from Greenland to Alaska.

6, 6a *Arca (Arca) noae* (Linné, 1758). **Noah's Ark Shell.** Longish with umbones directed forward, far apart from one another, and separated by a rhomboidal ligament surface. Hinge long and straight. With a chestnut-brown pattern. Lower shell edge gaping in the middle (byssus opening). Up to 70mm. Mediterranean (Istria) and adjacent Atlantic, attached by byssus to rocks. Edible.

7 *Larkinia grandis* (Broderip & Sowerby, 1829). Shell heavy, triangular, the umbones inflated. Up to 10cm. West coast of central America (Guaymas, Mexico).

8, 8a *Anadara (Anadara) antiquata* (Linné, 1958). Ribs flat, rounded, hinge straight. White with dark periostracum. Up to 90mm. Tropical Pacific (Japan), in shallow water.

9 *Cucullaea labiata* (Lightfoot, 1786). **Cowl Shell.** Left valve somewhat larger than the right. Interior with a lip-like septum for the rear adductor muscle. 70mm. Australia (Keppel Bay, Queensland).

10 *Senilia senilis* (Linné, 1758). Umbones directed forwards. Radial ribs broad. 45mm. West Africa (Senegal).

11 *Arca (Arca) zebra* (Swainson, 1833). **Turkey Wing.** Similar to No. 6, but with zebra pattern. 50-70mm. Caribbean.

12 *Barbatia (Acar) gradata* (Broderip & Sowerby, 1829). Prominent ornament. Up to 30mm. West coast of central America (Santa Cruz, Galapagos), down to 40m.

13 *Barbatia (Barbatia) virescens* (Reeve, 1843). Fine radial and coarse concentric ornament. Periostracum fibrous. 40mm. Indo-Pacific (Ceylon).

14 *Glycymeris gigantea* (Reeve, 1843). Almost circular, with ribs and a red-brown zigzag pattern. Up to 100mm. West coast of central America (La Paz, Mexico), 13m.

15, 15a *Glycymeris violascens* (Lamarck, 1819). Violet-grey with fine radial lines, and a periostracum. Up to 60mm. Mediterranean (Sicily). The related **Dog Cockle,** *G. glycymeris* (Linné, 1758), is circular with prominent growth lines and irregular brown markings. European coasts, Mediterranean.

16 *Limopsis sulcata* Verrill & Bush, 1898. Oblique-ovate, with concentric ornament. Periostracum shaggy at the edges. 20mm. Florida, West Indies.

53

1 *Modiolus (Modiolus) modiolus* (Linné, 1758). **Horse Mussel.** Shell inflated, the front rounded and the umbones rather far apart. Hinge smooth, periostracum brown and hairy in young shells. 70-100mm. European coasts, Arctic seas, U.S.A., Japan.

2 *Mytilus (Mytilus) edulis* Linné, 1758. **European Edible Mussel.** Shell pointed, with terminal umbones, and a periostracum. Violet to blue-black, often eroded. Inside white, with bluish zone at shell edge. Hinge with very small teeth. Up to 80mm. European coasts, but not Arctic, attached by byssus to rocks, piles, empty shells and to others of its own species.

3 *Lithophaga (Lithophaga) lithophaga* (Linné, 1758). **Date Mussel.** Umbones rather far apart. Periostracum brown. 70mm. Mediterranean (Marseilles), intertidal, boring smooth tunnels in hard limestone with help of an acid secretion. Edible.

4 *Mytilus (Mytilus) galloprovincialis* Lamarck, 1819. **Mediterranean Mussel.** Broader than No. 2, with pointed umbones. Up to 70mm. Mediterranean. Edible.

5 *Pinna (Pinna) nobilis* Linné, 1758. **Rough Pen Shell.** Wedge-shaped, gaping at the rear, and scaly. Up to 80cm. Mediterranean, embedded in sand.

6 *Atrina vexillum* (Born, 1778). Fairly smooth and considerably shorter and broader than No. 5, with the rear rounded. 20cm. Indo-Pacific (Moragalla, Ceylon).

7 *Musculus (Musculus) discors* (Linné, 1758). Shell thin with weak radial ornament in front and behind, smooth in the middle. Periostracum olive-brown. 16mm. Arctic to Cape Verde, under rocks around mid-tide and below.

8 *Malleus (Malleus) malleus* (Linné, 1758). **Black Hammer Oyster.** Shell with folded edges. Hinge elongated, the valves tapering towards the bottom. Mother-of-pearl inside. 15cm. West Pacific (Cebu).

9 *Mallus (Malleus) albus* Lamarck, 1817. **White Hammer Oyster.** 12cm. North Australia and southwestern Pacific.

10 *Pteria sterna* (Gould, 1851). **Western Wing Oyster.** Hinge elongated posteriorly. Exterior brown, inside mother-of-pearl. Periostracum shaggy. Up to 10cm. West coast of central America. Related species: *P. hirundo* (Linné, 1758), 90mm, Atlantic, Mediterranean.

11 *Pteria colymbus* (Röding, 1798). **Atlantic Wing Oyster.** Righ valve flat. 30mm. Florida, Texas, West Indies, on gorgonians.

12 *Pinctada maxima* (Jameson, 1901). **Golden or Silver Lip Pearl Shell.** Exterior yellowish-brown, interior mother-of-pearl with olive border. Up to 30cm. Between New Guinea and North Australia.

13, 13a *Pinctada margaritifera* (Linné, 1758). **Black Lip Pearl Shell.** Greenish-brown with radial ribs and scaly growth lamellae. Mother-of-pearl darker with the border black (No. 13) or yellowish-brown (No. 13a). Up to 25cm. Indo-Pacific.

54

1, 1a *Pecten (Pecten) maximus* (Linné, 1758). **Great Scallop.** Valves unequal. Left valve, concave at the umbo. Right valve convex. Yellowish, red or mottled. Ribs roundish, each with about 7 fine radial lines. Ears equal in size. Up to 13cm. Norway, Atlantic, Canaries. Edible. Often confused with No. 2.

2 *Pecten (Pecten) jacobaeus* (Linné, 1758). **Pilgrim Scallop.** Smaller than No. 1. Ribs angular, each with about 4 coarse ridges. Ears equal in size. About 10cm, usually less. Mediterranean, Canaries, Cape Verde. Edible. Pilgrims to the shrine of St. James of Compostella (N.W. Spain) carried a shell of this species, hence the specific name.

3 *Chlamys (Chlamys) islandica* (Müller, 1776). **Iceland Scallop.** Both valves convex. Anterior ear larger. Numerous radial ridges roughened by growth lines. Up to 10cm. Iceland, Greenland, North America, Arctic seas.

4 *Chlamys (Chlamys) multistriata* (Poli, 1795). Yellowish, orange, brownish-violet with numerous finely scaled radial ribs. Posterior ear truncated. Up to 35mm. Atlantic, Azores, Mediterranean (Costa Brava, Spain).

5 *Chlamys (Chlamys) varia* (Linné, 1758). **Variegated Scallop.** Right valve rather more convex than left. Numerous finely scaled radial ribs. Ears as in No. 4. Yellow, red, brown, usually dark purple, with variable pattern. Up to 60mm. Norway, European coasts, Mediterranean (Sardinia).

6 *Camptonectes tigrinus* (Müller, 1776). **Tiger Scallop.** Valves rather thin, almost equal, with weak radial ornament. Ears very unequal. Red to violet-red, often with white, transverse markings. Up to 30mm. European coasts Mediterranean. This species is sometimes placed in the genus *Palliolum*.

7 *Chlamyx (Flexopecten) flexuosa* (Poli, 1795). Valves almost equal with broad ribs. Ears almost equal. White, yellowish-brown, with brown and opaque white markings. 35mm. Mediterranean and adjacent Atlantic.

8 *Pseudamusseum septemradiatum* (Müller, 1776). Valves thin, fairly convex with broad radial folds. Ears small. Red to brown with pale dots. Right valve white. 40mm. North-east Atlantic to north-west Africa.

9 *Chlamys (Aequipecten) opercularis* (Linné, 1758). **Quin or Queen Scallop.** Valves almost equal, mottled reddish-brown. Radial ribs and intermediate spaces with fine ornament. Up to 80mm. North-east Atlantic, Mediterranean.

10 *Chlamys (Aequipecten) lineatus* (Da Costa, 1778). Pale, each rib marked with a brown line. Up to 70mm. England, French Atlantic coast. Possibly only a variety of No. 9.

55

1 *Chlamys (Chlamys) senatoria* (Gmelin, 1791). **Noble Scallop.** Valves almost equal, Radial ribs rounded, with rough, scaly growth lamellae. Anterior ear longer. Yellow, orange, red, violet, reddish-brown, often with pale mottling. Up to 10cm. West Pacific (Japan). Synonym: *C. nobilis* (Reeve, 1852).

2 *Chlamys (Chlamys) senatoria* (Gmelin, 1791). Two colour variants of the same species from Japan (Kii).

3 *Chlamys (Argopecten) circularis* (Sowerby, 1835). Valves unequal, very convex, with c. 21 rounded radial ribs. Ears almost equal. Coloration very variable: yellow, dark orange, purple, most frequently white. Up to 50mm. West coast of central America (Gulf of California) to Peru. The more northerly, larger and less brightly coloured *A. aequisulcatus* (Carpenter, 1864) should be a subspecies of *circularis*.

4 *Chlamys (Chlamys) delicatula* (Hutton, 1873). Valves almost equal. Posterior ear truncated. Numerous alternating large and small radial ribs. Only in tones of yellow. 50mm. Southern New Zealand (Timaru). Synonym: *C. subantarctica* Hedley, 1916.

5 *Chlamys (Cryptopecten) pallium* (Linné, 1758). Valves equal. Anterior ear larger. Radial ribs prominent with scaly growth lamellae. Cinnabar-red, purple or pale violet, whitish near the umbones, often with concentric bands. Up to c. 60mm. Tropical Pacific (Cebu, Philippines).

6 *Pecten (Pecten) albicans* Schröter, 1802. Valves unequal. Left valve flat, right convex. Ears almost equal. Up to 60mm. Japan (Aichi).

7 *Chlamys (Chlamys) squamosa* (Gmelin, 1791). Valves almost equal. About 10 coarsely scaled radial ribs, separated by finer ridges. Anterior ear longer. Red, orange, purplish-brown, often with white bands. Up to 60cm. Tropical Pacific (Japan).

8 *Chlamys (Swiftopecten) swifti* (Bernardi, 1858). Valves equal. Left valve with a few broad radial ribs with concentric ridges, pale reddish-purple. Right valve white, with broad ribs. Anterior ear longer. About 10cm. Central Japan northwards to Alaska.

9, 9a *Amusium japonicum* (Gmelin, 1791). **Japanese Sun and Moon Shell.** Disc-shaped, smooth outside, and with about 20 pairs of radial ridges inside. Left valve red-brown outside (sun), right valve yellowish-white (moon). 10cm. Japan. Edible. 9a is *A.j. balloti* Bernardi, 1861, up to 15cm with a concentric pattern. Australia. *A. pleuronectes* (Linné, 1758) is smaller, reddish, with 12 pairs of radial ridges inside. Taiwan to Australia.

10 *Hinnites multirugosus* (Gale, 1928). **Giant Rock Scallop.** Rough, brown with spiny scales, starting life free, but later becoming attached. Up to 15cm. West coast of U.S.A.

56

1 *Spondylus (Spondylus) gaederopus* Linné, 1758. **Thorny Oyster.** Shell very thick, valves unequal, the right one very convex with ribs and concentric lamellae, often spiny, white, and attached to the substrate. Left valve either with fairly fine ribs or irregular with coarse and fine ribs, and spines of unequal length. Ears very small. Brownish-violet to wine-red. Usually covered with algal growths. Inside porcelain-white. The valves close very tightly. Up to 80mm. Portuguese coasts to Cape Verde, Senegal, and in Mediterranean (Evboikos Kolpos, Greece), on large rocks even in shallow water.

2 *Spondylus (Spondylus) regius* Linné, 1758. **Regal Thorny Oyster.** Radial ribs with large, widely separated spines, the intermediate spaces with numerous finely scaled ridges. Orange to purplish pink, the ribs and spines orange to whitish. 90mm. Tropical Pacific (Zamboanga, Philippines). Related Pacific species: *S. decalis* Röding, 1798, purplish-red, ribs and spines white; *S. sinensis* Schreibers, 1793 with spatulate spines. See also No. 3.

3 *Spondylus (Spondylus) barbatus* Reeve, 1856. **Bearded Thorny Oyster.** Left valve with radial ribs carrying fine scales which become larger and spatulate towards the edge. Right (attached) valve with concentric growth lamellae. Pale purplish-red, young shells pale red at the umbones. 80mm. Tropical Pacific (Kii, Japan).

4 *Spondylus (Spondylus) americanus* Hermann, 1781. **Atlantic Thorny Oyster.** Usually white, with coloured markings towards the umbones, but may be orange or purplish-red. 70-100mm. Caribbean. Pacific species: *S. princeps* Broderip, 1833.

5 *Limaria (Limaria) tuberculata* (Olivi, 1792). Very convex, gaping, with small ears. Radial ornament, with a few small pustules. 45mm. French Atlantic coast to central Africa (Angola), Mediterranean. Synonym: *L. inflata* Chemnitz, 1784. Related species in West Indies.

6 *Lima (Lima) lima* (Linné, 1758). **Spiny Lima.** Ribs with prominent scaly spines. Anterior ear larger. 50mm. Mediterranean (Sardinia), Atlantic, West Indies, South Florida, attached to stones in shallow water.

7 *Lima (lima) nimbifer* (Iredale, 1929). Valves with rought scales, gaping. Ears unequal. Inside white, shiny. 25mm. South-west Australia.

8 *Ctenoides scabra* (Born, 1778). **Rough Lima.** Sides almost symmetrical. Ears equal. Ribs with fine scales which increase in breadth towards the edge. Periostracum brown. 60mm. West Indies, Florida (Miami). The similarly sized *C. s. tenera* (Sowerby, 1843) has minute scales giving a silky sheen.

9 *Lima (Lima) zelandica* Sowerby, 1876. 50mm. New Zealand. A deep-water form occasionally brought up by fishermen in Foveaux Strait.

57

1 *Placuna placenta* (Linné, 1758). **Window or Jingle Shell.** Round, flat, transparent with concentric and fine radial ornament. Inside shiny mother-of-pearl, with a central roundish muscle impression. Up to 15cm. Between Taiwan and Australia (Cebu, Philippines). The shells have been used as window glass in China.

2 *Anomia ephippium* Linné, 1758. **Saddle Oyster.** Shell thin with unequal valves. Right valve shaped to the substrate with a round hole for the byssus. Yellowish-white to horn-coloured, translucent. Left valve thick, convex, pale reddish-brown. Inside iridescent. Hinge without teeth. Up to 60mm. European coasts, Mediterranean, on rocks and larger bivalves in shallow depths.

3 *Anomia walteri* Hector, 1895. Right valve with hole, greenish-white, left valve transparent, golden-yellow. 90mm. New Zealand (Kahimaramara Beach).

4 *Ostrea edulis edulis* Linné, 1758. **Common European Oyster.** Shell consisting of numerous overlapping lamellae. Valves unequal, the left (lower) valve convex, with wavy ribs in the growth zone, attached to the substrate. Hinge short with triangular ligament groove. Right (upper) valve flat, lamellar, without ribs. Coloration dirty-white with violet areas. Inside iridescent. Usually up to 10cm. European coasts, Mediterranean, 30-80m, on various firm substrates with rocks, gravel, hard mud or sand, forming dense colonies. Cultivated on artificially prepared substrates in quiet waters.

5 *Neopycnodonte cochlear* (Poli, 1795). Shell thin, lamellar. Left (lower) valve deep, with wavy edge. Right valve flat, concave. Yellowish to reddish-brown. Inside whitish iridescent, with brown callus. Up to 80mm. Central Atlantic, Mediterranean, frequently on seaweeds and cables.

6, 6a *Crassostrea angulata* (Lamarck, 1819). **Portuguese Oyster.** Longish, lamellar, with somewhat angular outline, and radial wavy ornament. Lower valve very deep, upper slightly convex. Dirty-white to brownish-grey with violet. Periostracum thin. Up to 10cm. Parts of eastern Atlantic.

7, 7a *Hyotissa hyotis* (Linné, 1758). Lamellae with angular folds, forming tubular, hollow scales. Violet-brown. Up to 20cm. Indo-Pacific.

8 *Lopha cristagalli* (Linné, 1758). **Cock's-comb Oyster.** Angular and much folded, with a finely granular surface. Violet-brown. Inside iridescent, with violet edges. 80mm. Indo-Pacific.

58

1 *Venericardia purpurata* (Deshayes, 1854). Squarish-elliptical with rounded ribs. 30mm. New Zealand, intertidal in sand.

2 *Cardites laticostata* (Sowerby, 1833). Inflated, densely scaled, with almost square ribs and concentric bands. 35mm. West coast of central America.

3 *Neotrigonia margaritacea* (Lamarck, 1804). **Southern Brooch Shell.** Rounded triangular with dense scales. Outside reddish-brown, inside iridescent purple. 30mm. East and south Australia (Port Lincoln), Tasmania, in c. 70m. Used in the manufacture of jewellery.

4 *Carditamera (Carditamera) floridana* (Conrad, 1838). Longish-ovate, truncated to the rear, with strong, rough, scaly ribs. Coloration white with purplish-brown markings. 35mm. Florida (Fort Myers Beach), Texas, Mexico, in bays and lagoons.

5 *Cardita (Cardita) crassicostata* Lamarck, 1819. Longish with a slightly incurved base. Ribs with large, lamellar hollow scales. Colour variable: yellow, pink, red-brown. Inside porcelain-white. Up to 60mm. Japan to South Australia.

6 *Carditamera (Carditamera) marmorea* (Reeve, 1843). Ribs becoming broader, flatter and scaly towards the edge. Mottled whitish-brown. 40mm. North and west Australia (Broome).

7 *Pseudochama gryphina* (Lamarck, 1819). Valves unequal, very solid, with lamellae or scales. Right (lower) valve larger, deeper and attached, left valve like a lid. Off-white, the inside yellowish-orange to olive-green. 43mm. Mediterranean (Sardinia) and adjacent Atlantic. To be distinguished from *Chama gryphoides* Linné, 1758, 25mm, inside brownish-violet, from the same area, which is attached by the left valve.

8 *Astarte (Astarte) fusca* (Poli, 1785). Triangular-elliptical, thick, only moderately convex with finely toothed edge. With the concentric ridges becoming more widely separated towards the edge. Red-brown, inside brownish. 25mm. Mediterranean (Sicily) and adjacent Atlantic, 60-80m.

9 *Glossus (Glossus) humanus* (Linné, 1758). **Heart Cockle.** Umbones rolled inwards and towards the front. Periostracum brown. Up to 70mm. Norway to northern Africa, Mediterranean (Sardinia), on mud and sand. Edible. Synonym: *Isocardia cor* Lamarck, 1798.

10 *Glossus (Meiocardia) moltkianus* (Spengler, 1783). Back with keeled edge. Creamy-yellow, with concentric furrows. 35mm. Indo-Pacific.

11 *Arctica islandica* (Linné, 1767). **Black Clam, Iceland Cyprina.** Shell thick, white, with growth lines and brown to black periostracum. 50-90mm. North Atlantic, on mud, from 10m. Formerly under *Cyprina* Lamarck.

12, 12a *Chama lazarus* Linné, 1758. **Lazarus Jewel Box.** Left valve attached to substrate. Numerous frayed lamellae. White and brown. Up to 90mm. Indo-Pacific (Palawan, Philippines).

59

1 *Codakia (Codakia) tigerina* (Linné, 1758). Shell thick with reticulate ornament. White outside, yellow with a reddish edge inside. Up to 10cm. Indo-Pacific (Philippines), on coral sand, intertidal. Related species: *C. punctata* (Linné, 1758), with deeper radial furrows and fine growth lines, Indo-Pacific.

2 *Codakia (Codakia) distinguenda* (Tryon, 1872). Radial ornament dominant, and concentric lines. Yellowish inside with red edge. Up to 14cm. West coast of central America (Mexico). The east coast form *C. orbicularis* (Linné, 1758) has more prominent ornament, and is reddish inside. Up to 10cm. Caribbean.

3 *Codakia (Codakia) paytenorum* (Iredale, 1927). Smaller than No. 1, with fine reticulation. White with a reddish tinge. Inside yellow with a reddish margin. Up to 50mm. Australia, New Zealand (Middleton Reef).

4 *Ctena (Ctena) decussata* (O. G. Costa, 1830). Fine reticulation, the radial elements dominant. Whitish. 17mm. French Atlantic coast, Canaries, Mediterranean (Sardinia), intertidal.

5 *Lucinella divaricata* (Linné, 1758). With growth lines crossed obliquely by wavy furrows. White with a thin periostracum. European coasts (Morgat, Brittany), Mediterranean.

6 *Lucinoma borealis* (Linné, 1767). Numerous concentric growth lines separated by irregular spaces. White, with brown periostracum, which seldom adheres. 35mm. Arctic seas to northern Africa, Mediterranean.

7 *Fimbria fimbriata* (Linné, 1758).

Shell thick, inflated, with irregular concentric ridges overlying radial ornament. White inside and outside. Margin toothed. Up to 10cm. West Pacific (Barrier Reef), Hawaii.

8 *Anodontia (Anodontia) alba* Link, 1807. Shell thin, inflated, with dense growth lines. Creamy-yellow, the inside with an orange margin. 40mm. Florida (Tampa Bay), Texas, West Indies, various depths.

9, 9a *Linga (Linga) columbella* (Lamarck, 1819). Almost spherical, with concentric growth lines. Inner edge toothed. Up to 35mm. West Africa, Canaries (Lanzarote), 10-40m.

10 *Lucina (Lucina) pectinata* (Gmelin, 1791). Keeled at the rear. Creamy-orange. 60mm. Florida, Texas, West Indies. Formerly under *Phacoides* Blainville, 1825.

11 *Hippopus hippopus* (Linné, 1758). **Horse Shoe or Bear's Paw Clam.** Front edge with a horseshoe-shaped area containing the byssal gape. White with orange and brown markings. Up to 40cm. West Pacific, frequently on coral reefs.

12 *Tridacna (Chametrachea) maxima* (Röding, 1798). Longish-triangular, with wavy folds and hollow lamellar scales. Byssal gape wide, White, often with a yellow tinge. Up to 35cm. Indo-Pacific, except Hawaii, on coral reefs.

13 *Tridacna (Chametrachea) squamosa* Lamarck, 1819. **Scaly or Fluted Clam.** Roundish-triangular with a narrow byssal gape. Hollow scales and radial folds less dense. White, yellow, orange. Up to 40cm. Indo-Pacific, except Hawaii. Related species: *T. (Tridacna) gigas* (Linné, 1758), Giant Clam, up to 130cm. Indo-Pacific.

60

1 *Nemocardium (Discors) lyratum* (Sowerby, 1841). Primary ribs in front, becoming less prominent in centre and to rear, and overlaid by secondary ribs. Creamy-red, with red periostracum. 55mm. Indo-Pacific.

2 *Cerastoderma edule* (Linné, 1758). **Common European Edible Cockle.** Ribs scaly. Pale beige to ochre-coloured. 30mm. North-east Atlantic, in sand, close below the surface.

3 *Serripes groenlandicus* (Brugière, 1798). **Greenland Cockle.** Thin, with weak radial ribs. Reddish-brown. North Atlantic (Iceland), Arctic seas, Alaska, west coast of N. America.

4, 4a *Acanthocardia (Acanthocardia) aculeata* (Linné, 1758). **Spiny Cockle.** Ribs with pointed papillae. Ochre-coloured. 80mm. English west coast to Morocco, Mediterranean.

5 *Cardium (Bucardium) ringens* Bruguière, 1798. Ribs elongated at the rear end. 30mm. West Africa.

6 *Acanthocardia (Rudicardium) tuberculata* (Linné, 1758). Ribs with tuberculate thickenings. Yellowish-ochre with brown bands. 60mm. Southern England to Morocco, Mediterranean.

7 *Cardium (Cardium) costatum* Linné, 1758. Thin, white, with hollow keeled ribs. Inside showing ridges. 80mm. West Africa.

8 *Acanthocardia (Acanthocardia) echinata* (Linné, 1758). **Prickly Cockle.** Fewer ribs than in No. 4, and broader intermediate spaces. Small, pointed papillae, mainly in front and near the lower edge. Pale ochre to beige. Up to 50mm. North-east Atlantic, Mediterranean.

9 *Fragum (Fragum) fragum* (Linné, 1758). **White Strawberry Cockle.** Ribs with numerous scaly papillae. Creamy-white, shiny. White inside with yellow umbonal markings. 35mm. Tropical Pacific (Fitzroy Reef, Queensland). Related species: *F. unedo* (Linné, 1758), with purple scales, up to 60mm. Indo-Pacific.

10 *Clinocardium nuttalli* (Conrad, 1837). Ribs thick, periostracum thin, brownish. West coast of northern America, Bering Sea.

11 *Corculum cardissa* (Linné, 1758). **Heart Cockle.** Much compressed with a sharp, slightly toothed keel. Profile heart-shaped. 60mm. Tropical Pacific (Zamboanga, Philippines), coral sand.

12 *Clinocardium ciliatum* (Fabricius, 1780). **Iceland Cockle.** Similar to No. 10, but broader. Periostracum olive-brown with darker bands, often eroded. 50mm. Arctic seas, Norway to Alaska, Iceland.

13 *Laevicardium (Dinocardium) robustum vanhyningi* (Clench & Smith, 1944). **Great Heart Cockle.** Ribs prominent. Red-brown bands. 80mm. Florida. Nominate form rounder, Virginia to Texas.

14 *Trigoniocardia (Americardia) media* (Linné, 1758). **Atlantic Strawberry Cockle.** White with a pattern of brown markings. 30mm. Florida, West Indies.

15 *Laevicardium (Laevicardium) elatum* (Sowerby, 1833). **Giant Pacific Egg Cockle.** Umbo smooth, otherwise with weak ribs. Yellow. Up to 15cm. West coast of central America, California to Panama.

61

1 *Venus (Venus) verrucosa* Linné, 1758. Concentric ornament very prominent, warty to the rear. 50mm. North-east Atlantic, Mediterranean (Istria).

2 *Venus (Ventricoloidea) nux* Gmelin, 1791. Whitish to yellowish-white, with coarse concentric ornament. Up to 40mm. Mediterranean and adjacent Atlantic.

3 *Callista (Callista) chione* (Linné, 1758). Reddish-brown with darker areas. Periostracum shiny and persistent. 80mm. North-east Atlantic, Mediterranean.

4 *Timoclea (Timoclea) ovata* (Pennant, 1777). Radial ribs with fine scales. Yellowish. 17mm. North-east Atlantic, Mediterranean.

5 *Chamelea gallina* (Linné, 1758). Concentric, often with irregularly wrinkled ridges. 35mm. Mediterranean and adjacent Atlantic (Setubal).

6 *Irus (Irus) irus* (Linné, 1758). White with prominent lamellae. 20mm. Mediterranean and adjacent Atlantic.

7 *Callista (Costacallista) lilacina* (Lamarck, 1818). Beige and dark brown with strong concentric ornament. 80mm. Tropical Pacific.

8 *Chione (Chione) cancellata* (Linné, 1767). Creamy-white with prominent reticulate ornament 30mm. Florida, Texas, West Indies.

9 *Venus (Antigona) lamellaris* (Schumacher, 1817). Similar to No. 8. Creamy-white, with brown markings, inside reddish. 40mm. Indo-Pacific.

10 *Dosinia (Dosinia) stabilis* (Iredale, 1929). Shiny white and brown with concentric ornament. 30mm. Indo-Pacific (Port Hedland, N.W. Australia).

11 *Meretrix lusoria* (Röding, 1798). White with very glossy periostracum.

Up to 60mm. Taiwan, Japan, China.

12 *Periglypta reticulata* (Linné, 1758). Reticulate ornament, tuberculate at the intersections. Creamy-white and rust-brown. Up to 70mm. Tropical Pacific.

13 *Placamen flindersi* Cotton & Godfrey, 1938. Creamy-white, often red-striped, with up to 12 concentric lamellae. 20mm. East and south Australia.

14 *Tapes (Ruditapes) decussata* (Linné, 1758). **Carpet Shell.** Broad at the rear with radial and concentric ornament. Up to 60mm. Norway to Mediterranean. Formerly under *Venerupis* Lamarck, 1818.

15 *Dosinia (Pectunculus) exoleta* (Linné, 1758). Whitish or yellowish with dense lamellae. C. 40mm. Norway to Mediterranean. Also under *Orbiculus* Mühlfeld, 1811.

16 *Tapes (Tapes) literatus* (Linné, 1758). Outline as No. 14. Creamy-white with a brown pattern and weak concentric ornament. 80mm. Indo-Pacific.

17 *Tawera lagopus* (Lamarck, 1818). White with brown rays and concentric lamellae on basic radial ornament. 27mm. South Australia (Smoky Bay).

18 *Petricola (Rupellaria) lithophaga* (Retzius, 1786). Rounded and inflated in front, flattened behind. 25mm. Britain to Mediterranean. Bores in hard rock.

19 *Mysia undata* (Pennant, 1777). Thin, white, roundish, with fine irregular growth lines. 35mm. Norway to Mediterranean.

20 *Petricola (Petricolaria) pholadiformis* Lamarck, 1818. **American Piddock.** With tuberculate radial ribs in front, growth lines more prominent to the rear. 80mm. European coasts, Mediterranean, Caribbean, West Africa.

62

1 *Mactra (Mactra) corallina stultorum* (Linné, 1758). Inside of shell bright violet. 60mm. Mediterranean and adjacent Atlantic.

2 *Atactodea striata* (Gmelin, 1791). Triangular with concentric ornament. White with a thin periostracum. 25mm. Indo-Pacific (Sumatra).

3 *Mactra (Mactra) corallina corallina* (Linné, 1758). White inside and outside, with greyish periostracum. 50mm. Mediterranean.

4 *Spisula (Mactromeris) hemphilli* (Dall, 1894). White, with concave front edge and a yellowish periostracum. Up to 10cm. West coast of northern America.

5 *Mactra (Mactra) corallina cinerea* Montagu, 1808. Flatter than No. 1, and white inside. 60mm. North Sea, north-east Atlantic.

6, 6a *Spisula (Spisula) solida* (Linné, 1758). Ovate, whitish. Up to 40mm. North-east Atlantic.

7 *Notocallista kingi* (Gray, 1827). Creamy-white, with golden-brown markings and thin, shiny periostracum. 40mm. South and east Australia.

8, 8a *Spisula (Spisula) subtruncata* (Da Costa, 1778). Whitish, with periostracum usually remaining at the margin. 25mm. Norway to Morocco. 8a is an old shell washed ashore.

9 *Spisula (Spisula) elliptica* (Brown, 1827). Rear more pointed than in No. 6. Up to 30mm. North Atlantic, North Sea.

10 *Donacilla cornea* (Poli, 1791). Longer in front than behind. Yellowish-white with brown markings inside. 20mm. Mediterranean and adjacent Atlantic.

11 *Donax (Serrula) trunculus* Linné, 1758. White, the inside violet. Periostracum yellowish. 35mm. Mediterranean and adjacent Atlantic.

12 *Donax (Cuneus) vittatus* (Da Costa, 1778). **Banded Wedge Shell.** More pointed at rear. Edge finely toothed. 35mm. European coasts.

13 *Donacilla cuneata* (Lamarck, 1818). Ventral edge more curved. Inside white. Periostracum yellow. 25mm. South and east Australia.

14 *Donax (Chion) punctatostriatus* Hanley, 1843. Radial rows of dots (only visible under a lens). Inside with violet markings. 40mm. West coast of central America.

15 *Donax (Chion) denticulatus* Linné, 1758. **Common Caribbean Donax.** White with brown rays and radial ornament. Edge finely toothed. Up to 20mm. Caribbean (Venezuela).

16 *Donax (Latona) cuneatus* Linné, 1758. Brown rays, yellow periostracum, no violet markings inside. Edge without teeth. 35mm. South and east Australia.

17 *Donax (Grammatodonax) madagascariensis* Wood, 1828. With oblique furrows running parallel to the upper anterior edge. White, with yellowish-brown periostracum. Inside white, with violet markings. 25mm. South-east Africa (Natal).

18 *Pharus legumen* (Linné, 1758). Very thin, gaping at both ends. Umbones near the middle. 11cm. Norway to Senegal, Mediterranean.

19 *Ensis siliqua* (Linné, 1758). Shell gaping, umbones and hinge at the rear. 20cm. European coasts, not Mediterranean.

20 *Solen marginatus* (Pennant, 1777). 13cm. Norway to Angola, Mediterranean.

21 *Ensis ensis* (Linné, 1758). 13cm. North-east Atlantic, Mediterranean.

63

1 *Sanguinolaria (Nuttallia) nuttalli* Conrad, 1837. Right valve flatter, shell gaping at the rear. 90mm. West coast of North America (California).

2 *Solecurtus strigillatus* (Linné, 1758). Oblique, wavy furrows crossing the concentric growth lines. 80mm. Mediterranean and adjacent Atlantic.

3 *Asaphis (Asaphis) deflorata* (Linné, 1758). Yellow, pink or violet, with prominent radial ornament. 40mm. Florida, West Indies.

4 *Gari (Gobraeus) depressa* (Pennant, 1777). Rounded and truncated at rear. White to greyish-violet. 50mm. Britain to West Africa.

5 *Azorinus chamasolen* (Da Costa, 1778). Gaping in front and behind. White, the periostracum usually retained at the edge. 40mm. Britain to Canaries, Mediterranean.

6 *Tellina (Phylloda) foliacea* Linné, 1758. Much compressed, the rear edge toothed. Yellowish-orange. 80mm. Tropical west Pacific (Queensland).

7 *Tellina (Tellinella) virgata* Linné, 1758. The rear part pointed and turned to the right. 70mm. West Pacific.

8 *Tellina (Tellina) radiata* Linné, 1758. **Sunrise Tellin.** Shiny, whitish with purplish-red rays. 70mm. Texas, Florida, West Indies.

9 *Tellina (Cyclotellina) remies* Linné, 1758. Circular, white, thick-shelled with coarse growth lines. Periostracum greyish. 60mm. West Pacific.

10 *Tellina (Angulus) tenuis* Da Costa, 1778. Much compressed, white, yellow or pink, with fine growth lines. 25mm. Norway to Morocco. *T. (Laciolina) incarnata* Linné, 1758, Mediterranean, has the rear more elongated.

11 *Scrobicularia plana* (Da Costa, 1778). Flat, thin-shelled, whitish. 55mm. Norway to Senegal, Mediterranean.

12 *Tellina (Fabulina) fabula* Gronovius, 1781. Rear of shell curved to right. White. 23mm. Northeast Atlantic.

13, 13a *Macoma (Macoma) balthica* (Linné, 1758). Yellow to reddish. Up to 30mm. North Atlantic.

14 *Tellina (Arcopagia) crassa* (Pennant, 1777). White with concentric ornament, sometimes with reddish rays. 40mm. Norway to Senegal.

15 *Mya (Mya) truncata* Linné, 1758. **Blunt Gaper, Truncate Softshell Clam.** Up to 70mm. Circumpolar.

16 *Mya (Arenomya) arenaria* Linné, 1758. **Sand Gaper or Soft Clam.** Pointed at the rear. 13cm. East Pacific, North Atlantic.

17 *Hiatella arctica* (Linné, 1767). Up to 35mm. Circumpolar: Pacific, Arctic, North Atlantic. Synonym: *Saxicava* Fleuriau de Bellevue, 1802.

18 *Pholas (Pholas) dactylus* Linné, 1758. **Common Piddock.** Up to 10cm. North-east Atlantic, Mediterranean. Bores tunnels in rock, timber, etc.

19 *Zirfaea crispata* (Linné, 1758). **Oval Piddock.** 8cm. North-east Atlantic.

20 *Barnea (Barnea) candida* (Linné, 1758). **White Piddock.** 70mm. North-east Atlantic, Mediterranean.

21 *Cyrtopleura (Scobinopholas) costata* (Linné, 1758). 15cm. Florida, West Indies.

64

1 *Dentalium (Fissidentalium) vernedei* Sowerby, 1860. Shell slightly curved with very fine ornament. Shiny white, often with yellowish to yellow-brown rings. Apical opening narrowed, with a notch. 12cm. Japan (Kii), 20-40m.

2 *Dentalium (Laevidentalium) crocinum* Dall, 1907. Shell smooth, shiny, orange-yellow. Apical opening simple. 60mm. West Pacific, 50-100m.

3 *Dentalium (Dentalium) elephantinum* Linné, 1758. **Elephant's Tusk Shell.** With c. 10 strong ribs. Surface smooth, dark green in front, becoming paler behind and white at the tip. 90mm. Indo-Pacific (Sulu Archipelago).

4 *Dentalium (Antalis) vulgare* Da Costa, 1778. **Common Tusk Shell.** Fine stripes, disappearing towards mouth. Apical opening narrowed. Opaque white, the upper half reddish. Up to 60mm. European coasts, to 50m.

5 *Dentalium rossati* Caprotti, 1966. Shell smooth, translucent, white and brownish-red, with coarse growth zones. Apical opening simple. 48mm. Eastern Mediterranean (Israeli coast).

6 *Dentalium (Pseudantalis) rubescens* Deshayes, 1825. Shiny, scarlet with fine stripes. Apical opening with notch. 35mm. Mediterranean (Gulf of Genoa).

7 *Liolophura japonica* (Lischke, 1873). Girdle with numerous short, club-shaped spines. Brown and whitish. 50mm. Japan (Kusui), intertidal.

8 *Chiton (Chiton) tuberculatus* Linné, 1758. Shell plates ribbed laterally. Girdle granular. Grey-green. Up to 50mm. Florida, Texas, West Indies.

9 *Tonicella lineata* (Wood, 1815). **Lined Red Chiton.** Plates yellowish-brown, with darker wavy pattern. Girdle leathery. 40mm. West coast of northern America, Alaska to California.

10 *Chiton (Chiton) olivaceus* Spengler, 1797. Plates ribbed, yellow-brown and olive-grey. Girdle with pale and dark bands. 35mm. Mediterranean (Corsica). North Sea and Atlantic have *Lepidochiton cinereus* (Linné, 1767), on rocks, etc., in shallow water.

11 *Spirula spirula* (Linné, 1758). Spiral shell of a pelagic cephalopod, with numerous gas-filled chambers providing buoyancy. 35mm. All tropical seas.

12 *Argonauta argo* Linné, 1758. **Paper Nautilus.** Shell thin, translucent, without chambers, not firmly attached to the animal, but serving to hold the eggs. Up to 20cm. Male tiny, without shell. Pelagic in tropical seas.

13 *Argonauta hians* Lightfoot, 1786. Smaller than No. 12 with coarser wavy ribs. Up to 60mm. Same distribution.

14 *Nautilus pompilius* Linné, 1758. **Pearly Nautilus.** Shell with chambers separated by septa but intercommunicating by a tube (the siphuncle). Up to 20cm. Indo-Pacific.

BIBLIOGRAPHY

Handbooks

Moore, R. C. (editor) *Treatise on Invertebrate Paleontology* Geological Society of America and University of Kansas Press. Part I Mollusca 1 (General features, Scaphopoda, Amphineura, Monoplacophora, Archaeogastropoda), 1960 (1964). Part N (3 volumes) Mollusca 6 (Bivalvia), 1969.

Identification literature

EUROPE

Tebble, N. *British Bivalve Seashells* British Museum (Natural History). London, 1966.
McMillan, N. F. *British Shells* Warne, London. 1900.

AFRICA

Kennelly, D. H. *Marine Shells of Southern Africa* Books of Africa Pty. Ltd., Capt Town, 1969.
Kensley, B. *Sea-shells of Southern Africa : Gastropods* Maskew Miller Ltd., Cape Town, 1973.

AMERICA

Abbott, R. T. *American Seashells* Van Nostrand Rheinold, New York, U.S.A., 1974
Abbott, R. T. *Seashells of North America* Golden Press, New York, 1968.
Andrews, J. *Sea Shells of the Texas Coast* University of Texas Press, Austin, 1971.
Keen, A. M. & Cohn, E. *Marine Molluscan Genera of Western North America* (2nd edition) Stanford University Press, Stanford, 1974.
Keen, A. M. *Sea Shells of Tropical West America* (2nd edition) Stanford University Press, Stanford, 1971.
McLean, J. H. *Marine Shells of Southern California* Los Angeles County Museum of Natural History, Los Angeles, 1969.
Morris, P. A. *A Field Guide to Shells of the Atlantic and Gulf Coasts and the West Indies*, 1973. Houghton Mifflin Co., Boston.
Perry, L. M. and Schwengel, J. S. *Marine Shells of the Western Coast of Florida* Paleontological Research Institution, Ithaca, New York, 1955.
Rios, E. C. *Coastal Brazilian Shells* Museu oceanográfico de Rio Grande, Brazil, 1970.

INDO-PACIFIC AND JAPAN

Cernohorsky, W. O. *Marine Shells of the Pacific* Vol. I, 1971; Vol. I, 1972. Pacific Publications Pty. Ltd., Sydney.
Habe, T. *Shells of the Western Pacific in Color* Vol. II, 1964.

Hoikusha Publishing Co. Ltd., Osaka.
Kira, T. *Shells of the Western Pacific in Color* Vol. I, 1965.

AUSTRALIA AND NEW ZEALAND

Cotton, B. C. *South Australian Mollusca, Archaeogastropoda* 1959 and *Pelecypoda* 1961. W. L. Hawes, Government Printer, Adelaide.
Macpherson, J. H. and Gabriel, C. J. *Marine Molluscs of Victoria* Melbourne University Press, 1962.
Moon, G. J. H. and Penniket, J. R. *New Zealand Seashells in Colour* A. & W. Reed, Wellington and Auckland, 1970.
Powell, A. W. B. *Shells of New Zealand* Whitcombe & Tombs Ltd., Christchurch, 1967.
Wilson, B. R. & Gillett, K. *Australian Shells* A. & A. Reed, Sydney & Melbourne, 1971.

Monographs

Burgess, C. M. *The Living Cowries* A. S. Barnes & Co., New York, 1970.
Marsh, J. A. and Rippingale, O. H. *Cone Shells of the World* Jacaranda Press Pty., Ltd., Brisbane, 1968.
Weaver, C. S. and de Pont, J. E. *Living Volutes* Delaware Museum of Natural History, Greenville, Delaware, 1970.
Zeigler, R. F. and Porreca, H. C. *Olive Shells of the World* Published by Zeigler & Porreca, W. Henrietta, New York, 1969.
Johnsonia, Monographs of the Marin Mollusks of the Western Atlantic Museum of Comparative Zoology, Harvard University, Cambridge, Mass., U.S.A. (since 1941).
Indo-Pacific Mollusca, Monographs of the Marine Mollusks of the Tropical Western Pacific and Indian Oceans Delaware Museum of Natural History, Greenville, Delaware (since 1959).

SHELL COLLECTING

The American Malacological Union (see below) publishes (at $2-3 U.S.) a small booklet entitled *How to collect Shells*, which gives practical hints on collecting on the shore and in shallow water, dredging down to 100 feet, and diving, on the cleansing, preparation and arrangement of the shells, together with book lists and the addresses of malacological societies throughout the world. The Smithsonian Institution, Washington, D.C. 20560, U.S.A. publishes valuable information in its *Sources of Information on Molluscs*. Then there is the *International Directory of Conchologists* (revised every 2 years), which gives the names and addresses of more than 2,000 conchologists in over 100 countries; this publication can be obtained from The Shell Cabinet, P.O. Box 29, Falls Church, Virginia, 22046, U.S.A.

Collectors' Journals

Hawaiian Shell News, published by the Hawaiian Malacological Society, 2777 Kalabaua Avenue, Honolulu, Hawaii 96815. *Of Sea and Shore*, a quarterly published by Of Sea and Shore Publications, P.O. Box 33, Port Gamble,

Washington 98364, U.S.A.

Societies

Conchological Society of Great Britain and Ireland, C/o British Museum (Natural History), Cromwell Road, London, SW7, U.K.
American Malacological Union, Secretary, Mrs. M. S. Hubbard, 3957 Marlow Court, Seaford, New York, 11783, U.S.A.
Malacological Society of Australia, Australian Museum, Department of Molluscs, Sydney, N.S.W., Australia.
The Conchological Society of Southern Africa, P.O. Box 98, Howard Place, Pinelands, Cape, South Africa.

Scientific Journals

Basteria, published by the Netherlands Malacological Society, Zoological Museum, Plantage Middenlaan 53, Amsterdam C., Netherlands.
Malacologia, International Journal of Malacology, Museum of Zoology, University of Michigan, Ann Arbor, Michigan, U.S.A.
The Nautilus, published by Delaware Museum of Natural History, Delaware, U.S.A.
The Veliger, published by the California Malacozoological Society, 12719 San Vicente Boulevard, Los Angeles, California 90049, U.S.A.

Shell dealers

Eaton's Shell Shop, 16 Manette Street, London, W1V 5LB, U.K.
The Shell Cabinet, Falls Church, Virginia, 22046, U.S.A.
The names and addresses of other dealers can usually be obtained from one of the societies mentioned above.

SUBJECT INDEX

INDEX OF FAMILIES AND GENERA

The numbers in **bold** type refer to colour plates. Names in *italics* are synonyms.

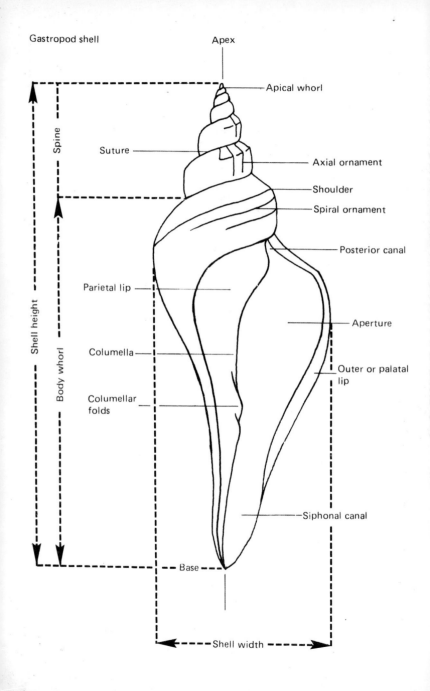

Gastropod shell

Apex

Apical whorl

Suture

Axial ornament

Shoulder

Spiral ornament

Posterior canal

Spine

Parietal lip

Aperture

Columella

Outer or palatal lip

Columellar folds

Shell height

Body whorl

Siphonal canal

Base

Shell width